TRAVELS
IN ASIA MINOR
1764–1765

RICHARD CHANDLER

TRAVELS
IN ASIA MINOR
1764–1765

Edited and abridged by
EDITH CLAY
with an Appreciation of
William Pars by
ANDREW WILTON

PUBLISHED BY
THE TRUSTEES OF THE BRITISH MUSEUM
LONDON 1971

SBN 7141 1230 5

Printed in Great Britain
by Alden & Mowbray Ltd at the Alden Press, Oxford

CONTENTS

TRAVELS
IN ASIA MINOR
1764–1765

vi

LIST OF ILLUSTRATIONS

INTRODUCTION

T HE main object of this book is to bring to public notice an account of the conditions of travel in Asia Minor two hundred years ago and to reproduce the contemporary watercolours of William Pars which have only appeared as engravings in *Ionian Antiquities*, Parts I and II published by the Society of Dilettanti.

This edition of Richard Chandler's *Travels in Asia Minor* is based on that published in 1825 which contained a memoir of Chandler by Ralph Churton and which included, as footnotes, remarks and amendments by Nicholas Revett. Revett's own copy of the original edition with this manuscript comments is now in the British Museum (ref. Cat. 1782b17). These include many interesting and often amusing remarks not always added by Churton. I have not reprinted Churton's memoir but have retained most of the footnotes of Chandler and Revett. Those of Chandler are confined to references to his own book on the inscriptions, to Classical and Byzantine texts and other relevant and contemporary sources. The footnotes by Chandler are indicated by [C] and those by Revett by [R]. All these references have been checked and the modern form given where possible. Unless otherwise stated the remaining notes are by the Editor.

Although considerably abridged, Chandler's text has not been changed nor has the spelling of place-names been altered unless these are obviously incorrect in modern usage. It has been thought best to retain, in general, the latinised form of place-names, e.g. Sigeum not Sigeion. The modern Turkish equivalents have been given where it has been possible to identify them. Chandler's old-fashioned spelling, quaint use of words, and his oddities in the use of italics and punctuation seem rather attractive and in general remain.

On studying Chandler's text it became apparent that the published account of his *Travels* had not been recorded in proper sequence of time. Chandler does however state, at the end of Chapter XXII in the 1825 edition, that for various reasons and because some of the ground had been covered twice, 'we shall unite them [the journeys] in our narrative'. It has therefore been thought best to re-arrange his text and to divide it into three parts. Part I being an account of the journey from England to Smyrna including the visit to the Troad in June to September 1764; Part II, the first journey from Smyrna during September and October 1764 and Part III, the second journey in March to May 1765. The mission was based on Smyrna, but exploration from there was often curtailed by the outbreak of plague: in fact, Chandler and his companions were confined in a small village near Smyrna from May to August 1765 on this account.

Chandler's visit to Asia Minor and Greece in 1764 to 1766 was carried out at the instigation and under the instructions of the Society of Dilettanti.

> In the year 1734 some gentlemen who had travelled in Italy, desirous of encouraging at home a taste for those objects which had contributed so much to their entertainment abroad, formed themselves into a society under the name of Dilettanti, and agreed upon such resolutions as they thought necessary to keep up the spirit of the scheme.[1]

Some thirty years later the Society decided to send out a mission 'to some parts of the East, in order to collect information and to make observations, relative to the ancient state of those countries, and to such monuments of antiquity as are still remaining'.

On 17th May 1764 they accordingly appointed Mr Richard Chandler (who had been introduced to the Society by Mr Robert Wood) to lead the mission, with Mr Nicholas Revett, as architect, and Mr William Pars, as artist, to be his companions. A sum of £800 was allocated for the project, £100 per annum being granted to Revett and £80 to Pars; the remaining £620 was entrusted to Chandler to 'be applied to the common purposes of the journey'. On the return of the mission £400 was left over from the total monies allocated, and the Society agreed that in view of 'the Grateful and

[1] *History of the Society of Dilettanti*, by Lionel Cust and Sidney Colvin (London, Macmillan, 1898), p. 4.

Proper Behaviour' of the three members this sum be divided equally between them 'on condition that they each of them in their respective departments do Promise to deliver their works in such Order and Arrangement as shall appear satisfactory to the Committee'. Further grants were made later to Revett and Pars for expenses connected with the completion of their work.

The Society's *Instructions to the Mission* and Chandler's *Dedication* to the Society preceded Chandler's main text in this edition as they did originally.

Although this edition of Chandler's *Travels* is confined to his explorations in Asia Minor only, he originally also published, at his own expense, the diaries of those he undertook in Greece. His first volume, *Travels in Asia Minor*, appeared in 1775 and *Travels in Greece* in the following year. There were several later editions including translations in French and German. I have been unable to trace the original diaries except for that part of them relating to the journey from England to Smyrna which is among the archives of the Society of Dilettanti at present housed in the British Museum. The scientific results of the Mission's explorations were published by the Society in two sumptuous volumes, *Ionian Antiquities; or Ruins of Magnificent and Famous Buildings in Ionia*, Part I in 1769 and Part II in 1797. Later three more volumes were issued—a new and revised edition in 1821 incorporating material collected by the mission led by Sir William Gell in 1812, and two further volumes in 1840 and 1881.

Richard Chandler was born at Elson in Hampshire in 1738 and was the second son of Daniel Chandler. He was educated on a foundation at Winchester College and entered Queen's College, Oxford on 9th May 1755; was elected to a demyship at Magdalen College on 24th July 1757, and was made a probationer fellow on 25th July 1770. In 1759, shortly after being admitted B.A., he published *Elegiaca Graeca*, but without his name; and in 1763 came *Marmora Oxoniensia*, a superb second edition of the Oxford or Arundel Marbles collected by Thomas Howard, 2nd Earl of Arundel and Surrey (1586–1646). From June 1764 to November 1766 he was away from England leading the Mission to Asia Minor and Greece. In 1772 he became senior proctor at Oxford, and in 1774 published

Inscriptiones antiquae etc., being the record of the inscriptions which he had collected during his tour abroad. In 1779 his College presented him to the living of East Worldham, West Tisted in Hampshire, and in 1875 he married Benigna, daughter of Liebet Dorrien by whom he had a son, William Berkeley, and a daughter, Georgina. He spent the winter after his marriage in France and Switzerland and in 1787 went on to Florence and Rome. In 1800 the living of Tilehurst, near Reading, was presented to him and he continued to reside there until his death, due to a stroke, on 9th February 1810. His published works are listed in Appendix C.

I must confess that the study of these *Travels* has left me with no vivid picture of the personality of Chandler nor of his personal relations with his companions apart from the following letter which he wrote to Mr Robert Wood from Smyrna on 5th January 1765 where he says:

> I am engaged on a thousand agreeable speculations in the Greek manners and superstitions, their connection with the Country, the introduction of Christianity, and the change that ensued, which takes in the downfall of the Temples, Theatres, etc., etc., and with my Engagements makes the time pass away too fast. My Companions desire their respects to you, we live very happily together.[1]

But one must bear in mind that travellers in those days were apt to be inarticulate where their emotions were concerned.

Chandler seems to have had a certain dry sense of humour, an obvious appreciation of the beauties of Nature and a lively curiosity about everything and every person he encountered—the traditional costumes of the women of Chios clearly took his fancy, for example. Certainly, he had many interests other than those of Classical remains.

He frequently comments on religious customs and local superstitions, and human incidents which he describes are often very touching:

> ... one evening, coming from the ruins, we found an old woman sitting by the church on the grave of her daughter, who had been buried two years. She wore a black veil, and pulling the ends alternatively, bowed her head down to her bosom; and at the same time lamented aloud, singing in an uniform dismal cadence, with very few pauses. She con-

[1] In the archives of the Society of Dilettanti.

tinued this above an hour, when it grew dark; fulfilling a measure of tributary sorrow, which the Greek superstitiously believe to be acceptable and beneficial to the souls of the deceased. The next morning a man was interred, the wife following the body, tearing her long dishevelled tresses in agony; calling him her life, her love; demanding the reason for his leaving her; and expostulating with him on dying, in terms the most expressive of conjugal endearment and affection.

Chandler's powers of observation were acute, and he tells us of the natural as well as the cultivated state of the countryside, commenting on the crops, vines and natural vegetation; and what he has to relate about the wild life is often described with sympathetic understanding:

> The cranes were now arrived at their respective quarters, and a couple made their nest, which is bigger in circumference than a bushel, on a dome close by our chamber. This pair stood, side by side, with great gravity, shewing no concern at what was transacting beneath them, but at intervals twisting their long necks, and clattering with their beaks turned behind them upon their backs. An owl, a bird also unmolested, was perched hard by, and as frequently hooted.

He remarks that the Turk calls a crane 'a friend and brother', and he had observed one 'hopping on a wall on a single leg, the maimed stump wrapped in linen'. In *Travels in Greece* (chap. xxvii), Chandler tells how 'he set at liberty a venerable and voracious prisoner' as he called a large horned owl which had been presented to him by a peasant.

Detailed, vivid and horrifying is the description we are given of the outbreak of plague at Smyrna which so greatly interfered with the activities of Chandler and his companions.[1] His remarks on the

---

[1] It is interesting to note that Lady Elgin writing to her mother from Smyrna on 15th August 1802 says:

> I think I never saw a place so calculated to contain contagion so perfectly as this: the streets are so narrow you can shake hands with your opposite neighbour. I was interrupted by the Père Luigi who came to pay us a visit; he told us some curious anecdotes. In the first place he said it is now 35 years since he had dedicated himself to the plague, and during all that period Smyrna had only 8 years been free of the plague, taking in this year which is not expired. He says it is a dreadful country to live in. I think if it were not for his vow he would be off.

Letters of Mary Nisbet, Lady Elgin, arranged by Lt. Col. Nisbet Hamilton Grant (London, John Murray, 1926), p. 214.

almost fatalistic attitude of the Turks at that period are penetrating:

> The Turk will not acknowledge the means [precautions] as efficacious, or will reject them as unlawful. A bigotted predestinarian, he resolves sickness or health, pleasure or pain, with all, even the most trifling, incidents of life, into the mighty power and uncontrollable will of the Supreme Being. .. He triumphs in superior courage and confidence, going out or coming in during the malady with a calm indifference as at other times; like the brute beast, unconscious of the road which leads to his security or destruction.

In spite of the difficulties of travel, the primitive conditions under which they lived, the monotony of the diet and the frequent and aggravating interruptions caused by approaching brigands, Chandler registers little complaint. He was, of course, only twenty-six years of age at the start of the mission, Revett being forty-three and Pars twenty-two. When they left Smyrna in August 1765 to continue their explorations in Greece, their return to England in November the following year was chiefly due to ill-health. Two years of hardships may perhaps have taken their toll.

There seems no doubt that Chandler had prepared himself well for his duties as leader of the Dilettanti Mission. Quite apart from his known academic achievements, he appears to have studied the published accounts of his predecessors in this field of travel and exploration. It is understandable that he made several mis-identifications of archaeological sites, such as Myus and Heracleia, and Tralles and Nysa. On these points Chandler is clearly in disagreement with Revett and it leads one to suppose that there was some personal as well as scholarly discord between them. There is a certain asperity in some of the manuscript notes by Revett in his copy of the *Travels in Asia Minor*, and it is most remarkable that Chandler apparently should not have consulted his companion before publishing the diaries of their travels.[1] Revett was, of course, much older than Chandler and had already spent some years in Italy and Greece studying Classical remains. Was Chandler too young, too obstinate

---

[1] One is reminded of the aspersions cast by Spon in his *Voyage* on the French traveller, de Guillet, who made his reply in his *Lettres Ecrites sur un dissertation d'un Voyage en Grèce, publié par J. Spon* (Paris, 1679). Spon's copy of this book containing his manuscript notes is in the Library of the University of London.

or too proud to consult his colleague, or did Revett resent having so much younger and less experienced a man as leader of the expedition? We cannot know. Certainly Revett's relations with the Society of Dilettanti, and with his former travelling companion, 'Athenian Stuart', were not of the happiest and on this I have touched in Appendix B.

Chandler's text was undoubtedly the most important description of Greece and Greek lands in the eighteenth century and was very widely used by scholars of that period. It superseded the published works of his English predecessors, Sandys, Chishull, Wheler and Spon which, however distinguished, were in no way the equal of Chandler's studies in the archaeological field.

In his account of Dr Chandler published in the 1825 edition of the *Travels*, R. Churton says that he had 'a mind, active, generous, clear and communicative', and although Chandler's old age was spent quietly and unpretentiously as a country parson, Churton describes how when Chandler 'adverted occasionally to the classical scenes, which he had visited in his travels, it was truly delightful, I had almost said enchanting, to my younger ears, to hear him tell, his bright eyes beaming with peculiar lustre, how, after a long lapse of ages of ignorance and barbarism, and under the cruel hand of Turkish tyranny and oppression, the lyre, though not now in the hands of a Tyrtaeus or Simonides, was still, however, cherished on the banks of the Ilissus'.

On the other hand, J. B. S. Morritt[1] writes of Chandler, 'He strikes me as a college fellow turned fresh out of Magdalen to a difficult and somewhat fatiguing voyage, for which he was as unfit as could be; and though very good at an inscription, was sure to go in the beaten track, and be bugbeared by every story or danger and every Turk that pleased to take the trouble.' And M. L. Clarke has remarked that Chandler's diaries 'though conscientious are flat and rather uninteresting'.[2]

A much more appreciative and sympathetic note is struck by T.

[1] *Letters of John B. S. Morritt of Rokeby, descriptive of journeys in Europe and Asia Minor in the years 1794–1796*, edited by C. E. Marrinden, 1914, p. 191.
[2] M. L. Clarke, *Greek Studies in England 1700–1830* (Cambridge University Press, 1945), p. 182.

Spencer[1] who says of the *Travels* that 'nothing so detailed and nothing so good had been published since Wheler and Spon, nearly a century before' and contained 'the most distinguished writing about Greece which had yet appeared in the English language'. Spencer also reminds us that Chandler had 'some skill in expressing his feelings' and obviously found 'the spectacle of the desolation of the Seven Churches profoundly moving'. Chandler's splendid description of Laodicea was also commended by Gibbon in his *Decline and Fall* (chap. ii, edited by J. B. Bury, 1896, i, 49).

Chandler's place in Hellenic travel is an assured one and moreover his books are still used by scholars studying the topography of the area he visited. As a recorder of inscriptions, in some cases he has provided the only text, or part of one, now lost. In general his work is accurate and he does not appear to have made any attempt to reconstruct. He was, I believe, the first Englishman to report the figures at Branchidae now in the British Museum and the site of Panionion has been located where Chandler thought it to have been.

Now that Chandler's *Travels in Asia Minor* have been abridged and arranged in better chronological order, and his rather scanty and often inaccurately printed footnotes have been securely identified and given here in modern form, it is hoped that his contribution to knowledge and scholarship will be more readily appreciated.

London, April 1967   EDITH CLAY

---

[1] Terence Spencer, *Fair Greece Sad Relic* (London, Weidenfeld and Nicolson, 1954), pp. 168—169.

ACKNOWLEDGEMENTS

I WOULD LIKE to express my gratitude to the Trustees of the British Museum for undertaking the publication of this book and for their permission to reproduce the water colours by William Pars which are in their custody; and to Sir Frank Francis, formerly Director and Principal Librarian, without whose interest and encouragement at its inception, I would not have ventured to carry out this project.

I am also most grateful to the Society of Dilettanti who gave me permission to undertake research in its archives and to publish any relevant material.

My warmest thanks go to Professor Donald Strong, formerly Assistant Keeper in the Department of Greek and Roman Antiquities in the British Museum, who at all stages of my work gave me most valuable assistance and advice; and to Professor George Bean who, from his unrivalled knowledge of the territory explored by Richard Chandler, has generously helped me over archaeological and topographical problems: many of the facts in my footnotes are given on his authority.

Mr Jeremy Harrison has assisted me in checking Chandler's references, especially those relating to the Inscriptions: to him I am very grateful as also to the Staff of the Library of the Societies for the Promotion of Hellenic and Roman Studies.

WILLIAM PARS

and his work in Asia Minor

BY ANDREW WILTON

Assistant Keeper in the British Museum
Department of Prints and Drawings

WHEN William Pars was chosen in 1764 by the Society of Dilettanti as artist to Richard Chandler's expedition to Asia Minor he was 22 years old.[1] It was his first important commission, and in the context of his work up to that time, it is a somewhat surprising one.

The range of Pars' activities as an artist in the early years of his career must have been extensive: the Preface to the *Ionian Antiquities*[2] states that 'the choice of a Proper Person for taking Views and copying Bass Reliefs, fell upon Mr. PARS a young Painter of promising Talents'. But unfortunately little evidence of this promise survives. Pars' father had been, according to Edward Edwards,[3] a chaser; his elder brother Henry was trained in their father's profession,[4] and it is likely that William received some instruction in draughtsmanship from them.[5] By 1756 he was at William Shipley's drawing school in the Strand,[6] for in that year he won the Society of Arts' 2nd premium for drawings by boys and girls under 14, and the 4th premium for textile design. He continued to win premiums annually, for life drawing, studies from the Antique and even for models in wax. Surviving examples of this work[7] do not demonstrate any great precocity. They are executed, generally, in chalks or black lead,

[1] Pars was born 28th February 1742. See biography.   [2] Vol. I, p. ii.

[3] Edward Edwards, *Anecdotes of Painters* (London, 1808), p. 89.

[4] Ibid, p. 91.

[5] William and Henry had a brother and sister, Albert and Anne, who were also artists: they are recorded as having won Society of Arts premiums in 1759, 1764 and 1765.

[6] William Shipley (1715–1803), the founder of the Royal Society of Arts, had been a practising painter in Northampton. For the history of his school see *Journal of the Royal Society of Arts*, March 1966, p. 320 and May 1966, p. 520.

[7] At the Royal Society of Arts.

rather clumsily; but they are, perhaps, superior in quality to the work of the majority of Pars' fellow-students.

Only one landscape drawing appears under Pars' name in the lists of premium winners: *Lambeth Ferry from Millbank*, in ink.[1] The date of the award is 1759, but it is inconceivable that the crude drawing at present identified with this[2] was executed by Pars, even at the age of 16 or 17. There is, then, little or no evidence of Pars' accomplishment as a landscape or topographical artist before the Ionian tour; and the only other evidence of his work at this period, in the catalogues of the Free Society and the Society of Artists from 1760, is almost exclusively of portraits.[3]

By 1763, Pars was a practising portrait painter, listed as living 'At the Twisted Pillars, opposite Beaufort-Buildings, in the Strand'.[4] It was near Beaufort Buildings that Shipley's school was held, by this time under the management of Pars' brother Henry. Thomas Jones, who entered the school in 1761, records[5] that Shipley had 'a little time before consigned [it] over to Mr. *Henry Pars* assisted occasionally by his brother William Pars . . .'; and in 1762 the *Public Advertiser* contained a notice announcing 'Drawing and Modelling in all branches taught by Henry and William Pars . . . and other proper masters, at Mr. Clarke's Great Room, near Beaufort Buildings in the Strand'.[6] Pars' occupation at his brother's school must have been the supervision of students in the same varied subjects as he had himself learned at Shipley's.

Edward Edwards[7] states that Pars also studied at the St Martin's Lane Academy; and a pen and ink sketch[8] showing some of its members includes a head inscribed 'Pars or Parker' which may therefore be a likeness of the artist, and testifies to his being a member of the group which was at the centre of artistic life in London before

[1] A. Dossie, *Memoirs of Agriculture* (London, 1782), vol. III, p. 413.

[2] At the Royal Society of Arts.

[3] See list in Algernon Graves, *Exhibitors at the Society of Artists of Great Britain and the Free Society of Artists* (London, 1907).

[4] Thomas Mortimer, *The Universal Director* (London, 1763), p. 21.

[5] Thomas Jones, *Memoirs*, Walpole Society, vol. XXXII (1946–1948), p. 8.

[6] See *Journal of the Royal Society of Arts*, May 1966, p. 524.

[7] Loc. cit. See also Ephraim Hardcastle, *Wine and Walnuts* (London, 1823), vol. I, pp. 177–178, note.

[8] Datable to the period 1762–1768; in the British Museum.

the foundation of the Royal Academy. Further evidence that Pars was already a fully-fledged artist is provided by a Society of Arts award for History Painting in 1764. The picture in question, *Caractacus before the Emperor Claudius*, was exhibited at the Free Society of Artists (under the patronage of the Society of Arts), and won the 3rd premium in that year. The conditions for the Historical premium were as follows: 'Painting in Oil Colours, Original Historical Pictures; the Subject taken from the British or Irish History; containing not less than three Human Figures as large as Life'.[1] History painting was regarded as the highest branch of Art in the eighteenth century and its exponents were looked upon with particular favour: the premiums in this field, 100 gns., 50 gns., and 20 gns., were far higher than those for any other class of painting.[2] Pars' success must have brought him to the notice of the Society of Dilettanti at the moment at which they were planning the Ionian expedition; and it alone was no doubt a sufficient recommendation of his ability.

But other factors must have determined the choice of the Dilettanti. The Ionian commission was one which obviously required watercolour rather than oil painting for its execution; an easily portable medium suitable for sketching and making finished drawings on the spot, which had been used for such purposes over the past hundred years in England.[3] It is clear from Pars' performance in Asia Minor that the medium was familiar to him; and, indeed, that he had to a great extent mastered it. Although no work has been traced some at least of the portraits mentioned in the catalogues were in watercolour—for example, two 'miniatures'[4] were no doubt in this medium; and 'A Lady, in watercolours' appears in the catalogue of the Free Society's 1761 exhibition (No. 145).[5]

[1] A. Dossie, op. cit., p. 431.

[2] Reynolds (in his Discourses *passim*) gives History painting the most important place and laments his own inaptitude for it (e.g. at the conclusion of Discourse XV, 1790). Benjamin Robert Haydon's recommendations for premiums for painting at the British Institution, proposed in April 1816, show the same preference, as does Haydon's Journal throughout.

[3] For a general survey of the early use of watercolour in England see Iolo A. Williams, *Early English Watercolours* (London, 1952), chaps. I and II.

[4] Society of Artists, 1761, No. 77; and Free Society, 1764, No. 133.

[5] A later portrait (*c.* 1771) in the British Museum, of *Miss Cronin of Killarney*, confirms that Pars used watercolour for such work.

The precedent for the kind of work which the Dilettanti planned to produce had been laid down in 1762 by the publication of the first volume of the *Antiquities of Athens* by James Stuart and Nicholas Revett. Revett had been responsible for the architectural drawings in that work, and his appointment to a similar office in connection with the *Ionian Antiquities* suggests that the Dilettanti, having engaged themselves actively in sponsoring the earlier book, were anxious that the new one should follow it closely in general format.

Certainly, for William Pars the existence of a precedent for what he was about to undertake must have been of enormous importance. Stuart himself had provided the views for the *Antiquities of Athens*: the published volume included six plates after his drawings, together with others from his studies of sculpture. It is reasonable to suppose that Pars looked at these before leaving for the Levant. He probably had access also to the complete series of drawings, in Stuart's possession. Despite the great difference of Pars' temperament from Stuart's, the work of the two artists in these series of views has many similarities, which suggest that Pars consciously took Stuart as his model, and copied his approach.

Stuart's views[1] were executed in body-colour, a medium perhaps more congenial to an architect and decorator than to most English artists. Stuart's preference for it may no doubt be traced to his training under Louis Goupy, a fan-painter who used it extensively;[2] and during his residence in Rome[3] he would have encountered and perhaps copied the common practice among Italian artists of making gouache views of ancient monuments for the tourist market. Marco Ricci's is perhaps the most distinguished name among these men. The brightness and generally hot tonality of body-colour is particularly appropriate to Mediterranean subjects and Stuart uses it with considerable dexterity. He states in his preface[4] that 'The Views were all finished on the spot; and in these, preferring Truth to every other

---

[1] Presented to the Royal Institute of British Architects by the executors of Thomas Howard, 1873.

[2] See Lesley Lawrence, *Stuart and Revett: Their Literary and Architectural Careers*, Journal of the Warburg Institute, 1938, p. 129; and J. T. Smith, *Nollekens and his Times* (London, 1828), vol. I, p. 21.

[3] From 1741 to 1749. See Lesley Lawrence, loc. cit.

[4] *Antiquities of Athens*, vol. I, p. viii.

consideration, I have taken none of the Liberties with which Painters are apt to indulge themselves, from a desire of rendering their representations of Places more agreeable to the Eye and better Pictures. Not an object is here embellished by strokes of Fancy. ... The Figures that are introduced in these views are from Nature, and represent the Dress and Appearance of the present Inhabitants of Athens.'

Although the execution is spontaneous and the subject-matter no doubt accurately rendered, Stuart nevertheless composes each scene with great care. The 'present Inhabitants of Athens' in their Turkish costumes are used repeatedly to introduce movement and colour into a static design. Often, as in the double-page plate which is the frontispiece to the first volume, Classical remains and topography are apparently a mere setting for lively human activity. The drawings represent a combination of factual accuracy and bold decoration which embodies the ideals of the topographical illustrators of the second half of the eighteenth century.

Pars was quickly to move away from Stuart's idiosyncratic influence. His own style is by no means absent from the Ionian drawings. The view of *The Stadium at Laodicea*[1] for example, is lit with an even bland light characteristic of Pars' watercolours throughout his life. The view comprehended by it is wide, its features are small in scale. The incidental variegation of texture, the jumble of rocks, plants and Classical fragments, is rendered in generalised masses worked up with a pen. In the distance sky and hills are rendered in a range of blue-greys which anticipates Pars' later extensive use of monochrome wash.[2] The drawing is given life by the delicate play of muted sunlight across the wide field of vision, brought into prominence by the group of figures in the foreground, which discreetly but decisively punctuates the unsurprising yet satisfactory sweep of the design.[3]

This easy, even expression of a fresh, if not original vision in simple formalised language is Pars' personal note; elsewhere in the series of views the washes of greyish blue-greens, ochre and russet-pink which were to become Pars' characteristic palette are already to

[1] Catalogue No. 22. Plate XVI.
[2] See also the view of *Heraclea* (Catalogue No. 21), which is largely in monochrome.   [3] See note 3, p. xxxiii, below.

be observed. These derive from the early eighteenth-century tradition of watercolour landscape, in which Pars' most significant predecessor was Jonathan Skelton. Skelton, like Pars, died in Rome, and it was in Italy that his style evolved away from the English topographical lessons of men like Lambert and Taverner.[1] The overall development of Pars' mature style follows a similar pattern. But, to a greater or lesser degree, the Ionian drawings, and the Greek ones made during the second half of the same tour, reflect Stuart's influence.

The tonality of the drawings is frequently intensified by means of touches of body-colour, indian ink shading, and, most significantly, gum arabic, which is often used to enrich foreground and occasionally covers the larger part of a drawing like a coat of varnish. In some instances these attempts to give weight to the designs have a perfunctory, disconnected quality (see, for example, the touches of sepia in the *Exterior of the Gymnasium at Troas*).[2] This may well indicate that Pars worked up the drawings later with the requirements of the engraver in mind. Several uncompleted compositions,[3] how-

---

[1] See *The Letters of Jonathan Skelton*, ed. Brinsley Ford, Walpole Society, vol. XXXVI (1956–1958), pp. 23 ff.

[2] Catalogue No. 1. Plate I.

[3] All views of Athens, in the British Museum. Versions of two of them, *The Erechtheum* and *A View of the Acropolis and Temple of Jupiter Olympius*, were presented to the American School of Classical Studies at Athens with the library of John Gennadius in 1926. See Francis R. Walton, *English Archaeological Drawings of the XVIIIth Century*, in Hesperia, vol. XXXI, No. 4 (Oct.–Dec. 1962), pp. 404 ff. The drawings are reproduced there (pls. 120a and 121a). Mr Walton argues that these watercolours are preliminary to the more fully worked out drawings in the British Museum from which the engravings were made (for the *Antiquities of Athens*, vol. II, chap. ii, pl. 1 and vol. III, chap. ii, pl. 1). From this it could be deduced that none of the Dilettanti views now in the British Museum was done on the spot, and that Pars made a whole series of complete studies which were later redrawn for presentation to his employers. Another drawing, an outline copy in pen and ink of Pars' view of *The Arch of Adrian and Temple of Jupiter Olympius* (British Museum, Department of Prints and Drawings), corresponding exactly with the composition and detail of the unfinished British Museum watercolour, and squared up, also suggests this. It is published by Mr Walton, loc. cit., p. 406 and pl. 119a. But the British Museum versions of the three subjects in Athens are evidently drawings done on the spot: none is finished; the *Erectheum* has notes and sketches in the uncompleted sky, and the *View of the Acropolis* bears traces in

ever, show that he generally brought them to a high degree of finish as he went along, apparently completing the figures at an early stage and washing in the sky lastly.

Pars' use of the pen is extensive and an important adjunct to his watercolour. It varies from the bold blocking-in of foreground masses to the most delicate indication of form in distant views. Hatching is frequently employed to suggest the texture and deepen the tonality of trees and stonework. For the most part the pen seems to have been dipped in a grey wash[1] rather than in ink, which is reserved for the darkest areas and foreground only, and usually has the dissonant effect noted above.

Body-colour is used sparingly, but imaginatively, to give a warm haze to distant mountains or clumps of foliage seen in full sunlight.[2] It is also used in the figures, to give them greater importance.

Although Pars' figures rarely play as prominent a role in the composition as do Stuart's, the Ionian drawings show a decided development in this respect from other archaeological topography—for example, the views of Palmyra and Balbec by Giovanni Battista Borra, with which Robert Wood illustrated his accounts of those cities.[3] There, figures, when they appear at all, are inconspicuous,

the architecture of careful preliminary measurement. None of the Gennadion drawings supplies any of the deficiencies of the incomplete versions; all follow exactly the whole composition of their respective originals down to the grouping and detail of the figures—unlikely in a preliminary sketch. Their drawing and colouring are also essentially different from the style of Pars himself. Another set of views in the Gennadion Library, versions of *The Temple of Jupiter Panhellenius in Aegina* (see note 4, p. xxxii, below); *The Temple of Jupiter Nemaeus*; *Heraclea*; *The Stadium at Laodicea*; and *Ruins of the Temple of Apollo Didymaeus* (second view), are published by Mr Walton, loc. cit., pls. 122, 123. The drawing of the *Stadium at Laodicea* is signed by John Thomas Serres (1759–1825) and dated 1781. Mr Walton gives details of the provenance of these drawings and concludes from these and from stylistic evidence that all are by Pars himself, save that signed by Serres. There are, however, strong affinities between the Serres work and the other, unsigned views, which suggest that Serres was probably responsible for all of them. They are, moreover, clearly in a different hand from that of the three Athenian views already discussed.

1 Perhaps a mixture of black ink and water.

2 E.g. in the *Sepulchral Monument at Mylasa* (Catalogue No. 15. Plate X).

3 Published in 1753 and 1757 respectively. Borra was responsible for some additional illustrations in the *Ionian Antiquities*, vol. I, chap. i, pl. 1; chap. iii, pl. 1.

dwarfed by the architecture which is presented in a formally decorative manner belonging to an earlier period: Borra's Turks strike attitudes like actors in a Baroque stage setting.

Even a small-scale group by Pars, such as that in the view of the *Exterior of the Gymnasium at Troas* shows the influence of Stuart. It is a factual record of Turks resting, in the spirit of Stuart's preference for 'Truth to every other consideration'.

The two views of the Gymnasium at Troas[1] were probably among the first to be executed; they are also among the least assured technically, although they do not look back to Stuart as much as some of the more accomplished later ones. They give a fair idea of what Pars was capable of in watercolours at the start of the commission, and help to gauge the extent of his development during the tour. They were probably followed by the *Gymnasium at Ephesus*,[2] in which the travellers are shown in their tent, pitched 'among its ruins'.[3] A pot boils on the fire, watched by Turks; arms, food and other equipment lie near by. Comparison with Borra's work, and with that of Continental topographers in Turkey of a later date,[4] show how new and how specifically English Pars' attitude to topography was. An accurate record of a place included the detail of its inhabitants, passenger or indigenous, shown for their own sake and not as trifling decorative adjuncts. Apart from Stuart, Pars' only predecessor with this preoccupation was Paul Sandby, although figures are treated with this kind of attention in few of Sandby's drawings before the 1760s.[5]

Pars' next view, chronologically, was probably the *Theatre at Miletus*.[6] Here the architectural subject is entirely subordinate to the interest provided by Turks and Europeans boarding the ferry on the Maeander. In spite of his training as a portrait painter, Pars' draughtmanship in the figures is not impeccable; but the group as a

---

[1] Catalogue Nos. 1 and 2. Plates I, II.

[2] Catalogue No. 6. Plate III.   [3] See Chandler's Diary, below, p. 81–2.

[4] E.g. Ignace-Antoine Melling, *Voyage Pittoresque de Constantinople et des Rives du Bosphore* (Paris, 1819); and Luigi Mayer, who contributed to vol. II of the *Ionian Antiquities*, 1797, pls. 56–59.

[5] For discussion of figure painting by Paul and Thomas Sandby see A. P. Oppé, *Sandby Drawings at Windsor* (1947), pp. 12 ff.

[6] Catalogue No. 9. Frontispiece.

whole is organised with gusto, making a very satisfactory integrated movement across the picture from the left. This procession is a development from a group in Stuart's drawing of *An Ionic Temple on the Ilyssus*,[1] and in scale and handling is very reminiscent of Stuart's work, as is the rich colouring of the horses' trappings and Turkish costume which contrasts poetically with the ruins of the Theatre, seen beyond the ferry in pale, dry sunlight against a distant blue peak.

The inclusion in this view of portraits of the tourists themselves may also stem from Stuart, who shows in two drawings a European clothed in a brilliant red Turkish robe and cap, sketching the Theatre of Bacchus[2] and the Erechtheum.[3] These are apparently Stuart himself, and, as an old pencil note under the print of the *Theatre of Bacchus* in the copy of the *Antiquities of Athens* in the British Museum Department of Prints and Drawings states, 'Mr. Revett'.[4] And Stuart's view of the *Arch of the Sergii at Pola* shows three men measuring the top of the arch with a red tape-measure. Similarly, Pars shows Revett measuring the ruins at Mylasa,[5] and at Branchidae, where the ruins of the Temple of Apollo must have been drawn next after the ferry at Miletus.

Of the two large views of this temple,[6] one is a dull composition, in which the uneventful terrain lies between a sky washed-in unconvincingly in stripes and a foreground obtrusively darkened with ink, out of key with the whole. The other, however, exemplifies all the delicacy of drawing and colouring of which Pars was capable. The architecture is stated with precision and conviction, dominating the picture not by emphasis but by careful placing. The heightened tonality of the foreground grass and group of Turks and goats offsets but never outweighs this dominance.

In the two smaller drawings which Pars did at the same site, the rich colour and large scale of Stuart is combined with Pars' own fine

---

[1] Engraved in the *Antiquities of Athens*, vol. I, chap. ii, pl. 1.

[2] *Antiquities of Athens*, vol. II, chap. iii, pl. 1.

[3] Ibid., vol. II, chap. ii, pl. 2.

[4] The engravings make the likenesses clearer, especially since that of Stuart is deprived of the moustache which he wears in the drawing. Pars, Chandler and Revett also wear moustaches in the *Miletus* view.

[5] Catalogue No. 14. Plate VIII. [6] Catalogue Nos. 10 and 11. Plates IV, V.

pen outlines and luminous glazes, giving the studies of fragments, especially that of the pilaster capital on which two Turks sit smoking, the intensity of a gem. The tight compositions are unusual for Pars, and effective in their engraved form as vignettes in the *Ionian Antiquities*.[1]

Another vignette, showing a capital from the Temple of Athene Polias at Priene,[2] is taken from a design which achieves a similar sense of scale, but which is contrastingly open in composition: the capital lies among tamarisk plants in the foreground of an extensive, map-like view of the course of the river Maeander. The design is contained within a circular cartouche of acanthus, tied as a wreath at the top. There are indications in the drawing that it was originally intended to be rectangular. Possibly the curving motif of the tamarisks closing the design at the right suggested the circular form, and the consequent deletion of the straight lines already bounding the drawing on its other three sides.

The device of the acanthus wreath is a conventional one,[3] reminiscent of Pars' exercises in textile design at Shipley's drawing school.[4] It is interesting in showing Pars' concern with the decorative as well as the purely topographical aspect of his illustrations. All these vignettes, in the richness of their designs, above all in the sense of scale which they convey,[5] anticipate the work of later archaeological topographers who were to lay particular stress on the subjective apprehension of grandeur and decay. One of these artists was John Peter Gandy, artist to the Society of Dilettanti's next Greek expedition under William Gell. His views for the *Unedited Antiquities of Attica*[6] and for the revised edition of the *Ionian Antiquities*[7]

[1] Vol. I, chap. iii, headpiece and tailpiece.

[2] Vol. I, chap. ii, tailpiece. Catalogue No. 20. Plate XIV.

[3] Compare for instance the oak-wreath frames used for Wilson's and Gainsborough's landscapes at the Foundling Hospital (1746–1748).

[4] An example in black lead touched with chalk is preserved by the Royal Society of Arts (reproduced in *Journal of the Royal Society of Arts*, May 1966, p. 523).

[5] In this connection it is worth noting that the small headpiece of the *Temple of Bacchus at Teos* (vol. I, chap. i, headpiece) was engraved again, for the 1821 edition of the *Ionian Antiquities* (chap. i, pl. 1), several times the size of the drawing (see Catalogue No. 17).   [6] Published 1817; see chap. viii, pl. 5.

[7] (See note 5, above) chap. iii, headpiece.

are very much in the mood of Pars' smaller studies.[1] John Peter was the brother of Sir John Soane's protégé, Joseph Michael Gandy, whose grandiose visions of Classical architecture are not as far removed as might be supposed from Pars' unexpected vignettes. In particular, Pars' inventive presentation of the two aspects of the pilaster capital foreshadows Gandy's fanciful multiple architectural subjects.

Both Pars and John Peter Gandy were employed not only to make views but also to sketch sculpture and other incidental material.[2] Stuart, as artist to his own expedition, had been responsible for the illustrations of sculpture in the first volume of the *Antiquities of Athens*; Pars supplied a great many of the drawings for the subsequent volumes of that work, both views and details of ornaments. The body of this material consists of drawings of reliefs on the Parthenon and the Theseum at Athens;[3] but some sketches were made in Asia Minor as well. Of these, only two were used in the published volumes of the *Ionian Antiquities*.[4] Others, like those of the Athenian reliefs, found their way into different books. Sir Richard Worsley's *Museum Worsleyanum*[5] made use of several of the Athenian drawings and included *A Basso Relievo in a Floor at Ephesus* engraved after Pars by Skelton, and *The Remains of an Ionick Temple in Asia Minor*, engraved, according to Worsley, 'from a very elegant drawing of the late Mr. Parr'[6] by Fittler.[7] The drawings for both these prints have disappeared, as have those used for an edition of Robert Wood's *Essay on the Original Genius and Writings*

---

[1] Two watercolours by J. P. Gandy, of *Myra* and *A Tomb at Myra*, for the *Unedited Antiquities of Attica*, are in the R.I.B.A. Another, in the collection of R. G. Searight Esq., also appears to be a scene at Myra and bears out the comparison with Pars.

[2] Drawings of bas-reliefs in black lead by J. P. Gandy are in the British Museum (Department of Prints and Drawings). Gandy was also responsible for many purely architectural drawings for Gell's expedition.

[3] See Chandler, *Travels in Greece* (Oxford, 1825), p. 64: 'Besides views and other sculptures, he [Pars] designed one hundred ninety-six feet of bass-relief in the Acropolis.'

[4] Vol. I, headpiece and tailpiece to Introduction.

[5] Published in 1794, with reference to a tour made in 1785–1786.

[6] Undoubtedly a mistake for Pars, whose name appears on the plate.

[7] See Catalogue Nos. 27, 28.

of Homer, published in 1775 with *A Comparative View of the Ancient and Present State of the Troade*. The title page and final page of this volume are embellished with engravings by Bartolozzi of reliefs 'Drawn at Ephesus in 1764 by W. Pars'. Chandler discusses them on p. 76 of the Diary. *The Comparative View* also includes a *View of the Ruined Bridge below the Junction of the two Rivers* (Simois and Scamander), engraved by Major after Pars.[1] Possibly another plate, a *View of the Ancient Bridge below Bornabaschi*,[2] which bears the name of neither engraver nor painter, is also after Pars. The somewhat perfunctory nature of the subjects, similar to that of some of the plates after Pars in the *Museum Worsleyanum*, suggests that in each case Pars' sketches, rather than finished designs, were being used. It is not possible to say how much casual sketching Pars did during the tour, since none that is certainly by Pars has survived.[3] These random engravings, however, testify to the existence of a number of drawings not now among the material related to the Ionian tour which was presented to the British Museum by the Society of Dilettanti in 1799.[4]

Apart from the two drawings used for the first volume of the *Ionian Antiquities*,[5] three unpublished studies of sculpture from Asia Minor remained with the Dilettanti. One is of side and front elevations of an altar mentioned by Chandler;[6] another is a small drawing of a relief showing a man leading a cart drawn by two mules, the mount of which is inscribed, probably by Pars himself, 'AT SCIO'.[7] The third, a finished study of a headless, draped figure, found in the Gymnasium at Ephesus[8] illustrates the technique which Pars evolved for this work and was to use extensively at

[1] Catalogue No. 23.   [2] Catalogue No. 24.

[3] The Victoria and Albert Museum possesses three fantasies which include Classical ruins and Turkish figures; but they are entirely imaginary and even if they could be given with certainty to Pars would not necessarily belong to his Ionian tour. A number of other drawings, which because of their 'Turkish' subjects have been attributed to Pars, are equally doubtful.

[4] Minutes of the Society of Dilettanti, 2nd June 1799. Incidentally, one of the views for the *Antiquities of Athens* is also missing: *The Temple of Jupiter Panhellenius in the Island of Aegina*, engraved by Newton for vol. II, pl. 2. A version of the subject exists in the Gennadion Library. See note 3, p. xxvi, above.

[5] See note 4, p. xxxi, above.   [6] Catalogue No. 8. See below, p. 83.

[7] Catalogue No. 4.   [8] Catalogue No. 7. See below, p. 81.

Athens. The fine pen outlines and discreet hatching of the views occur again here, drawn over a careful note of the forms in reddish-brown wash. There is a scientific precision in this record, combined with a stylish presentation, which fully justifies the Dilettanti Society's choice of artist, but which, once again, is quite unpredictable from the scant remains of Pars' early drawings from the Antique.[1]

The linear clarity and firm modelling of the sculpture studies provided particularly suitable material for engraving. Pars' water-colour views must have required greater modification in being transferred to the metal; for although in terms of his own palette he could achieve considerable richness of effect, even without the use of gum arabic or a high key of colour, the translation into black and white sometimes appreciably alters the whole mood of the design. It is notable that the engraved plates in the *Ionian Antiquities* which reproduce most closely the quality of Pars' originals are those from the intensely-coloured head- and tailpieces discussed above. These were engraved by various artists;[2] for the majority of the full-page plates William Byrne alone was responsible, producing work of high quality in which, for the most part, he compromises between Pars' cool vision and the richer tonal contrasts to which engraved illustration lends itself.[3]

The independent success of Pars' views as watercolours is demonstrated by another series of prints made after them in aquatint by Paul Sandby.[4] In spite of the relative crudeness of the aquatint medium, the sepia monochrome and fine etched outlines of these prints, approaching more closely than the engravings to Pars' own technique, show clearly the extent to which the watercolours succeed simply in terms of composition and the forceful presentation of

[1] The Royal Society of Arts possesses a *Dancing Faun*, in chalk, which won a premium in 1758.

[2] See Catalogue Nos. 12, 13, 17, 19, 20.

[3] N.B. Byrne's 'correction' of the weakly painted sky of *Ruins of the Temple of Apollo Didymaeus*, for vol. I, chap. iii, pl. 2*; and, conversely, Newton's introduction of sunbeams into the view of the *Stadium at Laodicea* (vol. II, pl. 48) in order to clarify Pars' delicate lighting. Compare Chandler's description of weather conditions at Laodicea, below, p. 180–1.

[4] Sandby applied for permission to aquatint Pars' views in 1776 and 1777. See Minutes of the Society of Dilettanti, March 1777. See Lionel Cust, *History of the Society of Dilettanti*, London, 1898, p. 97.

objects. The *Sepulchral Monument at Mylasa*, for example, and the *Temple at Iakli*, are vivid statements, both atmospheric and informative, in which architecture and landscape offset each other and contribute to an immediacy hardly to be found in topographical work before Pars, even including that of Stuart himself.

Stuart, too, must have approved of Pars' work, for in 1777[1] he applied to the Dilettanti for the use of that done in Greece, for a further volume of his *Antiquities of Athens*. It was in this second volume, and two subsequent ones,[2] that the majority of Pars' studies of sculpture appeared: the first comprehensive illustration of the Athenian marbles to be published; certainly the most painstaking survey ever attempted, and of importance as records of works which, by the time Lord Elgin reached them, were already further mutilated.

The marbles of the Parthenon were illustrated again in the *Museum Worsleyanum*[3] and some of Pars' drawings were borrowed for that publication. Three of the plates in this work[4] are of particular interest as they are inscribed: *Drawn and etched by Pars*. The plates are from drawings used in Volume II of the *Antiquities of Athens*; but the style of the etching is freer, with an assurance of needling which suggests that Pars was well acquainted with the medium, although other plates made by him are not recorded.

The Dilettanti themselves maintained their interest in Pars after the Ionian mission was completed. In 1770, the year in which Pars was elected A.R.A.,[5] one of their number, Henry Temple, Second Viscount Palmerston, engaged him to accompany his party on a tour to Germany and Switzerland. Pars produced a large number

[1] Minutes of the Society of Dilettanti, March 1777 (Cust, loc. cit.).

[2] Stuart did not live to complete vol. II which was published in 1788, the year of his death, or 1789. Vol. III, edited by Willey Reveley, appeared in 1795 and vol. IV, published by Josiah Taylor and edited by Joseph Woods, in 1816. [3] See above, p. xxxi.

[4] 'Basso Relievos on the Southern Side [of the Parthenon]', *Museum Worsleyanum*, vol. II.

[5] Pars had been admitted as a student in the drawing-schools of the newly-formed Royal Academy on 5th December 1769. (See Sidney C. Hutchison, *The Royal Academy Schools, 1768–1830*, Walpole Society vol. XXXVIII (1960–1962), pp. 123 ff.) He was elected Associate of the Academy on 27th August 1770 (he had eighteen votes).

of drawings, including many views of the Swiss Alps. Once again, he was confronted with topography almost unknown to English artists, and under the impact of the new experience his style evolved further. The exhibition of some of these Swiss views at the Royal Academy in 1771 was an important event in the history of topography and, indeed, of romantic landscape. Pars' characteristic broad, cool washes of subtle graded tones, and his fine pen outlines, had already appeared in the Ionian work, and in 1770 still anticipated Francis Towne and J. R. Cozens by a decade.

By the time that Towne arrived in Rome, in 1780,[1] Pars had been living there for five years. In 1775, after having travelled with Palmerston in Ireland and executed a number of commissions for him,[2] he was rewarded yet again by the Dilettanti, who granted him a student's pension on which he lived, travelling and drawing all over central Italy until his sudden death in 1782.[3]

The Ionian commission, then, provided Pars not only with a professional engagement which was to be of significance for his future career: it gave him an opportunity to develop technically under conditions demanding at the same time the greatest precision and the greatest facility. There are moments in his work at which one or other of these qualities may be wanting; but the work done in Asia Minor, even more than that done later on in the same tour, in Greece, must be thought of, in the context of Pars' whole career, as to some extent experimental. Its most remarkable achievement was, perhaps, that of deflecting an artist dedicated to figure painting and

[1] See A. P. Oppé, *Francis Towne, Landscape Painter*, Walpole Society, Vol. VIII (1919–1920), pp. 108 ff.

[2] And for other patrons, including Horace Walpole, who gave Pars a letter of introduction to Sir Horace Mann, the British Envoy at Florence, dated 23rd October 1775 (*Letters of Horace Walpole*, ed. Toynbee, vol. IX, p. 269): 'This will be delivered to you by Mr. Pars, a painter who is going to improve himself in Italy. He has already great merit, and has done several things for me, particularly washed drawings of Strawberry [Hill], of which he can talk to you very perfectly. This was his style originally. He executed an excellent volume full of them for Lord Palmerston, one of the Lords of the Admiralty, his protector. He has since taken to oil and portraits . . . He is very modest, sensible, and intelligent, and not mad, or I would not recommend him so strongly . . .'

[3] Pars died in October 1782, after catching cold from standing in water to draw at the Grotto of Neptune at Tivoli. See W. T. Whitley, *Artists and their Friends in England* (London, 1928), vol. II, p. 344, and Jones, *Memoirs*, p. 116.

portraiture into the profession of a successful landscape water-colourist. Thomas Jones, noting Pars' death,[1] referred to the effects of his longstanding engagements to the Dilettanti and, in particular, to Lord Palmerston: 'This habit of life, notwithstanding his affected Protestations to the Contrary, certainly gave him an inward bias in favour of Landscape, though brought up to Portrait—He executed his tinted Drawings after nature, with a taste peculiar to himself—And though, in a fit of Spleen, he would sometimes curse his fate, in being obliged to follow such trifling an Employment; as he called it—it was with the greatest difficulty his Friends could detach him from his favourite Study, and persuade him to apply to Portrait painting—in which line there was now a fair Opening.'

Pars did in fact continue to practise portraiture; Jones goes on: 'He took Our Advice at last, and the success he met with justified our Opinion';[2] and the *Memoirs* contain various references to Pars' activities in this field, and to his executing copies from the Old Masters in Rome and Naples.[3] Dossie's list of *Premiums Bestowed in the class of Polite Arts*, published in the year of Pars' death,[4] gives him as 'History Painter, Rome'; so that until the end of his life Pars maintained his standing as a practising artist in the 'higher branches of the profession', while being able to follow 'such trifling an Employment' as 'tinted drawings after nature', and to develop the 'taste peculiar to himself' to such a degree that he has been remembered for it while his more ambitious work is forgotten.

[1] Jones, *Memoirs*, loc. cit.
[2] See also Walpole's letter, note 2, p. xxxv, above.
[3] Jones, *Memoirs*, pp. 100, 106, 110. See Biography.
[4] A. Dossie, op. cit., p. 149.

CATALOGUE

*of Drawings Executed by William Pars
in Asia Minor*

I

EXTANT DRAWINGS

The order is chronological as far as deducible. All drawings, unless otherwise stated, were presented to the British Museum by the Society of Dilettanti in 1799. Nos. 3, 4, 5, 7, 8 are now in the Department of Greek and Roman Antiquities; the rest are in the Department of Prints and Drawings. Versions or copies of British Museum drawings are mentioned under the number of the original.

1   *Exterior of the Gymnasium at Alexandria Troas*
    Pen and grey ink and watercolour; some brown ink and gum arabic.
       29.4 × 50.8cm.
    Exhibited: ?R.A. 1769 (78); see 2.
    Engr: by William Byrne for *Ionian Antiquities*, vol. II, pl. 52.
       27.3 × 46.6cm.
    —— by Paul Sandby (aquatint) ?1777. 29.1 × 47.8cm.
    Plate I

2   *Interior of the Gymnasium at Alexandria Troas*
    Pen and grey and black ink and watercolour; some gum arabic. 30 ×
       55cm.
    Exhibited: possibly the drawing referred to R.A. 1769 (78); see 1.
    Engr: by William Byrne for *Ionian Antiquities*, vol. II, pl. 53. 26.5 ×
       45.4cm.
    —— by Paul Sandby (aquatint) ?1777. 28.8 × 49.9cm.
    Plate II

3   *Relief*
    Pen and wash and brown ink. 7 × 21.1cm.
    Inscr: on the artist's mount: *AT SIGEUM*; *Pars*.
    Engr: *Ionian Antiquities*, vol. I, p. i (headpiece). 7 × 20.7cm.
    Chandler identifies the subject as being the consignment of infants
       to the tutelary care of a deity (see vol. I, p. iv).

4   *Relief: A man leading a cart drawn by two mules*
    Pen and wash. 3.9 × 7.7cm.
    Inscr: on the artist's mount: *AT SCIO*; and *Pars*.
    Not engraved.

5   *Relief*
Pen and wash. 6.5 × 16.2cm.
Inscr: on the artist's mount: *BY THE BAZAR AT SCIO*; and *Pars*.
Engr: *Ionian Antiquities*, vol. I, p. iv (tailpiece). 6.4 × 16cm.
Chandler identifies the subject as being the death of Semele (see vol.
    I, p. iv).

6   *The Gymnasium at Ephesus*
Pen and black ink and watercolour; some gum arabic. 29.5 × 47.3cm.
Engr: by William Byrne for *Ionian Antiquities*, vol. II, pl. 39.
    25.7 × 45.7cm.
—   by Paul Sandby (aquatint) 1779. 28.1 × 47.6cm.
Plate III

7   *A Trunk in the Gymnasium at Ephesus*
Pen and brown ink and grey and red-brown wash. 35.4 × 23cm.
Inscr: with title; *Pars*; in the border: *8F 2I* (height of the figure).
Not engraved.

8   *An Altar at Ephesus*
Pen and brown ink and grey and red-brown wash. 17.7 × 13.9cm.
Inscr: 1 . . II . . 4 (height of column of altar); on mount: *Altar at
    Ephesus.*
Not engraved.
The drawing shows front and side elevations of the altar.

9   *The Theatre at Miletus*
Pen and grey ink and watercolour; some gum arabic. 29.6 × 47.1cm.
Exhibited: R.A. 1769 (83).
Engr: by James Newton for *Ionian Antiquities*, vol. I, p. 43 (detail
    only). 12.2 × 20.9cm.
—   by Paul Sandby (aquatint) *c.* 1778. 28.3 × 47.1cm.
Frontispiece

10 *Ruins of the Temple of Apollo Didymaeus from the North-East*
Pen and grey and black ink and watercolour; some gouache and gum
    arabic. 29.9 × 46.9cm.
Verso: rubbed over with black lead for transfer to plate. (No evi-
    dence of indentation survives on the drawing.)
Engr: by John Miller for *Ionian Antiquities*, vol. I, chap. iii, pl. 2.
    29.5 × 46.5cm.
—   by Paul Sandby (aquatint) 1779. 28.9 × 47.5cm.
Plate IV

11 *Ruins of the Temple of Apollo Didymaeus; another view*
Pen and black ink and watercolour; some gum arabic. 29.9 × 47.5cm.
Engr: by William Byrne for *Ionian Antiquities*, vol. I, chap. iii, pl.
    2*. 25.6 × 45.4cm.
A version of the subject by J. T. Serres, watercolour, 29.5 × 47cm.,
    is in the Gennadion Library of the American School of Clas-
    sical Studies at Athens.
Plate V

12 *Fragment from the Temple of Apollo Didymaeus*
Pen and grey ink and watercolour; some gum arabic. 13.9 × 21cm.
Inscr: ΑΓΑΘΗ ΤΥΧΗ ΑΠΟΛΛΩΝΟC ΔΙΔΥΜΕΩC
Engr: (in reverse) by George Sherlock and James Mason for *Ionian
    Antiquities*, vol. I, chap. iii (headpiece). 14.3 × 21.1cm.
Plate VI

13 *Capital of a Pilaster from the Temple of Apollo Didymaeus*
Watercolour and gouache; some pen and grey ink; on several small
    pieces of paper stuck together. 18.1 × 21.1cm.
Engr: by William Woollett and James Basire for *Ionian Antiquities*,
    vol. I, chap. iii (tailpiece). 18.1 × 21.1cm.
Collections: George Baker; sale Sotheby 16.6.1825ff. (844) bt.
    Thane. Bears mark of William Esdaile, from whose sale
    acquired by the British Museum, January 1857.
The capital is shown in two views, from the front and side.
Plate VII

14 *An Arch at Mylasa*
Watercolour; some gouache, pen and gum arabic. 29.6 × 47.1cm.
Exhibited: R.A. 1769 (77).
Engr: by William Byrne for *Ionian Antiquities*, vol. II, pl. 22. 26.3 ×
    44.3cm.
— by Paul Sandby (aquatint) 1780. 29 × 47.5cm.
Plate VIII

15 *Sepulchral Monument at Mylasa*
Pen and grey ink and watercolour; some gouache and gum arabic.
    29.7 × 47.1cm.
Engr: by William Byrne for *Ionian Antiquities*, vol. II, pl. 24. 26.5 ×
    45.2cm.
— by Paul Sandby (aquatint) 1777. 28.5 × 47.1cm.
Plate IX

16 *Temple at Iakli*
   Pen and grey ink and watercolour; some brown ink and gum arabic.
      29.9 × 47.5cm.
   Engr: by William Byrne for *Ionian Antiquities*, vol. I, chap. iv, pl. 1.
      26.8 × 46.7cm.
   —   by Paul Sandby (aquatint) 1779. 28.3 × 47.6cm.
   Plate **X**

17 *The Temple of Bacchus at Teos*
   Pen and grey ink and watercolour. 11.3 × 20.6cm.
   Engr: by J. P. Lebas for *Ionian Antiquities*, vol. I, chap. i (headpiece).
      11.3 × 20.5cm.
   —   and much enlarged for new edition of same work, 1821, chap.
      i, pl. 1. 22.3 × 34.5cm.
   Plate **XI**

18 *Ruins of the Temple of Athene Polias at Priene*
   Pen and grey and black ink and watercolour; some gouache. 29.9 ×
      47.2cm.
   Engr: by George Sherlock for *Ionian Antiquities*, vol. I, chap. ii,
      pl. 1. 28.8 × 46.9cm.
   Plate **XII**

19 *Capital from the Temple of Athene Polias at Priene*
   Watercolour, some pen and ink; black lead; gum arabic. 13 × 20.4cm.
   Verso: Sketch of the façade of a building, black lead; inscr: with a
      list, scratched out, and: *9 Inches ye Breadth of ye Letter Press*
      (this may refer to the layout of the *Ionian Antiquities*, where
      the letter-press is about 9¼ ins. wide).
   Engr: by James Mason for *Ionian Antiquities*, vol. I, chap. ii (head-
      piece). 13.3 × 20.6cm.
   Plate **XIII**

20 *Capital from the Temple of Athene Polias at Priene, with the Valley of
   the Maeander*
   Watercolour and gouache; some pen and brown ink; red chalk; gum
      arabic; the sheet of paper extended by a strip at the top. Circular:
      19.7 × 19cm.
   Engr: by Thomas White for *Ionian Antiquities*, vol. I, chap. ii (tail-
      piece). 19.5 × 18.5cm.
   Plate **XIV**

21　*The Lake and Theatre at Heraclea*
Pen and watercolour; some ink and gouache; gum arabic. 29.8 ×
47.4cm.
Engr: by William Byrne for *Ionian Antiquities*, vol. II, pl. 33 (as
Ruins near the Lake of Myüs, or Baffi). 26.1 × 44.8cm.
A version of the subject by J. T. Serres, watercolour, 29.5 × 47.5cm.,
is in the Gennadion Library of the American School of Classical
Studies at Athens.
Plate XV

22　*The Stadium at Laodicea*
Watercolour; some pen and grey and brown ink; gum arabic. 30 ×
47.6cm.
Engr. by James Newton for *Ionian Antiquities*, vol. II, pl. 48. 28.6 ×
47.6cm.
A version of the subject, watercolour, 30.5 × 48cm., signed and
dated *I. T. Serres* 1781, is in the Gennadion Library of the
American School of Classical Studies at Athens.
Plate XVI

II

DRAWINGS NOW KNOWN ONLY FROM ENGRAVINGS

23　*View of the Ruined Bridge below the Junction of the Two Rivers*
Engr: by Thomas Major for Robert Wood's *Essay on the Original
Genius and Writings of Homer: with A Comparative View of the
Ancient and Present State of the Troade*, London, 1775 (opp. p.
324). 15.3 × 19.4cm.
Inscr: with title; *Pars del*; *Major sculp.*

24　*View of the Ancient Bridge below Bornabaschi*
Engr: for Wood's *Essay on . . . Homer*, etc. (opp. p. 326).
Not inscribed. Perhaps, like No. 23 above, by Major after Pars.
Borra contributed to the same work (opp. p. 341, engr. by
Lebas).

25　*Relief near Ephesus*
Engr: by Bartolozzi for Wood's *Essay on . . . Homer*, etc. (title-page
vignette). 8.8 × c. 15cm.
Inscr: *Drawn at Ephesus in 1764 by W. Pars*; *Engrav'd by F.
Bartolozzi.*
The subject is identified by Chandler as being the death of Patroclus.

26 *Relief near Ephesus*
Engr: by Bartolozzi for Wood's *Essay on ... Homer, etc.* (p. 342, tailpiece). 8.8 × *c.* 16.8cm.
Inscr: as No. 25 above.
The subject is identified by Chandler as being the Trojans mourning over the body of Hector.

27 *Bas-relief found at Ephesus*
Engr: by William Skelton for *Museum Worsleyanum*, 1794, vol. I, pl. 20, opp. p. 39. 10.6 × 14.3cm.
Inscr: *A Basso Relievo in a floor at Ephesus*; *Pars delt. Skelton sculpt.*

28 *Ruins of an Ionic Temple*
Engr: by James Fittler for *Museum Worsleyanum*, 1794, vol. II, opp. p. 91. 16.8 × 25.1cm.
Inscr: *The Remains of an Ionick Temple in Asia Minor*; *Pars delin.; Fittler sculp.*

BIOGRAPHY

1742   Born 28th February, the second son of a metal chaser probably of Dutch origin.

1756   At William Shipley's drawing school in the Strand. Society of Arts' 2nd premium for drawings by candidates under 14: a *Head of Laocoön* (in chalks); 4th premium for textile design.

1757   1st premium for an Academy figure, in chalks.

1758   3rd premium for a drawing of the *Dancing Faun* in the Duke of Richmond's Gallery of casts. 1st premium for a composition in wax: *Cattle in a landscape.*

1759   2nd premium for a drawing of Sansovino's *Bacchus* in the Duke of Richmond's Gallery. 1st premium for a *Festoon of Flowers* in wax; 1st premium for (?)textile design by candidates under 18. 4th premium for a view after Nature (*Lambeth Ferry from Millbank*, in ink).

1760   Whole premium for drawing of a horse from life by candidates under 20. A portrait exhibited at the Society of Artists (No. 41). At about this time became a member of the St Martin's Lane Academy.

1761   1st premium for a composition of birds, beasts, etc. or a still life. A miniature exhibited at the Society of Artists (No. 77), and two portraits at the Free Society (Nos. 1, 145, the second 'in water-colours'). Henry Pars master of Shipley's drawing school, assisted by William.

1762   4th premium for a drawing of the human figure from life by candidates under 24. Exhibited four portraits at the Free Society (Nos. 67, 79, 128, 195).

1763   Practising portraiture at the Twisted Pillars, Strand. Two pictures exhibited at the Free Society (Nos. 148, 149).

1764   3rd premium for history painting: *Caractacus before the Emperor Claudius*, exhibited at the Free Society (No. 134).

        May: the Society of Dilettanti resolved to commission Richard Chandler, Nicholas Revett and William Pars to visit and record Classical remains in Asia Minor, according to instructions drawn up by Robert Wood.

        24th June: Sailed from Falmouth, landing at the Dardanelles 25th August.

        11th September: reached Smyrna. Drawing in Asia Minor.

1765   Drawing in Asia Minor.

        20th August: left Smyrna; arrived Athens 31st August, having visited Sunium and Aegina. Drawing in Greece.

1766   Drawing in Greece.

11th June: left Athens for Corinth. Further travelling prevented by illness among the party.

31st August: sailed for England, arriving at Bristol 2nd November.

2nd December: views and drawings of bas-reliefs submitted to the Society of Dilettanti, who resolved that their expectations of the commission were fulfilled.

1767 7th February: engraving of the drawings begun.

1768 Copper plates completed.

1769 May: *Ionian Antiquities* published. Seven of Pars' views of Asia Minor and Greece exhibited at the Royal Academy (Nos. 77–83). Entered R. A. schools 5th December.

1770 View of the Parthenon exhibited at the Royal Academy (No. 138). Pars asked to accompany Lord Palmerston (a member of the Society of Dilettanti) on his tour to Italy, Switzerland, etc.

27th August: elected Associate of the Royal Academy.

1771 Eight views in Switzerland and Luxembourg exhibited at the Royal Academy (Nos. 143–150) together with a *Portrait of a Gentleman* (No. 151). Continued in the service of Lord Palmerston, accompanying him to Ireland, the Lake District, etc.

1772 Two watercolour views in Ireland and the Lake District exhibited at the Royal Academy (Nos. 180, 181); together with *A Philosopher* (No. 179). Employed by Horace Walpole to make drawings of Strawberry Hill.

1773 Two portraits and *A View on the Lake of Como* exhibited at the Royal Academy (Nos. 220–222).

1775 Two portraits exhibited at the Royal Academy (Nos. 215, 216). Copies of various earlier watercolour views executed.

March: appointed to go as a student to Italy under the protection of the Society of Dilettanti. Travelled with the wife of John Smart, miniature painter, with whom he had formed an intimate but ill-defined association, taking a letter of introduction from Horace Walpole to Sir Horace Mann, British Envoy at Florence. Arrived in Rome 21st December.

1776 Portraits of children exhibited at the Royal Academy (Nos. 216, 217). Application by Paul Sandby to the Dilettanti for permission to aquatint Pars' views in Asia Minor and Greece.

27th November: meeting of Pars and Thomas Jones in Rome.

1777 Pars working in and around Rome. Application by Stuart to the Dilettanti for permission to use Pars' drawings in Volume II of the *Antiquities of Athens*.

1778 6th June: death of 'Mrs. Pars'.

1779 Sharing lodgings with Jones in Salvator Rosa's house, Strada Gregoriana, where Mengs died 29th June. Engaged in copying

Guido Reni's *Aurora* in the Palazzo Rospigliosi, the size of the original.

1780 October: in Naples to copy Titian's *Danaë* in the Capodimonte Gallery.

1781 Copies of Pars' views in Asia Minor and Greece executed by John Thomas Serres.

1782 October: death of Pars after a short illness contracted while standing in water to draw at Tivoli.

TRAVELS
IN ASIA MINOR
1764–1765

DEDICATION

TO THE
SOCIETY OF DILETTANTI

My Lords and Gentlemen,

THE relation of a journey into a remote country, performed at your expense, naturally claims the honour of your patronage, on its being submitted to general inspection. Indeed, justice requires that the author should point out the sources of his intelligence; and, if information or amusement result from his undertaking, that the approbation of the public should be referred principally to his employers.

But, besides this motive for addressing you, the author is happy in an opportunity of avowing the pride and pleasure which he feels in having served a Society composed of such illustrious and distinguished personages as the Dilettanti, and in recording one remarkable instance of your munificent attention to letters and the arts.

The countries to which his researches were particularly directed by your committee, have made a most conspicuous figure in history. The changes they have undergone, with their present state and remaining antiquities, were deservedly regarded by them as proper objects of inquiry. Your traveller, on his part, was solicitous, while abroad, to execute to your satisfaction his share in the enterprise, which you so generously supported; and has since been assiduous in rendering the materials confided to him not unworthy of the Society, and of a favourable reception from the curious and learned.

The spirit of discovery which prevails in this nation will ever be reckoned among its most honourable characteristics; and when the various attempts to which it has given rise shall be enumerated, and their produce examined, this, it is presumed, will be found of no inconsiderable value, but will receive its portion of praise, and reflect some lustre on the name of the Society of Dilettanti.

I have the honour to be, with the greatest respect and deference,

My Lords and Gentlemen,
Your most obliged
and most obedient
humble Servant,
RICHARD CHANDLER.

PREFACE

THE following Work cannot perhaps be more suitably prefaced than with the Instructions of the committee of Dilettanti, which the author has the leave of the Society to lay before the public; and with a succinct account of the materials which the tour produced.

"INSTRUCTIONS FOR MR. CHANDLER, MR. REVETT, "AND MR. PARS.

"Whereas the Society of Dilettanti have resolved, that a person or "persons, properly qualified, be sent with sufficient appointments "to some parts of the East, in order to collect informations, and "make observations, relative to the ancient state of those countries, "and to such monuments of antiquity as are still remaining; and the "Society having further resolved, that a sum, not exceeding two "thousand pounds, be appropriated to that purpose, and having "also appointed you to execute their orders on this head; we, the "committee intrusted by the Society with the care and management "of this scheme, have agreed upon the following instructions for "your direction in the discharge of that duty to which you are "appointed.

"1 You are forthwith to embark on board the Anglicana, captain "Stuart, and to proceed to Smyrna, where you will present to consul "Hayes the letters which have been delivered to you, from one of "His Majesty's principal secretaries of state, and from the Turkey "company, and you will consult with Mr. Hayes about the most "effectual method of carrying those instructions into execution.

"2 Our principal object at present is, that, fixing upon Smyrna

"as your headquarters, you do from thence make excursions to the
"several remains of antiquity in that neighbourhood, at such
"different times, and in such manner, as you shall, from the informa-
"tion collected on the spot, judge most safe and convenient, and
"that you do procure the exactest plans and measures possible of the
"buildings you shall find, making accurate drawings of the bass-
"reliefs and ornaments, and taking such views as you shall judge
"proper; copying all the inscriptions you shall meet with, and
"remarking every circumstance which can contribute towards
"giving the best idea of the ancient and present state of those
"places.

"3   As various circumstances, best learnt upon the spot, must
"decide the order in which you shall proceed in the execution of the
"foregoing article, we shall not confine you in that respect, and shall
"only observe in general, that, by a judicious distribution of your
"time and business, you may, with proper diligence, in about twelve
"months, visit every place worth your notice, within eight or ten
"days journey of Smyrna: it may be most advisable to begin with
"such objects as are less distant from that city, and which may give
"you an opportunity of soon transmitting to the Society a specimen
"of your labours. You will be exact in marking distances, and the
"direction in which you travel, by frequently observing your
"watches and pocket compasses, and you will take the variation as
"often as you can.

"4   Though the principal view of the Society, in this scheme, is
"pointed at such discoveries and observations as you shall be able
"to make with regard to the ancient state of those countries, yet it
"is by no means intended to confine you to that province; on the
"contrary, it is expected that you do report to us, for the information
"of the Society, whatever can fall within the notice of curious and
"observing travellers; and, in order to ascertain more fully our
"meaning on this head, we do hereby direct, that from the day of
"your departure from hence, to that of your return, you do, each of
"you, keep a very minute journal of every day's occurrences and
"observations, representing things exactly in the light they strike

"you, in the plainest manner, and without any regard to style or "language, except that of being intelligible; and that you do deliver "the same, with whatever drawings you shall have made, (which are "to be considered as the property of the Society,) to Mr. Hayes, to "be by him transmitted, as often as conveyances shall offer, to us, "under cover to William Russell, esq. secretary to the Levant "company, and you shall receive from us, through the same chan-"nel, such further orders as we shall judge necessary.

"5   Having ordered the sum of two hundred pounds to be "invested in Mr. Chandler's hands, to defray all expenses which may "be incurred till your arrival at Smyrna, we have also ordered a "credit in your favour, to the amount of eight hundred pounds per "annum, to commence from the day of your arrival at that place, "you giving drafts, signed by Mr. Chandler, and Mr. Revett or Mr. "Pars; the whole to be disposed of as follows: viz. one hundred "pounds a year to Mr. Revett; eighty pounds a year to Mr. Pars, "who are each of them to be paid one quarter in advance; the re-"maining six hundred and twenty is to be applied to the common "purposes of the journey, by Mr. Chandler, who is to be treasurer, "paymaster, and accomptant, and may appropriate to his private "use such part of that sum as he shall find necessary, informing us "of his management of the common stock, and transmitting to us "his account from time to time.

"6   And though our entire confidence in your prudence and "discretion leaves us no room to doubt, but that perfect harmony "and good understanding, which is so necessary, as well to your "own happiness, as to the success of the undertaking, will subsist "among you; yet, in order to prevent any possible dispute, which "might arise about different measures, in the course of this expedi-"tion, we expressly declare, that the direction of the whole is "hereby lodged in Mr. Chandler, assisted by Mr. Revett: and though "Mr. Revett and Mr. Pars should protest against any measure pro-"posed by Mr. Chandler, it is our meaning, that any such difference "of opinion should not in the least interrupt or suspend your "operations, but that, at the same time that such persons as dissent

7

"from or disapprove of what is proposed, shall transmit to us their
"reasons for such dissent, they do notwithstanding continue to
"pursue Mr. Chandler's plan, till they receive our further orders for
"their conduct.

"Given under our hands, at the Star and Garter, this seventeenth
"day of May, 1764.

"CHARLEMONT
"ROB. WOOD
"THO. BRAND
"WM. FAUQUIER
"JAMES STUART
"MIDDLESEX
"LE DESPENCER
"J. GRAY
"BESSBOROUGH."[1]

[1] See Appendix A.

PART I

9 June–September 1764

Gravesend — Falmouth — Lisbon — Gibraltar —
Genoa — Leghorn — Cape Matapan — Sigeum —
Eleûs — Tenedos — Alexandria Troas—Colonae —
Yenikoy — Cape Baba — Cape Mastusia — Mytilene —
Chios — Cape Kara-burun — Smyrna.

[Ref. 1825 edition, chaps. I–XXI]

I

WE embarked at Gravesend on the 9th of June, 1764, in the Anglicana, a ship carrying sixteen guns, and thirty-two men, burden about three hundred tons. The commander was captain John Stewart; the price of our passage to Turkey sixty guineas. We had a fair wind; but our pilot, being in liquor, did not sail that evening.

On Whitsunday, early in the morning, we got under way with a brisk gale, and arrived in the Downs about four in the afternoon. The next day we weighed anchor again, and proceeded to Falmouth to complete our cargo. We were detained there from the 17th to the 24th, when we recovered our anchor with some difficulty, and got clear of the harbour. A signal was made for a pilot, but he did not come on board soon enough to be of use.

The wind had been very high while we were in the port of Falmouth, and the weather was still unsettled. Black louring clouds rendered the morning of our departure uncommonly gloomy and awful. After a heavy shower of rain we were becalmed in the mouth of the channel, the water heaving prodigiously, with the surface quite smooth and unbroken. We were carried along by the current, and land soon disappeared. We now encountered foul weather and contrary winds. The ship seemed but a wherry, and was agitated exceedingly by the sea, pitching and rolling, the waves frequently bursting over, and the swell affecting some of our oldest mariners.

On the 3d of July we made the rock of Lisbon. We had then a strong gale, and sailed at the rate of nine knots, or miles, in an hour. We had run one hundred and seventy knots in the last twenty-four hours. We here saw a grampus or whale spouting up water, which, in falling, formed a mist not unlike the smoke from a flash of gunpowder. It blew hard in the night, and the next evening we could discern cape St. Vincent.

As we now approached near to the Mediterranean, some of the sailors had got a strong new rope, and prepared it for ducking such of the crew as were novices in this sea. They were to be let down from the yard-arm, with their hands and feet tied to two bars of wood, placed at convenient distances; but when everything was ready, they all preferred the alternative, which is a small forfeit to be deducted from their pay.

Our passage through the strait of Gibraltar was amusing and delightful beyond imagination. The coast on each side is irregular, adorned with lofty grotesque mountains of various shapes, the majestic tops worn white with rain, and looking as crowned with snow. From one of the narrow valleys a thick smoke arose. The land is of a brown complexion, as sunburnt and barren. On the Spanish shore are many watchtowers, ranging along to a great extent, designed to alarm the country by signals on the appearance of an enemy. We had Spanish and Moorish towns in view, with the rock and fortress of Gibraltar. Sea-birds were flying, and numerous small-craft moving to and fro on every quarter. We had a gentle breeze, and our sails all set, with the current from the western or Atlantic ocean in our favour. In this, the water was agitated and noisy, like a shallow brook running over pebbles; while in the contrary currents, it was smooth and calm as in a mill pond, except where disturbed by albicores, porpoises, and sea-monsters, which sported around us, innumerable. Their burnished sides reflected the rays of the sun, which then shone in a picturesque sky of clear azure, softened by thin fleecy clouds, imparting cheerfulness to the waves, which seemed to smile on us.

Our entry into the Mediterranean is here faintly described, as no words can convey the ideas excited by scenes of so much novelty, grandeur, and beauty. The vast assemblage of bulky monsters, in particular, was beyond measure amazing; some leaping up, as if aiming to divert us; some approaching the ship, as it were to be seen by us, floating together, abreast, and half out of the water. We counted in one company fourteen of the species called by the sailors, *the bottle nose*,[1] each, as we guessed, about twelve feet long. These

---

[1] A genus of whale.

are almost shapeless, looking black and oily, with a large thick fin on the back, no eyes or mouth discernible, the head rounded at the extremity, and so joined with the body, as to render it difficult to distinguish where the one ends or the other begins; but on the upper part is a hole about an inch and a half in diameter, from which, at regular intervals, the log-like being blows out water accompanied with a puff audible at some distance.

To complete this wonderful day, the sun before its setting was exceedingly big, and assumed a variety of fantastic shapes. It was surrounded first with a golden glory, of great extent, and flamed upon the surface of the sea in a long column of fire. The lower half of the orb soon after immerged in the horizon, the other portion remaining very large and red, with half of a smaller orb beneath it, and separate, but in the same direction, the circular rim approaching the line of its diameter. These two by degrees united, and then changed rapidly into different figures, until the resemblance was that of a capacious punch-bowl inverted. The rim of the bottom extending upward, and the body lengthening below, it became a mushroom on a stalk, with a round head. It was the next meta-morphosed into a flaming caldron, of which the lid, rising up, swelled nearly into an orb, and vanished. The other portion put on several uncircular forms, and, after many twinklings and faint glim-merings, slowly disappeared, quite red; leaving the clouds, hanging over the dark rocks on the Barbary shore, finely tinged with a vivid bloody hue...

The Anglicana being freighted for Genoa and Leghorn, we now shaped our course for the former port. We were becalmed, on the 7th of July, near the coast of Spain, off cape de Gatte. We then had heavy showers and hard gales, by which we were driven out of our way, and our masts endangered. Light airs and clear weather fol-lowed; the sky blue, and spread with thin fleecy clouds. We had a view of several Spanish towns, and of St. Philip's castle in the island of Minorca. We found the days lengthen as we advanced northward; and the wind, with a bright sun, very cold, coming from the Alps. We stood for Corsica with a brisk gale and a great swell, which took us on the weather side; the waves distinct, vast, and black, breaking with white tops. In the night it blew hard. We shipped several large seas, and rolled and tossed prodigiously. The gulf of Lyons almost equalled in turbulence the bay of Biscay.

We were becalmed, on the 17th of July, off cape de Melle; and then had a fine gale, and approached Italy at the rate of twelve miles an hour. The pharos of Genoa appeared as a tall pillar, the coast picturesque and mountainous, its slopes covered with white houses, looking from the sea as one continued city . . .

Early the next day we came to an anchor in the port . . .

We were delighted at Genoa with the magnificent churches, the marble palaces, the pieces of excellent sculpture, and the many noble pictures, which adorn so profusely that admired city. But this splendour is contrasted by the general poverty and misery of the people. Beggars pestered us exceedingly; and a great number of persons occurred, variously, and often most shockingly deformed, witnessing early violence; nature, when uncontrolled, rarely failing to be regular, if not beautiful in her productions. One evening we saw a man amuse the populace by performing on a slack rope, which crossed the street; and, among other extraordinary feats, he hung by the neck, swinging, and clapping his hands at intervals.

We tarried at Genoa until the 25th of July, when we weighed anchor and got out of the mole in the night . . . and the next night were becalmed about three leagues from Leghorn . . .

We had been advised to carry with us money, for our journey, in crownpieces of silver, called imperial tallerie, from Leghorn. Mr. Rutherford, an English merchant, accepted our bills on a banker in London; and, on our arrival at Smyrna, we found that we gained more than five per cent, on the money we had imported, not including insurance, freight, and consulage, which, by the Anglicana, would have amounted to about two per cent. and that drawing on Leghorn from Smyrna would be nine and a half per cent. better, according to the then exchange, than drawing directly from Smyrna on London, exclusive of the beforementioned expenses.

We were detained at Leghorn by foul weather, the wind south, with thunder, lightning, and rain; the air thick and hazy. Some ships, which had put to sea, were forced back again. We went daily on shore . . .

II

THEY sailed from Leghorn on 10th August, and after passing the Sicilian coast, were becalmed beyond Malta. On the 19th they continued their voyage and entered the Ægean sea rounding Cape Matapan on the 21st and catching sight of the temple of Cape Sunium on the 23rd.[1] On they sailed sighting Chios, Mytilene, Tenedos and Lemnos until finally on August the 25th,] the sun rising beautifully behind M. Ida, disclosed its numerous tops, and brightened the surface of the sea. We were now entering the Hellespont, with the Troad on our right hand, and on the left the Cherronese, or peninsula of Thrace. About six in the morning we were within Sigeum, and the opposite promontory Mastusia. They are divided by a very narrow strait. We then passed between the two castles erected by Mahomet the Fourth in 1659; that on the European side stands high, the other low; and by each is a town. These structures, with the houses, the graceful minarees or turrets of the mosques, the domes and cypresses, the mountains, islands, and the shining water, formed a view exceedingly delicious. The cocks crowed ashore, and were answered by those in our coops on board, the waves broke on the Asiatic beach with an amusing murmur, and the soft air wafted fragrance.

We now saw a level and extensive plain, the scene, as we conceived, of the battles of the Iliad, with barrows of heroes, and the river Scamander, which had a bank or bar of sand at the mouth. The stream was then inconsiderable, but, we were told, is in winter frequently swollen to a great size, and discolours the sea far without

---

[1] Chandler remarks in a letter to Mr Robert Wood (in the archives of the Society of Dilettanti) dated 25th August 1764 that 'to my inexpressible delight, we had yesterday by the help of our Reflecting Telescope a distant view of the Temple at the Sunian Promontory'.

the promontories. The shore of the Cherronese, as we advanced, was steep, of a dry barren aspect, and contrasted by the Asiatic coast, which rises gently, M. Ida terminating the view. The width of the Hellespont, the smoothness of the water, and the rippling of the current, reminded us of the Thames. Xerxes but slightly degraded it, when he styled it a salt river.

We now approached the inner castles, which were erected by Mahomet the Second, and command a very narrow strait, dividing the two continents. By each is a town;[1] and at that in Asia was hoisted a white flag, near the sea-side, and also a red one with the cross. These belonged to the English and French nations. As we had agreed to land here, the captain, when we were abreast with the Asiatic castle, brought the ship to, and made a signal for a scheick, or wherry to come along side. Our baggage was lowered into it with great expedition, and we quitted the ship, which fired three guns, and sailed away.

After leaving the Anglicana, we had scarcely time to contemplate the savage figures of our boatmen, who had their necks and arms bare, and their faces yellow from the sun, before we reached land. The current carried us below the castle, where we saw on the shore two Turkish women. But what figures! each wrapped in a white sheet, shapeless, and stalking in boots. A company of Turks, assembled on the beach to view the ship, seemed, as it were, a new species of human beings. They were in general large and tall; some with long, comely or venerable beards, of a portly mien and noble presence, to which their high turbans and loose garments, of various lively colours, greatly contributed; adding, besides their majesty, to the apparent bulk of the wearers.

We were received on shore by the English consul, a fat well-looking Jew, who, after bidding us welcome in broken Italian or Lingua Franca, conducted us through the town to his house, in the quarter assigned to that nation. We ascended some stairs into a room, which had a raised floor, covered with a carpet. Round three sides was a low sofa with cushions for leaning. The cooling breeze entered at the wooden lattices of the windows. Their law not permitting the Jews to touch fire on their sabbath, our host was in

[1] Evidently Canakkale on the Asiatic side, Kilitbahir on the European.

distress about our entertainment. However we were soon presented with the customary refreshments, a pipe of lighted tobacco; a spoonful of sweetmeat, put into our mouths; and coffee in a china cup, which was placed in one of filigree work, to prevent it from burning our fingers. The consul then introduced to us a young man, his brother, and his wife and daughter; the latter a girl in a long white vest, with a zone[1] about her middle, her feet naked, her nails dyed red, her hair platted, and hanging down her back. She came to us, and taking the right hand of each separately, kissed and gently moved it to her forehead.

We found some difficulty in complying with the oriental mode of sitting cross-legged, but at dinner it was necessary, the table being only a large low salver, placed on the carpet. A variety of dishes were served up in quick succession, and we were supplied as rapidly with cups of wine. We had no plates, or knives and forks, but used our fingers. The whole repast and the apparatus was antique. It concluded with fruits of wholesome quality and exquisite flavour, figs and melons, such as are peculiar to hot climates, and grapes in large and rich clusters, fresh from the vineyard. The consul ate with us, while his brother waited, with another Jew. When we had finished, we washed, one of our attendants bringing an ewer, a basin and a towel, and pouring water on our hands. We then received each a cup of coffee, and our host, who was much fatigued with the sultry walk to the beach, and afterwards to the governor, to inform him of our arrival, retired with the whole family to sleep, as is the universal practice toward noon, when the heat becomes exceedingly intense.

In the evening we went with the consul to view the town. We found the houses numerous, mostly of wood, and mean, and the streets very narrow. We saw the manufactory of earthen ware, which is considerable; and we supposed the fashion had never altered, the jars and vessels, in general, retaining the old shapes, and being formed, it seems, by ancient models. The situation of the place is low, and subject to epidemical disorders. Besides these, the plague, which commonly visits the inhabitants every year, is remarkably destructive, and seldom fails to make a long stay. The cemeteries are

[1] A girdle.

17

swelled to a great extent round the town, and filled with broken columns, pieces of granite, and marble fragments, fixed as grave-stones; some carved with Turkish characters in relievo, gilded and painted. In the Armenian burying-ground we discovered a long Greek inscription, on a slab of white marble, but not legible. On a rocky eminence, on the side next the Propontis, is a range of windmills.

The town and castle has on the south a river which descends from M. Ida with prodigious violence after snow or rain upon the summits. Its source, as we were told, is seven hours up in the country. A thick wall has been erected, and plane-trees disposed, to keep off the torrent when it overflows, and to protect the buildings from its assaults. At the mouth, like the Scamander, it had then a bar of sand. The bed was wide, stony, and intersected with green thickets; but had water in the cavities, at which many women, with their faces muffled, were busy washing linen, and spreading it on the ground to dry.

This river enables us to ascertain the site of the inner castles, a point of some consequence in the topography of the Hellespont. Its ancient name, as appears from Strabo, was Rhodius, and it entered the sea between Dardanus and Abydos.[1] The remnants of marble, which we saw in the burying grounds about the town, have been removed thither, chiefly from the ruins of these cities, particularly of the latter, which was the most considerable ... On the European side, opposite to the Rhodius, was Cynossema, *The Barrow of Hecuba*, which is still very conspicuous, and within or close by the castle.

We returned, when we had finished our survey, to our lodgings,[2]

[1] Now Koca Ç. and enters the sea at Canakkale.
[2] Chandler writes to Mr Robert Wood (in the archives of the Society of Dilettanti) from Smyrna on 26th September 1764: 'The fire having rendered it difficult to procure lodgings here at any price, we are constrained to live with the consul, but as I believe it contrary to the Intensions of the Committee that we should be a burthen to him or anyone, I have insisted on paying, and agreed with him for a detached Sett of Rooms, and our Diet on reasonable terms. I must do him the justice to say that he shows us every civility in his power.' Later on 2nd November he says, 'In consequence of the fire, we are constrained to continue with the Consul, but we live in his house on such terms and in such a manner as I flatter myself would meet with your approbation, than which nothing can afford me greater pleasure and satisfaction.'

where we supped cross-legged, about sunset. Soon after, when it was dark, three coverlets, richly embroidered, were taken from a press in the room which we occupied, and delivered one to each of us; the carpet or sofa and a cushion serving, with this addition, instead of a bed. A lamp was left burning on a shelf, and the consul retired to his family, which lay, in the same manner, in an adjoining apartment. We pulled off our coats and shoes, and expected to be much refreshed by sleeping on shore. We had not been apprised of a nightly plague, that of bugs, which haunts the place, or perhaps rather the houses of the Jews. Two of us could not obtain rest for a moment, but waited the approach of dawn with a degree of impatience equalled only by our bodily sufferings, which cannot be described.

III

WE had agreed in the evening to visit some neighbouring places on the continent, with the principal islands near the mouth of the Hellespont. Early in the morning the consul asked for money to purchase provisions, which, with other necessaries, were put into a scheick or wherry. He embarked with us, between the hours of eight and nine by our watches. We had six Turks, who rowed; a janizary, and a Jew servant. The two latter, with the consul, sate cross-legged before us on a small carpet; as the rais or master of the boat did behind, steering with the handle of the helm over his shoulder.

We soon crossed the Hellespont, and coasting by the European shore, saw several solitary kingfishers, with young partridges, among vast single rocks. The winter torrents had worn deep gullies; but the courses were dry, except a stream, which we were informed turns a mill. A narrow valley or two was green with the cotton plant and with vines, or sowed with grain.

After passing the mouth of a port or bay called anciently Cœlos[1] we landed, about eleven, on the cherronese or peninsula of Thrace, near the first European castle, within the entrance of the Hellespont, and ascended to the miserable cottage of a poor Jew in the town. Here a mat was spread on the mud floor of a room by the seaside, and the eatables we had provided were placed on it. The noontide heat at this place was excessive. The consul retired, as usual, to sleep; while we also rested, or were amused with the prospect from the window. Beneath us was the shining canal, with cape Mastusia on the right hand; and opposite, the Asiatic town and castle, with the

---

[1] This must be the little bay at the extremity of the peninsula which was called Morto Bay. Chandler would appear to be mistaken in thinking this Coelus, which is recorded by Mela as being the site of a naval battle, presumably the battle of Cynossema in 411 B.C. which took place further north.

noble plain divided by the Scamander; and the barrows mentioned before, two standing by each other not far from the shore, within Sigeum, and one more remote.

The ancient name of this town, which is exceedingly mean and wretched, was Eleûs. The streets or lanes are narrow and intricate. It is on the north side of the castle,[1] and ranges along the brink of a precipice . . .

The Turks, after we were landed, had rowed the wherry round Mastusia, and waited for us without the point. [After refreshing themselves in the Governor's garden they set out to rejoin the boat, by the castle-wall where] we saw a large Corinthian capital; and an altar with festoons, made hollow, and used as a mortar for bruising corn. Near the other end of the town is a bare barrow. By this was formerly the sacred portion of Protesilaus[2] and his temple, to which perhaps the marble fragments have belonged. He was one of the leaders in the Trojan expedition, and was killed by Hector. Afterwards he was worshipped as a hero, and reputed the patron or tutelar deity of Eleûs.

On our arrival at the wherry, which was behind the castle, we found our Turks sitting on the ground, where they had dined, chiefly on ripe fruits, with ordinary bread . . . We had intended to visit Lemnos, and the principal places in that quarter; but the wind proving contrary, we now steered for Tenedos . . .

The island Tenedos is chiefly rock, but fertile. It was anciently reckoned about eighty stadia, or ten miles in circumference, and from Sigeum twelve miles and a half. Its position, thus near the mouth of the Hellespont, has given it importance in all ages; vessels bound toward Constantinople finding shelter in its port, or safe anchorage in the road, during the etesian or contrary winds, and in foul weather. The emperor Justinian erected a magazine to receive the cargoes of the corn ships from Alexandria, when detained there. This was a lofty building, two hundred and eighty feet long, and ninety broad. The voyage from Egypt was rendered less precarious, and the grain preserved until it could be transported to the capital. Afterwards, during the troubles of the Greek empire, Tenedos

[1] An old Turkish fort.
[2] A conspicuous tumulus is still called the Tomb of Protesilaus, see Schliemann, *Troja*, pp. 254–262.

experienced a variety of fortune. The pirates, which infested these seas, made it for many years their place of rendezvous; and Othman seized it in 1302, procured vessels, and from thence subdued the other islands of the Archipelago.

The port of Tenedos has been enclosed in a mole, of which no part now appears above water, but loose stones are piled on the foundations to break the waves. The basin is encompassed by a ridge of the mountain. On the south side is a row of windmills and a small fort; and on the opposite a castle by the shore. This was taken in the year 1656 by the Venetians in four days, but soon after abandoned as not tenable. The houses, which are numerous, stand at the foot, or on the slope, of an acclivity; with a flat between them, and the sea, formed by weeds and slime from the water, and by soil washed down from above. They reckon six hundred Turkish families and three hundred Greek. The church belonging to the latter is decent.

We found here but few remains of antiquity worthy notice. We perceived on our landing a large and entire sarcophagus, or stone coffin, serving as a fountain, the top-stone or lid being perforated to admit a current of water, which supplies the vent below; and on one side is an inscription . . .[1] Near this was part of a fluted column converted into a mortar for bruising corn; and in a shop was a remnant of tessellated pavement then recently discovered. In the streets, the walls, and burying-grounds, were pieces of marble, and fragments of pillars, with a few inscriptions . . .[2]

We were lodged, much to our satisfaction, in a large room, with a raised floor matted, on which we slept in our clothes, in company with two Jews and several Greeks; a cool breeze entering all night at the latticed windows, and sweetening our repose.

In these countries, on account of the heat, it is usual to rise with the dawn. About daybreak we received from the French consul, a Greek with a respectable beard, a present of grapes, the clusters large and rich, with other fruits, all fresh gathered. We had, besides, bread and coffee for breakfast, and good wines, particularly one sort, of an exquisite flavour, called Muscadel. The island is deservedly famous for the species of vine which produces this delicious liquor.

[1] *Inscriptiones Antiquae*, pp. 3, 4. [C]. *CIG*, 2, p. 875, no. 3583.
[2] Ibid. [C]. *CIG*, 2, pp. 185, 877, nos. 2165, 3590.

IV

AFTER some delay we got on board our wherry, and leaving the port of Tenedos, coasted, with the island on our right hand. We soon passed a creek, which is frequented by small-craft during the vintage, and has near it a solitary church, with a fountain or spring of excellent water, and at some distance a quarry of stone or marble. The gullies and the slopes of the hills were green with vines. We doubled a craggy point, and saw some cliffs inhabited by wild pigeons; with some partridges; a few cattle; and a church, by which, we were told, is a water noted for its purgative qualities. We landed about ten on a fair beach, having gone almost half round the island.

We were now near the building which we had purposed to examine on the north of the island. It proved a small arched room, the masonry ancient, underneath a mean ruined church. You descend to it by a few steps, with a light. The floor was covered with water. Near it was a figtree or two, and a fountain, with an inscription, in modern Greek characters, fixed in the wall.

The reader, as we proceed, will find frequent mention of fountains. Their number is owing to the nature of the country and of the climate. The soil, parched and thirsty, demands moisture to aid vegetation. The verdure, shade, and coolness, its agreeable attendants, are rendered highly grateful to the people by a cloudless sun and inflamed atmosphere. Hence they occur not only in the towns and villages, but in the fields and gardens, and by the sides of the roads and of the beaten tracks on the mountains. Many of them are the useful donations of humane persons while living; or have been bequeathed as legacies on their decease. The Turks esteem the erecting of them as meritorious, and seldom go away, after performing their ablutions or drinking, without gratefully blessing the name and memory of the founder.

The method of obtaining the necessary supplies of water used by the ancients still prevails. It is by conveying the fluid from the springs or sources, which are sometimes very remote, in earthen pipes or paved channels, carried over the gaps and breaks in the way on arches. When arrived at the destined spot, it is received by a cistern with a vent; and the waste current passes below from another cistern, often an ancient sarcophagus or coffin. It is common to find a cup of tin or iron hanging near by a chain; or a wooden scoop with a handle, placed in a niche in the wall. The front is of stone or marble; and in some, painted and decorated with gilding, and with an inscription in Turkish characters in relievo.

The women resort to the fountains by their houses, each with a large two-handled earthen jar on their back, or thrown over the shoulder, for water. They assemble at one without the village or town, if no river be near, to wash their linen, which is afterwards spread on the ground or bushes to dry. To these also the Turks and Greeks frequently repair for refreshment; especially the latter on their festivals, when whole families are seen sitting on the grass, and enjoying their early or evening repast, beneath the trees, by the side of a rill . . .

We agreed to let the heat of noon be passed before we proceeded on our voyage. A carpet was spread for us under a shady holme [oak], and a fire kindled at some distance. We now received each a lighted pipe and a dish of coffee. A kettle was then filled with water, and some fowls, which we had provided, made ready to be boiled. The French consul, who had joined us, undertook to furnish grapes . . .

We dined and slept in the shade; and soon after, the French consul took leave of us. About two in the afternoon we sailed with a brisk gale, steering for Eski-Stamboul, anciently called Troas and Alexandria Troas. The distance of this city from Tenedos was reckoned forty stadia or five miles. Some of its ruins are in view, standing on an eminence; the uneven summits of mount Ida covered with trees rising beautifully behind.

V

O N the way from Tenedos we were amused by vast caravans or companies of cranes, passing high in the air from Thrace, to winter, as we supposed, in Egypt. We admired the number and variety of the squadrons, their extent, orderly array, and apparently good discipline. About a quarter after three we landed near the ancient port of Troas.

We immediately began a cursory survey of this deserted place; ascending to the principal ruin, which is at some distance from the shore. The whole site was overspread with stones and rubbish intermingled with stubble, plantations of cotton and of Turkey wheat, plats of long dry grass, thickets and trees, chiefly the species of low oak, which produces valanea, or the large acorns the husks of which are exported for tanning hides. A solemn silence prevailed, and we saw nothing alive but a fox and some partridges. In the meantime, the Turks, who were left in the wherry, removed about three miles lower down, towards the promontory Lectos,[1] where the beach afforded a station less exposed to the wind, and more secure.

The evening coming on, we were advised to retire to our boat. By the way we saw a drove of camels feeding. We came to a shed, formed with boughs round a tree, to shelter the flocks and herds from the sun at noon; and under it was a peasant, who had an ass laden, besides other articles, with a goatskin containing sour curds, on which, and some brown bread, our Turks made their evening meal. A goatskin, with the hair on, served likewise for a bucket. It was distended by a piece of wood, to which a rope was fastened. He drew for us water from a well not far off, and promised to bring us milk and a kid the next day. We found our cook, a Jew, busy by the seaside preparing supper; his tin kettle boiling over a fire in the open air.

[1] Cape Baba.

The beauty of the evening in this country surpasses all description. The sky now glowed with the rich tints of the setting sun, which, skirting the western horizon, raised, as it were, up to our view the distant summits of the European mountains. We saw the cone of Athos distinctly ... This top is so lofty, that the sun rising is beheld on it three hours sooner than by the inhabitants of the seacoast.[1] The shadow of the mountain at the solstice reached into the agora or *market-place* of Myrina, a town in Lemnos, which island is distant eighty-seven miles eastward ...[2]

We had here no choice, but were forced to pass the night on the beach which was sandy. The Turks constructed a half-tent for us near our boat with the oars and sail. We now discovered that we had neglected to procure wine and candles at Tenedos. We did not, however, remain in the dark. An extemporary lamp supplied one omission. It was a cotton-wick swimming in oil, on a bit of cork in a drinking-glass, suspended by a string. By this light, the Turks, sitting before us on the ground, cross-legged, endeavoured to amuse us, by teaching us the numbers in their language, or by learning them in English. Some desired us to distinguish each by his name, *Mahmet, Selim, Mustapha* and the like. They were liberal of their tobacco, filling their pipes from their bags, lighting and presenting them to us, as often as they saw us unprovided. Our janizary, who was called Baructer Aga, played on a Turkish instrument like a guitar. Some accompanied him with their voices, singing loud. Their favourite ballad contained the praises of Stamboul or Constantinople. Two, and sometimes three or four, danced together, keeping time to a lively tune, until they were almost breathless. These extraordinary exertions were followed with a demand of bac-shish, *a reward* or *present*; which term, from its frequent use, was already become very familiar to us. We were fatigued by our rough hot walk among the ruins, and growing weary of our savages, gladly lay down to rest under the half-tent. The Turks slept by us, upon the ground, with their arms ready in case of an alarm, except two who had charge of the boat. The janizary, who watched sate smoking cross-legged by the fire. The stars shone in a clear blue sky, shedding a calm serene

[1] Strabo, *Frag.*, 6.33. [C].
[2] Pliny, *Nat. Hist.*, IV.xii.73. [C].

light; the jackals howled in vast packs, approaching near us, or on mount Ida; and the waves beat gently on the shore in regular succession . . .

[They rose at dawn, ready dressed, and set out for the great ruin at Troas.]

VI

Alexander the Great instead of marking his progress by devastations, widely provided more lasting and honourable monuments of his passage through the countries which he subdued; causing cities and temples to be erected, and forming plans for their improvement and future prosperity. As his stay was commonly short, the execution of his noble designs was committed to the governors, whom he appointed; men of grand ideas, fitted to serve so magnificent a master. Alexandria Troas was one of eighteen cities which bore his name.

This city was begun by Antigonus, and from him first called Antigonia; but Lysimachus, to whom as a successor of Alexander, it devolved, changed the appellation in honour of the deceased king. In the war with Antiochus it was eminent for its fidelity to the Romans, who conferred on it the same privileges as the cities of Italy enjoyed. Under Augustus, it received a Roman colony, and increased. It was then the only considerable place between Sigeum and Lectos, and was inferior to no city of its name, but Alexandria in Egypt.

Alexandria Troas[1] was seated on a hill, sloping toward the sea, and divided from M. Ida by a deep valley. On each side is an extensive plain, with water-courses. The founders, it is probable, were aware, that, like Tenedos, it would derive many advantages from its situation on the coast, near the mouth of the Hellespont.

The port of Troas, by which we landed, has a hill rising round it in a semicircle, and covered with rubbish. Many small granite pillars are standing, half buried, and much corroded by the spray. It is likely the vessels were fastened to them by ropes. A sand-bank, at the entrance, had cut off the communication with the sea, and the smaller

[1] Now Eski Istanbul. For description of site and plan see W. Leaf, *Strabo on the Troad*, pp. 233–240.

basin was dry. The larger had water, but apparently shallow. Its margin was incrusted with spontaneous salt. Both were artificial, and intended for small-craft and galleys; ships of burden anchoring in the road without the mole.

The city wall is standing, except toward the vineyard, but with gaps, and the battlements ruined. It was thick and solid, had square towers at regular distances, and was several miles in circumference. Besides houses, it has enclosed many magnificent structures; but now appears as the boundary of a forest or neglected park. A map belonging to Mr. Wood, and made, as we supposed, by a Frenchman, in 1726, served us as a guide. The author, it is imagined, believed, as other travellers had done, that this was the site of Troy, or of a more recent city named Ilium, instead of Alexandria Troas.[1]

Confusion cannot easily be described. Above the shore is a hollow, overgrown with trees, near which Pococke saw remains of a stadium or place for races, sunk in the ground; and higher up is the vaulted substruction or basement of a large temple.[2] We were told this had been lately a lurking-place of banditti; who often lay concealed here, their horses tied in rows to wooden pegs, of which, many then remained in the wall. It now swarmed with bats, much bigger in size than the English, which, on our entering, flitted about innumerable; and settling, when tired, blackened the roof. Near it is a souterrain; and, at some distance, vestiges of a theatre and of an odeum, or music theatre. These edifices were toward the centre of the city. The semicircular sweep, on which their seats ranged, is formed in the hill, with the ends vaulted. Among the rubbish, which is of great extent, are a few scraps of marble and of sculpture, with many small granite pillars.

The principal ruin, which is that seen afar by mariners, commands a view of the islands Tenedos and Lemnos; and, on one side, of the plain to the Hellespont, and of the mountains in Europe. Before it is a gentle descent, woody, with inequalities, to the sea distant by computation about three miles. It was a very ample building, and,

[1] For Robert Wood's book on the Troad see Appendix A, p. 229.

[2] More likely of some other fabric, it bearing no resemblance to the basement of the temple [R]. Correct. The temple lies further to the south-east and above the theatre. The vaulted substructure seen by Pococke above the stadium must have been the baths.

as we supposed, once the gymnasium,[1] where the youth were instructed in learning and in the exercises. It consists of three open massive arches, towering amid walls, and a vast heap of huge materials. They are constructed with a species of stone, which is full of petrified cockle-shells, and of cavities, like honeycomb ... The piers have capitals and mouldings of white marble, and the whole fabric appears to have been incrusted. Some remnants of the earthern spouts or pipes are visible. A view of it, which belonged to Mr Wood, has been lately published. On one side is a ruin of brick; and behind, without the city wall, are sepulchres. One of these is of the masonry called *reticulated*, or *netted*.

A city distinguished and flourishing by Roman favour, would not be tardy in paying the tribute of adulation to its benefactors. The peasant shewed me a marble pedestal inscribed in Latin, the characters large, plain, and well-formed. We found, near this, two other pedestals, one above half buried in rubbish; but the Turks cleared the front with their sabres to the eighth line. All three were alike, and had the same inscription, except some slight variations. They had been erected by different cities in honour of Caius Antonius Rufus, flamen or high-priest of the god Julius and of the god Augustus ... We made diligent search for inscriptions, but discovered, besides the abovementioned, only a small fragment of a pedestal, on which the name of Hadrian occurs.

An aqueduct begins behind the city, not far from the sepulchres, and is seen descending and crossing the country on the side next the Hellespont, extending several miles. The piers, which we measured, are five feet nine inches wide; three feet and two inches thick: the void between them, twelve feet and four inches. The arches are all broken.

The history of this noble and once useful structure affords an illustrious instance of imperial and private munificence. An Athenian, Tiberius Claudius Atticus Herodes, presided over the free cities of Asia. Seeing Troas destitute of commodious baths, and of water, except such as was procured from muddy wells or reservoirs made to

[1] This building is not a gymnasium but baths, although on a different plan from the Roman type, and the aqueduct has been found to lead straight to them. See Plates I and II.

receive rain, he wrote to the emperor Hadrian not to suffer an ancient and maritime city to be destroyed by drought, but to bestow on it three hundred myriads of drachms for water, especially as he had given far greater sums even to villages. Hadrian readily complied, and appointed him overseer of the building. The expense exceeded seven hundred myriads,[1] and it was represented to the emperor as a grievance, that the tribute from five hundred cities had been lavished on one in an aqueduct. Herodes, in reply, begged him not to be displeased, that, having gone beyond his estimate, he had presented the overplus of the sum to his son, and he to the city . . .

The Christian religion was planted early at Troas. In the beginning of the fifth century, the bishop, Silvanus, was required to deliver a vessel from a demon, which was believed to detain it, as it could not be launched. It was intended for transporting large columns, and was of great size. Going down to the beach, he prayed, and taking hold of a rope, called on the multitude to assist, when the ship readily obeyed him, and hurried into the sea.[2] But the churches have been so long demolished, that the traces of them are uncertain.

The desolation of this place was begun, and probably completed, before the extinction of the Greek empire. Many houses and public structures at Constantinople have since been raised with its materials. We found only a few inconsiderable remnants of white marble by the principal ruin, where formerly was a vast heap. Some pieces in the water by the port, and two large granite columns, were perhaps removed to the shore to be ready for embarkation. The magazine is yet far from being exhausted. The name Troas was not become obsolete in the year 1389.

[1] 500 myriads amounted to £161,458 6s. 8d. in 1764. [C]
[2] Sozomen, vii.i. [C]

VII

WE were employed at Troas chiefly in taking a plan and two
views of the principal ruin.[1] We dined under a spreading tree
before the arcade; and on the second day had just resumed
our labour, when we were almost reduced to fly with precipitation.
One of the Turks, coming to us, emptied the ashes from his pipe,
and a spark of fire fell unobserved in the grass, which was long,
parched by the sun, and inflammable like tinder. A brisk wind soon
kindled a blaze, which withered in an instant the leaves of the
bushes and trees in its way, seized the branches and roots, and
devoured all before it with prodigious crackling and noise, and with
a thick smoke, leaving the ground black, and the stones hot. We
were much alarmed, as a general conflagration of the country
seemed likely to ensue. The Turks with their sabres cut down boughs
and we all begun buffetting the flames, which were at length subdued;
the ruins somewhat retarding their progress, and enabling us to com-
bat them more effectually. The struggle lasted about an hour, and a
considerable tract of ground was laid waste. .. The sun shone
exceedingly hot, and we were all covered with smoke and smut.

In the evening we returned to the vineyard, and found our cook,
with two or three of the Turks, busy in a hovel, roasting a kid on a
wooden spit or stake. We sate down with our Jew and janizary, and
the flesh proved excellent. Our table was a mat on the ground,
beneath a spreading vine. Our men formed a like group at a little
distance from us. Soon after we fell asleep, and the starry heaven was
our canopy.

Early in the morning the ass was loaded again. We passed the day
at the ruins, with some discontent from keen appetites not duly
gratified. The wine and provisions, which we expected from Tenedos,

[1] Plates I and II.

did not arrive in time; and the peasant, whom we had sent to a village named Chemali, could procure only a couple of fowls, with some eggs, which he broke in bringing. This accident compelled our Jews to fast, their law not permitting them to eat of what we had, and which supplied us with a very scanty meal . . .

When we lay by the seaside, we had observed a fire blazing on an eminence before us, or toward Lectos. We were told it was a signal for a boat designed to be laden clandestinely with corn, the exportation of which is prohibited under severe penalties. One of the men had approached and viewed us with a degree of attention which we disliked, the people of this district bearing a very bad character. At midnight the aga of Chemali, who was concerned in this contraband business, had come prancing along the shore with two Turks, armed, on long-tailed horses, to inquire who we were. The janizary entertained him apart by the fire with a pipe and coffee, after which he mounted and gallopped back, leaving us an invitation to see an old building at his village. Our host informed us, that by the way were hot baths worthy our notice, and that Chemali was distant about two hours. This mode of computing by time prevails universally in these countries, and is taken from the caravans, which move an uniform pace, about three or four miles in an hour.

In the morning, after breakfasting on grapes, figs, white honey in the comb, and coffee, we set out in a body for the village, a Turk or two remaining with the boat, and our janizary, whose right eye was inflamed, at the vineyard. We entered a narrow track worn by camels, the sand deep and loose; and saw several of these animals single, lying down, feeding with their burdens on their backs, or moving pensively in a long train, the leader mounted on a low ass; and also a flock of goats, and a few sheep and oxen. We came to a river, which winds from the deep valley behind Troas, and has been mentioned before. The stream here was now shallow, but abounded in small fish. It had overflowed nearer the sea, and formed a little marsh.

The hot spring rises in the slope of the hill of Troas, about four miles from the shore . . . The bed resembles rusty iron in colour, and the edges were incrusted with white salt. After running a few paces, it enters a basin about nine feet square, within a mean hovel roofed with boughs. This is the bath appropriated to women. In a gully there, Fahrenheit's thermometer rose to one hundred and thirteen. The current passing from hence, unseen, is admitted by channels into another basin ... It was before in the air and shade at eighty-two. The water has the colour of whey; the taste is brackish, and this quality it communicates to the river below. We supposed it to be strongly impregnated by iron ore. One of the basins was choked up in 1610; and not long ago, we were told, the spring had entirely disappeared for nine years, after an earthquake. It is reckoned very efficacious in the rheumatism, the leprosy, and all cutaneous disorders. They first scour the skin by rolling in the bed of the river, which is a fine sand, and full of holes or cavities, like graves, made for the body. By each inclosure is a shed, where they sleep after bathing. In the court-wall of one is inserted the trunk of a large statue; and higher on the hill are the ruins and vestiges of the ancient sepulchres of Troas.

We crossed the river again, and in fifteen minutes entered among the roots[1] of mount Ida, which hitherto had been on our right hand, but now faced us ...

The mosque, which we had taken this long walk to examine, instead of proving, as we had hoped, some ancient building or temple, contained nothing to reward our labour. The portico, under which we stopped, is supported by broken columns, and in the walls are marble fragments. The door is carved with Greek characters so exceedingly complicated, that I could neither copy nor decipher them. We suppose it had formerly been a church. In the court was a plain chair of marble, almost entire; and under the post of a shed, a pedestal, with a moulding cut along one side, and an inscription in Latin, which shews it once belonged to a statue of Nero, nephew of the emperor Tiberius ...

Colonae,[2] *the Hills*, was a town on the continent opposite to Tenedos. Antigonus removed the inhabitants to Troas, but the place was not entirely abandoned. It seems to have recovered under the Romans, and has survived the new city; still, as may be collected from the site and marbles, lingering on in the Turkish village Chemali.

[1] Foothills. [2] Now perhaps Kösederesi, 3 miles south of Alexandria Troas.

1   Exterior of the Gymnasium at Alexandria Troas. (Cat. 1)

II   Interior of the Gymnasium at Alexandria Troas. (Cat. 2)

VIII

From Chemali we returned to the vineyard, purposing to embark as soon as possible; the danger from banditti increasing with our stay in these parts, which had already produced a general uneasiness ... We hastened to get on board, coasted by Troas in the dusk, and, after rowing about five miles, landed, and slept on the beach. The solemn night was rendered yet more awful by the melancholy howlings of numerous jackals, in packs, hunting, as we supposed, their prey.

We embarked again three hours before the break of day, and rowed by a bold rocky shore until near seven. We then landed at Enekioi,[1] or *New Town*, now a Greek village, so miserable, as scarcely to furnish grapes, wine, eggs, and oil to fry them, sufficient for our breakfast. It stands very high, and has been more considerable. By the church door is a Latin sepulchral inscription; and Pliny mentions a town in the Troad, called Nea, or *New Town*, which perhaps was on this spot. There was an image of Minerva, on which no rain ever fell; and it was said that sacrifices left there did not putrefy.

We left Enekioi, and landed again about mid-day on the beach without the Hellespont, not far from the Sigean promontory, and ascended by a steep track to Giaurkioi, a Greek village, once the city Sigeum,[2] high above the sea, and now resembling Enekioi in wretchedness as well as in situation. We were here accommodated with a small apartment in one of the cottages; but it required caution to avoid falling through the floor. The family to which it belonged was as poor as oppressed. The thin-voiced women scolding and howling in the court, we inquired the reason, and were told they had paid a piaster for the privilege of keeping a hog; that the Turk, who had collected this money for the aga, demanded ten pereaus as his

---

[1] Now Yenıköy.   [2] Sigeum lies at the now ruined village of Yenişehir.

fee; that they were unable or unwilling to gratify him, and he was carrying the son to prison.

The high hill of Giaurkioi was the acropolis or citadel of Sigeum; and a mean church on the brow, toward mount Ida, occupies the site of the Atheneum, or temple of Minerva, of which the scattered marbles by it are remains. The famous Sigean inscription lies on the right hand as you enter it; and on the left is part of a pedestal of fine white marble; each serving as a seat. The latter is carved in basso relievo.[1] The Greeks were accustomed to consign their infants to the tutelar care of some deity; the midwife, dressed in white, with her feet bare, carrying the child to be presented on the fifth day after its birth. The Romans had the same superstition; and Caligula is on record as having placed his daughter Livia Drusilla in the lap of Minerva.[2] That usage is the subject of the sculpture. The goddess is sitting, as described by Homer, in her temple in Troy. A little chest, borne by one of the figures, may be supposed to contain incense, of the offerings which accompanied this ceremony. A marble, once reposited in the precincts of the temple, and now preserved in the library of Trinity College in Cambridge, was found within the same building.[3] It contains a decree, made by the Sigeans, two hundred and seventy-eight years before the Christian era, in honour of king Antiochus; and enacts, among other articles, the erecting in the temple a golden statue of him on horseback, on a pedestal of white marble; with an inscription commemorating his religious regard for the temple, and stiling him the saviour of the people. This, in the year 1718, was purchased of the papas, or Greek priest, by Edward Wortley Montague, esq. then going ambassador to Constantinople.[4] The place in the wall from which it was removed is still visible.

[1] *Letters of the Right Honble Lady Mary Montague*, vol. iii, Letter XLIV, pp. 58–60 and L. H. Jeffery, *The Local Scripts of Archaic Greece* (Oxford, 1961), No. 43, p. 371, pl. 71; B.M.Cat. Ins. No. 1002.

[2] Suetonius, c.25. [C]. *Gaius Caligula*, XXV.

[3] I am indebted to Dr F. H. Stubbings and Dr A. G. Woodhead for the following information: This marble is still at Trinity College and sits in the stairwell of the Library. It was presented to the College by E. W. Montague's daughter, Mary Countess of Bute as is stated on an inscription set above it. See *CIG*, 2, p. 878 no. 3595.

[4] Chishull, *Antiq. Asiat.*, pp. 49–52. [C]. *CIG*, 2, p. 878, no. 3595.

The city Sigeum stood on a slope, now bare, opposite to the part where we ascended. It was founded by the Mityleneans of Lesbos . . .

The temple at Sigeum was of remote antiquity, if not coeval with the city, which is said to have been built from the ruins of Troy . . . The celebrated inscription is on part of a pilaster, eight feet seven inches long, one foot and something more than six inches wide, and above ten inches thick. It is broken at the bottom. In the top is a hole three inches and a half long, three wide, and above two deep. This served to unite it firmly with the upper portion, or the capital, by receiving a bar of wood or metal; a customary mode of construction, which rendered the fabric as solid as the materials were durable. The stone was given to the temple, as appears from the inscription on it, by Phanodicus of Proconnesus, a city and island not far from Sigeum, famous for its quarries of marble. . . .

The Greek alphabet, as imported by Cadmus from Phoenicia, consisted of sixteen letters. Palamedes, the rival of Ulysses, who was put to death in the Greek camp before Troy, added four. Simonides of Ceos increased the number to twenty-four. This person was a favourite of Hipparchus, brother of Hegesistratus, the tyrant of Sigeum, and lived with him at Athens.

We may infer from the first inscription on the pilaster, that Phanodicus and the temple, to which he contributed, existed before the improvement made by Simonides; for it exhibits only Cadmean and Palamedean characters: and also that the structure was raised under the Mityleneans; for it is in their dialect, or the Æolian.

The second inscription has the letters of Simonides, and was engraved under the Athenians, as may be collected from its Atticisms; and, it is likely, about the time of Hegesistratus; the methods of arranging the lines not being changed, nor the memory of the person whom it records, if he were not then living, become obsolete.

We copied these inscriptions very carefully,[1] and not without deep regret that a stone so singularly curious, which has preserved to us a specimen of writing antiquated above two thousand years ago, should be suffered to lie so neglected and exposed. Above half a century has elapsed since it was first discovered, and it still remains

[1] Inscript. Ant. pl. 1. [C]. B.M. 1, 1002; Jeffery, op. cit., no. 43, p. 371, pl. 71.

in the open air, a seat for the Greeks, destitute of a patron to rescue it from barbarism, and obtain its removal into the safer custody of some private museum, or, which is rather to be desired, some public repository.[1]

[1] It is to be wished that a premium were offered, and the undertaking recommended to commanders of ships in the Levant trade. They have commonly interpreters to negociate for them, with men, levers, ropes, and the other requisites; besides instruments or tools, by which the stone might be broken, if necessary. By a proper application of all-prevailing gold, it is believed they might gain the permission or connivance of the papas and persons concerned. It should be done with secrecy. The experiment is easily made when they are at Tenedos, or wind-bound near the mouth of the Hellespont. [C]

IX

From the brow by the church [at Sigeum] we had in view
several barrows, and a large cultivated plain, parched, and of
a russett colour, excepting some plantations of cotton. On it
were flocks of sheep and of goats; oxen unmuzzled treading out
corn; droves of cattle and horses, some feeding, others rolling in the
wide bed, which receives the Scamander and Simois united. Near the
mouth was lively verdure, with trees; and on the same side as Sigeum,
the castle, and Chomkali. By the water many women were employed,
their faces muffled, washing linen, or spreading it to dry; with
children playing on the banks. It is proper here to inform the reader,
that Ilium, or New Troy, stood above the junction of the two
streams; and that the Simois, which has been mistaken for the
Scamander, was the river next Sigeum and cape Baba or Lectos.

... We descended from the church into the plain, and crossing
the river above the women, to avoid giving offence, walked about
two hours up into the country. We saw in this ramble some villages,
consisting of a few huts; and were worried more than once by the
dogs, which are kept to guard the flocks and herds from wild beasts.
They were very fierce, and not easily repelled by our mussulmen.
The ground in many places appeared to have been swampy, and
had channels in it worn by floods and torrents. The Turkey wheat
standing in the fields had the ears turned yellow, and seemed ripe.
Pieces of marble and broken columns lay scattered about. The bed
of the river was very wide, the banks steep, with thickets of tamarisk
growing in it. We saw small fish in the water; and on the margin
found a live tortoise, the first I had seen. I passed the stream several
times without being wet-shod. We had advanced in sight of some
barrows, which are beyond the Scamander, and of a large conical
hill, more remote, at the foot of mount Ida, called anciently Callico-

lone, when the sun declining apace, to my great regret, we were obliged to go back.

A rumour had prevailed that the consul, after parting from us at Tenedos, had been attacked by robbers in his way to Gallipoli. At our return to the village we found this intelligence confirmed, and our Jews in affliction. He had gone with company in a boat from the Dardanell. They landed to dine, as usual, ashore; when the banditti rushed suddenly down upon them, and soon overcame them. The consul, as we were told, ran into the water up to his chin, where they still fired at him, and he was much hurt ...

[They had intended to stay several days at Sigeum but fear of bandits caused them to return to] our cottage not far from the brow of the hill on which the church stands, and we repaired thither to enjoy again, before sunset, the delicious prospect. A long train of low carriages, resembling ancient cars, was then coming as it were in procession from mount Ida. Each was wreathed round with wicker work, had two wheels, and conveyed a nodding load of green wood, which was drawn through the dusty plain by yoked oxen or buffaloes, with a slow and solemn pace, and with an ugly screaking [sic] noise.

Early in the morning we descended the slope, on which Sigeum stood, going to our boat, which waited at Chomkali, distant about half an hour from Giaurkioi by land. After walking eight minutes, we came between two barrows standing each in a vineyard or enclosure.[1] One was that of Achilles and Patroclus; the other, which was on our right hand, that of Antilochus, son of Nestor. This had a fragment or two of white marble on the top, which I ascended; as had also another on our right hand, not far off, which, if I mistake not, was that of Peneleus, one of the leaders of the Boeotians, who was slain by Euryplyus. We had likewise in view the barrow of Ajax Telamon; and at a distance from it on the side next Lectos, that of Æsyetes, mentioned in Homer. From thence the road was between vineyards, cotton-fields, pomegranate, and fig-trees; the verdure and freshness about the mouth of the river contrasted with

[1] These so-called Tombs of Achilles, Patroclus and Antilochus lie at the north end of the Sigeion ridge where it falls to the low sandy promontory of Kum Kale. See Leaf, op. cit., pp. 165–166.

the parched naked plain surrounding it, and as agreeable as striking.

The town of Chomkali appeared to advantage after the wretched places in which we had lately been; but is mean, and not large. We tarried there at a coffeehouse, while our men purchased the necessary provisions. We saw in the street two capitals of columns excavated, and serving as mortars to bruise wheat in. The water-cisterns are sarcophagi or ancient coffins, with vents. On one was a Greek inscription, not legible; the stone rough. All these have been removed from adjacent ruins; for even the site of Chomkali and its castle is of modern origin.

X

WE had intended to return by the coast of Asia, hoping it might afford us something worthy observation; but when we came to the wherry, the rais or master refused, preferring the European side of the Hellespont, because, as he urged, the stream there is less violent. This point being settled, not much to our satisfaction, we were rowed over to the Cherronese, where we landed above Eleûs, within a point nearly parallel to Mastusia and its castle, and at the mouth of the hollow bay Cœlos, which lies between them, and has been mentioned before. We could discern some buildings among trees at the bottom of the bay, with piers of an aqueduct; and on the rock near us were vestiges of a fortress.

We had not been long on shore, before our attention was engaged by the appearance of many boats, on the Hellespont, steering towards us, and full of people. The passengers landing, as they arrived, ascended a ridge near us in a long train, men and boys, women with infants, and persons decrepit from age. On inquiry, we were informed that this was a great holyday among the Greeks, none of whom would be absent from the panegyris or *general assembly*. The feast of Venus and Adonis by Sestos did not occasion a more complete desertion of the villages and towns on both sides the Hellespont, when Leander of Abydos first beheld and became enamoured with his mistress Hero.

It is the custom of the Greeks on these days, after fulfilling their religious duties, to indulge in festivity. Two of their musicians, seeing us sitting under a shady tree, where we had dined, came and played before us, while some of our Turks danced. One of their instruments resembled a common tabour, but was larger and thicker. It was sounded with two sticks, the performer beating it with a slender one underneath, and at the same time with a bigger, which had a round knob at the end, on the top. This was accompanied by a pipe with a reed for the mouthpiece, and below it a circular rim of wood, against which the lips of the player came. His cheeks were much inflated, and the notes were so various, shrill, and disagreeable, as to remind me of a famous composition designed for the ancient aulos or flute, as was fabled, by Minerva.[1] It was an imitation of the squalling and wailing, made by the serpent-haired gorgons, when Perseus maimed the triple sisterhood, by severing from their common body the head of Medusa . . .

We went up to the place at which the Greeks were assembled. It was about a quarter of a mile from the shore by a church of the *Panagia*, or Virgin Mary, for so they called some walls of stones piled, without a roof, and stuck, on this solemnity, with wax candle lighted, and with small tapers. Close by was an aperture in the surface of the ground, with a spring running under the rock. This cavity, at which a portrait hung of the Virgin, painted on wood, was also illuminated; and some priests, who took money of those who came for water, were preparing to perform mass near it. We were told it was a place of great sanctity. The multitude was sitting under half-tents, with store of melons and grapes, besides lambs and sheep to be killed, wine in gourds and skins, and other necessary provisions. . .

We left this lively scene with some regret, and re-coasting the rough European shore, landed not far from the town and castle. . . . Here a fire was presently kindled, and coffee made, and the whole company seemed to experience much self-enjoyment. We then returned on board, and our men tugged against the stream, until we were considerably above the two castles and their towns, when the tide set us over, and we landed in Asia, on the beach, from which we had embarked on our expedition.

On quitting the boat, we took leave of our mussulmen, upon the whole well satisfied with their attention and civility. The rais was an obstinate hairy savage, as rough in figure as a bear. In their disputes some had displayed great ferocity, drawing their sabres and threatening; but some were of far gentler manners. They were all temperate in their diet; cheerfully sating their hunger with fruits, hard coarse

[1] Pindar, *Pyth.*, XII.8. [C]

43

bread, salt cheese, or sour curds called *caimac*; and contentedly quenching their thirst with water. Our janizary, Baructer-Aga, often requested we would speak well of him and his nation in England. He was tall, and polished in person and dress, and an excellent singer. Our Turks respected him, and he quelled their animosities, interposing with authority. He was exact and regular in performing the customary ablutions, and failed not to rehearse his prayers at the stated times, then spreading his cloak on the ground, prostrating his body, and touching it with his forehead; or standing in a suppliant posture, with his hands composed, deeply intent on his duty, and to appearance equally devout and humble.

The banditti, which infested these parts, were represented to us as numerous and cruel ... The consul had been attacked going to Gallipoli, about two hours from home. We had been told of ruins, which we supposed to be remains of Abydos, on that side; but were warned not to venture that way by his recent peril ... We were much perplexed by our situation, and unable to determine how to proceed ...

The wind in the morning proved high, but we were too impatient, under present grievances, to tarry at this place, and resolved to get to Chomkali, the town we had lately left, and to pass on by sea to Smyrna. It remained only to purchase provisions, with utensils for cooking, and other necessaries for the voyage, and to engage a boat, with proper servants and an interpreter; when a messenger from the beach announced the arrival of a ship with English colours.

We had scarcely time to congratulate each other on this unexpected news, before the captain, whose name was Jolly, entered the room. He informed us that he had sailed with his ship the Delawar, not many hours since, from Gallipoli, where the Anglicana had entered not long before; that he was come to an anchor in the road, all vessels from Constantinople stopping there, to be searched for contraband goods or fugitive slaves; that he was bound for Cyprus and England, but should touch at Scio, from whence we might easily get to Smyrna.

We were now relieved from our embarrassment and in the afternoon we embarked on board the Delawar. We were followed by a stately well-dressed Turk in a boat. The captain, while the hold was examined, entertained him and some of his officers in the cabin, with pipes, coffee, and sherbet. When this ceremony was ended, we set sail with the wind fresh and fair . . .

The satisfaction we derived from the sudden change of our situation for the better, received great addition from the liberal behaviour of our new captain, by whom we were elegantly entertained, and after supper accommodated with clean bedding, on the cabin-floor, which afforded us much refreshment. The prosperous gale continued, and the ship made great way. We sailed by the western side of the island Mitylene [sic] in the night; and passing the mouth of the gulf of Smyrna, entered the channel of Scio, and before mid-day cast anchor in the road off the city.

XI

THE island of Chios, now Scio, is by Strabo reckoned nine hundred stadia, or one hundred and twelve miles and a half, in circuit; and about four hundred stadia, or fifty miles, from the island Mitylene. The principal mountain, called anciently Pelinaeus,[1] presents to view a long, lofty range of bare rock, reflecting the sun; but the recesses at its feet are diligently cultivated, and reward the husbandman by their rich produce. The slopes are clothed with vines. The groves of lemon, orange, and citron-trees, regularly planted, at once perfume the air with the odour of their blossoms, and delight the eye with their golden fruit. Myrtles and jasmines are interspersed, with olive and palm trees, and cypresses. Amid these the tall minarees rise, and white houses glitter, dazzling the beholder.

Scio shared in the calamities which attended the destruction of the Greek empire. In the year 1093, when robbers and pirates were in possession of several considerable place, Tzachas, a Turkish malecontent, took the city. The Greek admiral endeavouring to reduce it for the emperor Alexis, made a breach in the wall; and he came to its relief from Smyrna with a fleet and eight thousand men, but soon after abandoned it in the night. In 1306 this was one of the islands which suffered from the exactions of the grand duke Roger, general of the Roman armies. The city was then seized by the Turks, who came before it with thirty ships, and put the inhabitants to the sword. In 1346 it was taken by some galleys, fitted out by thirty noble Genoese. A fleet of sixty vessels was sent by the sultan in 1394 to burn it and the towns adjacent, and to ravage the islands and seacoast. The city purchased peace from Mahomet the Second in 1455; giving a sum of money, and agreeing to pay tribute yearly. Scio experienced evil, but if it be compared with the sufferings of some

[1] Now [Mount] Ayıos Ilias.

other places, in these times of rapine and violence, fortune will seem to have concurred with the partiality of nature, and to have distinguished this as a favourite island.

The Genoese continued in possession of Scio about two hundred and forty years. They were deprived of it in 1566, during the siege of Malta, by the Turkish admiral, who garrisoned it for sultan Solyman; but the Chiotes in general were still indulged with numerous and extraordinary privileges. They consisted of two parties, differing in their religious tenets; one of the Greek persuasion, which acknowledge the patriarch of Constantinople as their head; the other of the Latin, or papists, which enjoyed a free toleration under the Turks, their priests celebrating mass as in Christendom, bearing the sacraments to the sick, going in solemn procession, habited, beneath canopies, with censers in their hands, to the year 1694. The Venetians then attacked and took the castle, but abandoned it on a defeat of their fleet near the Spalmador islands, which lie in the channel between Scio and the continent. The Latins, who had assisted them, dreaded the punishment, which their ingratitude deserved; and the prime families, with the bishop, fled and settled in the Morea, which had been recently conquered by the Venetians. The Turks seized the churches, abolished the Genoese dress, and imposed on their vassals badges of their subjection; obliging them, among other articles, to alight from their horses at the city gate, and at the approach of any, even the meanest, mussulman.

The town of Scio[1] and its vicinity, resembles from the sea Genoa and its territory, as it were in miniature. The ancient city had a good port, and stations for eighty ships. The present, which occupies its site, beneath Pelinaeus, is large, well built, and populous. A naked hill rises above it, with a house or two on the summit, where was the acropolis or citadel of the Greeks, and afterwards of the Genoese. We found men at work there, digging up the old foundations for the materials.[2] The port has an ordinary or ruinous mole, like that of

[1] See *Views*. Le Brun, p. 168 [C]. Pl. 61, *p. 120: see Bibliography*.

[2] I am indebted to Mr Sinclair Hood for this note. Since the Mediaeval and modern towns have occupied the same site as the ancient city virtually no traces of the latter are now visible above ground apart from loose stones and fragments of pottery. Soundings have been made at various points by the local Antiquities officers, as a result of chance discoveries, and excavations on a small

Tenedos, almost level with the water. The mouth is narrow, and beset with lurking rocks and shoals. It was about noon when we landed. We went to the house of the English consul, who was in the country. A Greek, called Antonio, his servant, and the dragoman or interpreter belonging to the captain, who was with us, procured some fowls and eggs, with wine and fruit, for our dinner. In the evening we walked over the town, which appeared to us as a collection of petty palaces, after the hovels of mud we had lately seen on the continent.

The beautiful Greek girls are the most striking ornaments of Scio. Many of these were sitting at the doors and windows, twisting cotton or silk, or employed in spinning and needlework, and accosted us with familiarity, bidding us welcome, as we passed. The streets on Sundays and holydays are filled with them in groups. They wear short petticoats, reaching only to their knees, with white silk or cotton hose. Their headdress, which is peculiar to the island, is a kind of turban, the linen so white and thin it seemed snow. Their slippers are chiefly yellow, with a knot of red fringe at the heel. Some wore them fastened with a thong. Their garments were of silk of various colours; and their whole appearance so fantastic and lively, as to afford us much entertainment. The Turks inhabit a separate quarter, and their women are concealed.

We returned to the ship at night, the drugoman and Chiote lighting us with long paper lanterns to the boat, which waited at the beach . . .

The next morning we were set on shore again. I accompanied captain Jolly to the principal bagnio [sic], or public bathing-place, a very noble edifice, with ample domes, all of marble; and shall attempt to give an account of the mode of bathing. We undressed in a large square room, where linen is hung to dry, and the keeper attends with his servants. We had each a long towel given us to wrap round our middle, and a pair of tall wooden pattens to walk in. We were led through a warm narrow passage into the inner room, which is yet more spacious, and made very hot by stoves, which are concealed. In this was a water-bath, and recesses, with partitions, on the sides. The pavement in the centre under the dome was raised,

scale were carried out by the British School at Athens in open ground on the Kofina ridge on the north side of the ancient city. (*BSA*, 49 (1954), pp. 123–182.)

and covered with linen cloths, on which we were bid to lie down. We were soon covered with big drops of sweat, and two men naked, except the waist, then entered, and began kneading our flesh; tracing all the muscles and cleansing the pores. By the time they had finished, our joints were sufficiently suppled, and they commenced the formidable operation of snapping all of them, not only the toes, ancles, knees, fingers, and the like, but the vertebrae of the back, and the breast; one while wrenching our necks; then turning us on our bellies, crossing our arms behind us, and placing their right knee between our shoulders. The feats they perform cannot easily be described, and are hardly credible. When this was over, we were rubbed with a mohair-bag fitted to the hand, which, like the ancient strigil, brings away the gross matter perspired. We were then led each to a recess, supplied by pipes with hot and cold water, which we tempered to our liking. The men returned with soap-lather and tow in a wooden bowl, with which they cleaned the skin, and then poured a large quantity of warm water on our heads. Our spirits were quite exhausted, when they covered us with dry cloths, and led us back to the first room, where beds were ready for us. On waking after a gentle slumber, we were presented each with a lighted pipe and a dish of coffee. We rose much refreshed, and as the ladies of the aga or Turkish governor were expected there, hastened away ...

On our return from the bath we found the consul at home. He was a spare shrewd Greek, a direct contrast to the fat, open, hospitable Jew, our host at the Dardanell. He presented us with pomegranates, of a particular species, for which the island is noted. The kernels are free from stones. It is usual to bring them to table in a plate, sprinkled with rose water. These are excellent fruit, but accounted astringent. An English gentleman named Bracebridge[1] had

[1] I am indebted to Dr Philip Argenti for the following information. When exploring various orange groves and properties in 1930, Dr. Argenti came across a marble slab, or plaque, half-buried and face downwards in the earth at Tallaros, about a couple of miles south of Chios town. This plaque bore the inscription *Hic jacet Samuele Bracebridge Anglus 1796*. The property at Tallaros formerly had belonged to a member of Giustiniani family and at some time had passed to Bracebridge. Bracebridge was born in 1693 and died in Chios in 1786. It is curious to find a tombstone not in a cemetery and it would appear that Bracebridge had been buried *in* his property. He is referred to under various spellings: Baimbridge, Bainbridge, Bradbridge by other travellers, see E. D.

come with the consul to visit us. He was an elderly person, and had been absent some years from his native country, for the benefit of a warmer climate. After much wandering, he gave the preference to this island above any of the places which he had tried . . .

We soon found that the old religious parties still subsist with unextinguished animosity, each sect cherishing insuperable hatred, and intriguing to ruin its adversary. We saw the Latins at their worship in the chapel of the vice-consul of the French nation, which was very neat, well filled, especially with women, and handsomely illuminated. The English consul, who served some other European powers, was much haunted by priests of that church, and had a patent of knighthood from the pope.

The wines of Scio have been celebrated as aiding digestion, as nutritive and pleasant. They were much esteemed by the Romans; and red wine, with the method of making these liquors, was invented by the Chians. A rugged tract, named Arvisia, was particularly famous for its produce, which has been extolled as ambrosial, and stiled a new nectar. Mr. Bracebridge, whom we visited at his house near the town, treated us with a variety of choice specimens; and it may be questioned, if either the flavour or qualities, once so commended, be at all impaired. In several we found the former truly admirable.

To the peculiar possession of the Arvisian vine, now no longer talked of, has succeeded the profitable culture of the lentiscus, or mastic-tree. This employs, as we were told, twenty-one villages, which are required to provide as many thousand okes[1] of gum annually, for the use of the seraglio at Constantinople. They procure it by boring the trunks with a small sharp iron, in the summer months. In October their harvest is conveyed with music into the city, and lodged in the castle. The cadi and officers, who attend while it is weighed, have each a certain portion for their perquisite. The remainder is delivered to the farmer or planter, to

Clarke, *Travels in various countries* (London, M.D.CCC.XVII), vol. III, chap. vii, p. 237; W. Wittman, *Travels in Turkey, Asia Minor, Syria* . . . (London, 1803), p. 453, and John Galt, *Voyages and Travels in the years* 1809, 1810, 1811 (London, 1812), p. 189.

[1] An oke is a Turkish weight of about two pounds three quarters avoirdupois. [C]

III   The Gymnasium at Ephesus. (Cat. 6)

be disposed of for his own advantage. The Greeks of these villages have a separate governor, and enjoy many privileges. In particular, they are allowed to wear a turban of white cotton [sic], and their churches have each a bell to call them to prayers, an indulgence of which they speak with much glee. The Asiatic ladies are excessively fond of this gum, which they chew greedily, believing it good for the breath, and attributing to it various other excellent properties.

Prosperity is less friendly to antiquity than desertion and de-population. We saw no stadium, theatre, or odeum; but so illustrious a city, with a marble quarry near it, could not be destitute of those necessary structures, and perhaps some traces might be discovered about the hill on which the citadel stood. A few bass-reliefs and marbles are fixed in the walls, and over the gateways of the houses.[1] We found by the seaside, near the towns, three stones with inscrip-tions, which had been brought for ballast from the continent of Asia. The Chiote, our attendant, was vociferous in his inquiries, but to little purpose. We were more than once desired to look at a Genoese coat of arms for a piece of ancient sculpture; and a date in modern Greek for an old inscription.

The most curious remain is that which has been named, without reason, *the School of Homer*.[2] It is on the coast at some distance from the city, northward, and appears to have been an open temple of Cybele, formed on the top of a rock. The shape is oval, and in the centre is the image of the goddess, the head and an arm wanting. She is represented, as usual, sitting. The chair has a lion carved on each side, and on the back. The area is bounded by a low rim or seat, and about five yards over. The whole is hewn out of the mountain, is rude, indistinct, and probably of the most remote antiquity. From the slope higher up is a fine view of the rich vale of Scio, and of the channel, with its shining islands, beyond which are the mountains on the mainland of Asia.

[1] *Inscript. Ant.*, p. 4. [C]. *CIG*, 2, p. 209, no. 2239; p. 211, no. 2243; p. 207, no. 2226.

[2] This has been identified as a *naiskos* with a seated Kybele and figures on either side of the goddess which may have been human attendants. It is dated to the early fifth, if not sixth century B.C. See J. Boardman, *Antiquaries Journal*, 1959, pp. 195–196, pl. xxxiv.

XII

THE inconveniences under which we had laboured for some time rendered us impatient to get as fast as possible to Smyrna. We had been advised not to carry servants with us from England, and had made our way thus far alone. Besides the want of proper attendants, we were without our bedding, which, in our hurry at quitting the Anglicana, had been left on the quarter-deck. The weather was unfavourable to our departure from Scio. Thick clouds covered the mountains, and the southerly wind called sirocco prevailed. It thundered very much, with lightning, and rained hard in the night. We had hired a boat manned with Greeks, and our baggage was carried to the customhouse to be inspected; but it blew so violently, we were advised not to go on board. The next day the wind still continued high and contrary; but as it seemed not likely to change, and our boat was stout, we resolved to venture, and accordingly about noon embarked with a rough sea.

Leaving the mole of Scio, we buffetted the waves across to the continent, where we took in more ballast. We then stood to and fro the whole afternoon, but made little way. Our boat carried a large unhandy sail, which, when we tacked about, did not readily clear, and once we barely escaped being overset. In the evening we entered a small creek, and moored by two other vessels. In the rock close by were caverns black with smoke. These afford shelter to mariners and fishermen, in dark nights and tempestuous weather, when the sea is not navigable. We landed very wet from the salt spray, and half-starved with hunger. We had endeavoured, when we stopped before, to make the crew understand, that our keen appetites required present gratification, but did not succeed. Some of them now made a fire on the shore, and boiled the fowls which we had provided. We supped in a manner sufficiently disgusting, and retired to the boat, where the fresh ballast was our bed.

We were under sail again as soon as the morning dawned; plying between mount Mimas on the continent and the Spalmadore islands, called anciently Œnussæ. They belonged to the Chians, who had refused to sell them to the Phoceans. About two we weathered the southern promontory of the gulf of Smyrna, formerly called Acra Melæna, or *Black Point*. The Turkish name, which now prevails, signifies nearly the same. It is Kara-bornu, or *Black Nose*.

Smyrna is situated at the end of a long bay. As soon as we had gained the mouth of this gulf, the wind called inbat began to waft us pleasantly along. This, which is a westerly wind, sets regularly in, during the hot months, in the daytime; and is generally succeeded by a land-breeze in the night. The city was in view before us, when evening came on, and the gale died away.

We arrived at the Frank Scale, or key [sic] for Europeans, early in the morning, and beheld Smyrna, no longer remote, spreading on a slope, the summit of the hill crowned with a large solitary castle; domes and minarees, with cypress-trees interspersed, rising above the houses. On the south side, where the Armenians and Jews have extensive burying-grounds, on flats one above another, the surface of the acclivity appeared as covered with white marble. The quarter assigned to the Franks is on the north side; and by the shore, not far from us, the English flag was hoisted. Soon after, the consul, then Antony Hayes, esq. sent an Armenian, one of his dragomen, or interpreters, to be our guide to his house.

We landed, and passed through the bezesten, or market, which is "in form like a street, shutting up at each end, the shops being little "rooms with cupolas leaded, and the holes on the top with glass to "let the light in".[1] We then entered the street of the Franks, which had a dirty kennel, was of a mean aspect, and so narrow, that we could scarcely get by a camel laden with charcoal. It was partly in ruins, a terrible fire having happened and some of the consuls and merchants were now rebuilding, or had recently finished their houses, which in general extend from the street backward to the beach, and have an area or court. The apartments are in the upper

[1] Wheler, Bk. III, p. 247. [C]

story, spacious and handsome, with long galleries and terraces, open to the sea and the refreshing inbat. Beneath them are large and substantial magazines for goods.

We were received by the consul, and visited by Mr. Lee, one of the principal merchants, and by other gentlemen, with great civility. As we were likely to make some stay, we inquired for lodgings, but were told that the families which had been burned out occupied all, and were distressed for room. The consul politely offered us a detached part of his house, which consists of a large quadrangle, with a court behind it. We were here much at our ease, and close by an ample gallery, where we might enjoy the grateful inbat, with a full view of the shipping and of the long fair canal within Kara-bornu, which is bordered by woody mountains and dusky olive-groves; the surface of the water shining, and smooth; or ruffled by the wind; the waves then coming toward Smyrna as it were in regular progression, and breaking on the beach.

Among the new objects, which first attracted our attention, were two live chameleons, one of the size of a large lizard. They were confined each on a long narrow piece of board suspended between two strings, and had for security twisted their tails several times round. We were much amused with the changes in the colour of these reptiles, and with seeing them feed. A fly, deprived of its wings, being put on the board, the chameleon soon perceives its prey, and untwirling its tail, moves toward it very gently and deliberately. When within distance, it suddenly seizes the poor insect, darting forward its tongue, a small long tube furnished with glutinous matter at the end, to which the fly adheres. This is done so nimbly and quietly, that we did not wonder it remained unobserved for ages, while the creature was idly supposed to subsist on air. One of these made its escape, the other perished with hunger.

XIII

IT is related of Alexander the Great, that after hunting he fell
asleep on mount Pagus beneath a plane-tree, which grew by a
fountain, near a temple of the Nemeses; and that the goddesses
directed him in a vision to found there a city for the Smyrneans, a
people from Ephesus, then living in villages. The work was begun
by Antigonus, and finished by Lysimachus. The Clarian oracle was
consulted on the removal of the Smyrneans,[1] and answered in an
heroic couplet, that those, who should dwell on mount Pagus,
beyond the sacred Meles, would experience great prosperity. Afterwards the Ephesians,[2] remembering their common origin, procured,
with the concurrence of king Attalus and of Arsinoe his queen, their
admission as members of the Ionic body; an honour which they had
coveted long before, when it was first constituted . . .

The site selected by Alexander for this people was such as the
ancient founders commonly preferred. Their cities in general were
seated by some hill or mountain, which, as this did, supplied them
with marble, and was commodious as well for defence as ornament.
The side or slope afforded a secure foundation for the seats of the
stadium and theatres, lessening both the labour and expense. It
displayed the public and private structures, which rose from its
quarry, to advantage; and rendered the view as captivating as noble . . .

Smyrna flourished, as Apollo had foretold; and, under the
Romans, was esteemed the most beautiful of the Ionian cities. The
wall comprised a portion of mount Pagus, but more of the plain by
the port, by the metroum or temple of Cybele, and by the gynmas-
ium. The streets were as straight as the site would admit, and
excellently disposed. The ways were paved. Both above and below

[1] Pausanias, vii.5.2. [C]
[2] Vitruvius, IV.c.1.4, who says 'Smyrnians' not Ephesians. [C]

were large quadrangular stoas or porticoes. There was also a library, and, besides the other requisites of a noble city, a port which shut up; but from an omission of the architects, the want of sewers occasioned a great nuisance. It was much frequented by the sophists, and, with Ephesus, became renowned as a school of oratory and science. It has been exalted with high encomiums, and styled *the lovely, the crown of Ionia, the ornament of Asia.*

In the year 1084, Tzachas, a Turkish malecontent, who assumed the title of king, seized and made Smyrna his capital. His fleet took Clazomene, Phocea, Scio, Samos, Mitylene, and other places. In 1097 this city was besieged by John Ducas, the Greek admiral: and on its surrender, Caspaces, who had been sent to attack it by sea, was appointed governor; but a Turk stabbed him, and his death was revenged by the massacre of ten thousand inhabitants. The whole coast of Asia, from Smyrna to Attalia, had been desolated by the wars, when the Greek emperor sent Philokales, in 1106, to restore its cities. Adramyttium, which had been utterly destroyed, was then rebuilt, and peopled with peasants and strangers.

At the beginning of the thirteenth century, Smyrna lay in ruins, except the acropolis or citadel, which then served as a fortress. This was repaired and beautified by the emperor John Angelus Comnenus,[1] who died in 1224. Smyrna, thus restored, was a small town chiefly on the summit of mount Pagus, or within the present castle.

In 1313, Atin had subdued Lydia, and extended his conquests to this place. In 1332, Amir or Homur, his son and successor, was sultan of Smyrna. In 1345, while he was absent with his fleet, ravaging the coasts of the Propontis, some galleys of the Latins, and of the knights of Rhodes, burnt several vessels in the port. Amir arrived in time to save the town, but could not dislodge the enemy from a fort which they had seized, nor prevent their making of a settlement at the mouth of the port, at a distance from the Turkish town. The next year the pope sent thither a nominal patriarch of Constantinople, escorted by twelve galleys; but Amir, while mass was celebrating in the church, attacked and drove the Italians into their citadel, called fort St. Peter, before which he was afterwards killed by an arrow.

[1] Ducas, C.7. [C]

Tamerlane, who ravaged Anatolia, or Asia Minor, in 1402, hearing that the Christians and Mahometans had each a stronghold at Smyrna, and were always at war, required the former to change their religion; but the governor soliciting aid from the European princes, Tamerlane marched in person to subdue a place which sultan Morat had attempted in vain, and which his son Bajazet had besieged or blockaded for seven years. He attacked it by sea and land; and, to ruin the port, ordered each soldier to throw a stone into the mouth, which was soon filled up; but the ships had got away. He took the town in fourteen days, with great slaughter of the inhabitants, and demolished the houses. The knights had fled into the castle of St. Peter, and thence to their galleys, which lay near. He is said to have cut off a thousand prisoners, and to have caused a tower to be erected with stones and their heads intermixed.

Cineis, who had long been governor of the Turkish town, continued in possession, when it was thus freed from its enemy and rival. He was much esteemed by the Ionians, and, after a variety of fortune, rose to be a sovereign in Asia. Sultan Mohammed the First marched against him in 1419, and deprived him of Nympheum, the city Cyme, and a fortress in the field of Menomen. He was assisted by the governors of the islands, who hated Cineis, by several princes on the continent, his neighbours, and even by the grand master of Rhodes, who was then rebuilding fort St. Peter, which Tamerlane had destroyed. He demolished the fortification of Smyrna, but spared the inhabitants; and, on a complaint that the Ionian slaves, who escaped from their owners, found shelter in the fort, ordered it to be ruined; permitting another to be erected on the borders of Lycia and Caria. Smyrna was again taken in 1424 by sultan Morat, Cineis retiring to the mountains.

When the conquering Turk had gained complete possession of the Greek empire, and peace was restored, commerce revived, and again settled at Smyrna. The inhabitants, delivered from their apprehensions of danger, by degrees abandoned the castle, and the town slid, as it were, down the slope towards the sea; leaving behind it a naked space, where they now dig for old materials, and also ordinary ruins below the castle, which overlooks the buildings and the bay, at a distance.

The reader will not be surprised if few traces of the ancient city remain.[1] From a survey of the castle, which is extensive, we collect, that after being reedified by John Angelus Comnenus, its condition, though less ruinous than before, was far more mean and ignoble. The old wall, of which many remnants may be discovered, is of a solid massive construction, worthy of Alexander and his captains. All the repairs are mere patchwork. Near the western gateway, at which you enter from the town, was once a fountain, now dry; by which is a marble colossal head, the face much injured, of Apollo, or, as some have supposed, of Smyrna, an Amazon, from whom the people derived their name. Within is a deserted mosque, rubbish of buildings, and a large reservoir for water; the roof arched, and supported by piers. On the marble arch of the gateway fronting the north is inscribed a copy of verses, giving an elegant and poetical description of the extreme misery from which the emperor John, before mentioned, had raised the city; and concluding with an address to the omnipotent Ruler of heaven and earth, that he would grant him and his queen, whose beauty it celebrates, a reign of many years. On each side is an eagle, rudely cut. The river Hermus may be seen from this eminence, which also affords a view of a fine champaign country round about, covered with vines.

Going down from the western gate of the castle toward the sea, at some distance is the ground-plat of the stadium, stripped of its marble seats and decorations. One side was on the slope of the mountain; the opposite, or that next to the town, was raised on a vaulted substruction, which remains. It appears as a long dale, semi-circular, or rounded at the top. The area, when we first saw it, had been reaped; and, another time, some men were busy ploughing in it. Going from the northern gate of the castle, over which is the inscription, you come to vestiges of a theatre, in the side of the hill, near the brow, and fronting the bay. Farther down is a quarry. Below the theatre is part of a slight wall, which, with a foss round the hill, was begun about the year 1736, to protect the town from Soley Bey Ogle, a famous rebel, by whom it had been much distressed.[2]

[1] For discussion of site and map see Bean, *Aegean Turkey*. An *Archaeological Guide* (London, Ernest Benn, 1966), pp. 41–67.

[2] Pocock, vol. II, pp. 35–36. [C]

The port, which shut up, reached once to the foot of the castle-hill, but is now dry, except after heavy rains, when it receives water from the slopes. It forms a spacious recess within the present town, and has houses along the margin. Tamerlane, by depriving the sea of its free ingress, contributed to this change, and the mud washed from above has gradually completed it. Like some of the Italian havens, it required perhaps to be cleansed, and deepened by machines contrived for that purpose. It is mentioned as the galley port at the beginning of this century.[1] A small mean castle still in use, on the north side of the entrance, is supposed to occupy the site of fort St. Peter.

The city wall, which, descending from the castle, included the stadium on one hand, and the theatre on the other, has been long since demolished; and even its ruins are removed. A small remnant of it, on the hill above the stadium, consists of hard cement of rubble; but has been faced with better materials ... This side comprehended a large portion of the burying-grounds without the present town. The side next the theatre may be traced a considerable way along the brow, from its junction with the north-east angle of the castle. In the Armenian quarter, by *The Three Corners*, or near the Frank street, are remnants of a thick and massive wall, which has a large V cut on each stone; and in 1675 the foundations of a great and solid fabric, probably the gymnasium, were visible in that part. Beyond the deep valley, in which the river Meles winds, behind the castle, are several portions of the wall of the pomœrium, which encompassed the city at a distance, but broken. The facings are gone, and masses only of hard cement and rubble are left.

The ancient sepulchres were chiefly in the *pomœrium*, without the city ...

The ancient city has supplied materials for the public edifices erected by the Turks. The bezesten, or market, which was unfinished in 1675, and the vizir-khan, were both raised with the white marble of the theatre ...

In the history of St. Polycarp, the first bishop of Smyrna, it is related, that he was burnt here in the amphitheatre. The Asiatic cities used the stadium for the diversions of the Roman amphitheatre; and that, it is probable, was the scene of his martyrdom.

[1] Tournefort, vol. III, pp. 341–343. [C]

XIV

SMYRNA continues a large and flourishing city. The bay, besides numerous small-craft, is daily frequented by ships of burden from the chief ports in Europe; and the factors, who are a respectable body, at once live in affluence and acquire fortunes.

The conflux at Smyrna of people of various nations, differing in dress, in manners, in language, and in religion, is very considerable. The Turks occupy by far the greater part of the town. The other tribes live in separate quarters. The protestants and Roman catholics have their chapels; the Jews a synagogue or two; the Armenians a large and handsome church, with a burying-ground by it. The Greeks, before the fire, had two churches. They applied, by their bishop at Constantinople, for leave to rebuild that which was destroyed, but the sum demanded was too exorbitant to be given. By this policy the Turks will in time extirpate Christianity from among their vassals.

The factors, and other Europeans settled at Smyrna, generally intermarry with the Greeks, or with natives of the same religion. Their ladies wear the oriental dress, consisting of large trowsers or breeches, which reach to the ancle; long vests of rich silk, or of velvet, lined in winter with costly furs; and round their waist an embroidered zone, with clasps of silver or gold. Their hair is platted, and descends down the back, often in great profusion. The girls have sometimes above twenty thick tresses, besides two or three encircling the head, as a coronet, and set off with flowers, and plumes of feathers, pearls, or jewels. They commonly stain it of a chesnut colour, which is the most desired. Their apparel and carriage are alike antique. It is remarkable that the trowsers are mentioned in a fragment of Sappho.[1] The habit is light, loose, and cool, adapted to the climate. When they visit each other, they put over their heads a thin transparent veil of muslin, with a border of gold tissue. A janizary walks before, and two or more handmaids follow them, through the streets. When assembled, they are seen reclining in various attitudes, or sitting cross-legged on a sofa. Girls of inferior rank from the islands, especially Tino[s], abound; and are many of them as beautiful in person, as picturesque in their appearance. They excel in a glow of colour, which seems the effect of a warm sun, ripening the human body as it were into uncommon perfection. The women of the Turks, and of some other nations, are kept carefully concealed; and when they go out, are enwrapped in white linen, wear boots, and have their faces muffled.

The principal buildings in Smyrna are the mosques, the public baths, the bezesten or market, and the khans or inns. Some of these are very ample and noble edifices. The khans have in general a quadrangle or square area, and sometimes a fountain in the middle. The upper story consists of an open gallery, with a range of apartments, and often a small mosque, or place of worship, for the use of the devout mussulmen. Below are the camels with their burdens, and the mules, or horses. A servant dusts the floor of a vacant chamber when you arrive, and spreading a mat, which is all the furniture, leaves you in possession. The gates are shut about sunset, and a trifling gratuity is expected by the keeper at your departure . . .

The Turks bury chiefly without the town, where the enclosures are very extensive, it being their custom not to open the grounds filled with bodies, until a long term of years has elapsed. The graves have stones or pillars at the head and feet, and are sometimes shaded with cypress-trees. In their cemeteries, and in those of the Christians and Jews, are found many marble slabs and fragments of architecture. The English ground, which is at a distance from the Frank quarter, at the opposite end of the town, is walled in, and contains some monuments worthy notice for the beauty of their sculpture. These were brought from Italy. Mr. Bouverie, the friend

[1] Warton's *Theocritus*, p. 304. [C]

and companion of Mr. Dawkins and Mr. Wood,[1] is interred there, and has over him a plain marble, with a long Latin inscription. He died at Guzelhissar or Magnesia by the Mæander.

Smyrna is well supplied with provisions. The sheep have broad tails, hanging down like an apron, some weighing eight, ten, or more pounds. These are eaten as a dainty, and the fat, before they are full grown, accounted as delicious as marrow. The flesh of wild hogs is common, and in esteem among the Europeans and Greeks, who purchase the animal, when killed by the Turks. Fine fish is taken in the bay. Hares, with game and fowl, are cheap. The partridges are bigger than the English, of a different colour and species, with red legs. The olive groves furnish doves, fieldfares, thrushes, quails, snipes, and the like, in abundance. A variety of excellent wines are produced in the country, or imported from the islands. The fruits are of an exquisite flavour. Among those of the gourd kind, the water-melon, which grows to a great size, is not only highly palatable, but so innocent as to be allowed to the sick in fevers. The figs are deservedly famous. The rich clusters of grapes are as wholesome as beautiful. Many on the stalk are found converted by the sun into raisins. We were shewn one species which had no stones. Large and heavy bunches are hung on strings, and preserved in the shops for sale in the winter. Lemons and oranges, with citrons, are in plenty. The sherbets made with the juice of the two former, newly gathered, in water, sweetened with white honey, are as cooling as grateful to the taste. Coffee is brought from Arabia. We partook almost daily of eatables unknown to us before. It is the general custom to sleep after dinner; and this indulgence is recommended as conducing, and even necessary, to health in that climate.

Our situation was not, however, without grievances. We were much infested by a minute fly, which irritates by its puncture, and, settling on the white wall, eludes the angry pursuer with surprising activity. But this species, and the other insects which annoyed us,

[1] James Dawkins (1722–1759). Travelled with Robert Wood in Asia Minor and Greece, also to Palmyra and Baalbec. M.P. for Hindon Borough, 1754. Was noted for his Jacobite sympathies. Elected to the Society of Dilettanti 1755.
John Bouverie: travelled with Wood and Dawkins in Asia Minor and died at Magnesia a. M. in 1751; was buried at Smyrna.

were petty offenders compared with the musquittoes [sic], or large gnats, which tormented us most exceedingly by their loud noise, and by repeated attacks on our skin, where naked or lightly clothed, perforating it with their acute proboscis, and sucking our blood, till they were full. A small fiery tumour then ensues, which will not soon subside, unless the patient has been, as it were, naturalized by residence; but the pain is much allayed by lemon-juice. At night they raged furiously about our beds, assaulting the gauze veil, our defence, which, thin as it was, augmented the violent heat to a degree almost intolerable. Their fondness of foreign food is generally but too visible, in the swollen and distorted features of persons newly arrived.

XV

SMYRNA has on the south-east a fine plain, in which are villages, and the houses of the principal factors, who reside in the country in the summer. Norlecui and Hadjelar are toward the east. On the north side is Bujaw, distinguished by tall cypress-trees; and about a league from the sea Bonavre.

The Meles was anciently the boast of the Smyrneans. This most beautiful water, as it has been stiled, flowed by the city-wall, and had its sources not remote. The clear stream is shallow in summer, not covering the rocky bed, but winding in the deep valley behind the castle, and murmuring among the evergreens. It receives many rills from the sides; and, after turning an over-shot mill or two, approaches *the gardens* without the town, where it is branched out by small canals, and divided and subdivided into lesser currents, until it is absorbed, or reaches the sea, at the end of the Frank street, in ditches, unlike a river: but in winter, after heavy rains on the mountains, or the melting of snow, it swells into a torrent, rapid and deep, often not fordable, or with danger.

On the north of Smyrna the sea enters a recess, in which is the road where ships careen. This inner bay is called by the English sailors, *Peg's hole*. The Meles, when full, pursues its way thither, instead of losing itself in the gardens. There also the first Smyrna was situated.

Old Smyrna[1] was about twenty stadia, or two miles and a half, from the present city, and on the other side of the river. It is described as near the sea, with the clear stream of the Meles running by, and existed in the second century . . .

[1] The site of the ancient city has been located at Bayraklı and was excavated in 1948–1951 by the British School at Athens and the University of Ankara. (*BSA* (53–54), 1958–1959, pp. 1–181; *BSA* (59), 1964, pp. 39–49; *BSA* (60), 1965, pp. 114–153.) It lies on a low spur at the foot of Yamanlar Dağı at a distance of 450 metres east of the present coast line. See Bean op. cit., pp. 45–47 for discussion of the location of the river Meles. Turkish archaeologists conducted excavations here from 1966–69.

Pococke[1] has described several very ancient sepulchres on the side of the hill, more to the west than Bonavre, and near the corner of the bay, which, I should suppose, are relics of old Smyrna. The plainest sort consists, as he relates, of a raised ground in a circular form, of stones hewn out, or laid in a rough manner. In these are generally two graves, sunk in the earth, made of hewn stone, and covered over with a large stone. The others are circular mounts, from twenty to sixty feet in diameter, walled round, as high as their tops, with large rusticated stones: and have within, under ground, a room, which in some is divided into two apartments. The walls are all of good workmanship, constructed with a kind of brown bastard granite, the produce of the country, wrought very smooth; the joinings as fine as in polished marble . . .

The Smyrneans were originally of Ephesus, but had seceded, and, after dispossessing the Leleges, founded the city above mentioned. They were expelled in turn by the Æolians of Cyme, and retired to Colophon; but a party, pretending to be fugitives, obtained re-admission, and, while the people were celebrating a feast of Bacchus without the walls, shut the gates. A general war was likely to follow between Æolia and Ionia, but it was at length agreed, that the town should deliver up all the effects of the late inhabitants, who were to be distributed among the Æolian cities. The territory of Smyrna had supplied corn for exportation, and the place was then become a considerable emporium. The Lydians destroyed this city, and the Smyrneans subsisted four hundred years as villagers, before they settled on mount Pagus.

It was the Æolian Smyrna which claimed the glory of producing Homer. Critheis, his mother, it is related, going in company with other women out of the town, to observe a festival, was delivered of him near the Meles, and named him Melesigenes. This story is dated ten years after the building of Smyrna, and one hundred and fifty-eight after the war of Troy. We may regret that the pleas of all the cities, which disputed the honour of his birth, are not on record. The place and time are equally unascertained; and it has been observed, that the poet has mentioned neither the Meles nor Smyrna.[2]

The history of Homer, it is remarkable, is scarcely more obscure

[1] Pococke, vol. II, p. 39. [C]   [2] Strabo, 12.3.27. [C]

than that of another poet of Smyrna, who had likewise written on the Trojan war. This person indeed tells us, in an address to the Muses, that he had been inspired by them with his whole song before the down covered his cheeks, while he fed sheep in the territory of Smyrna, by the temple of Diana, on a mountain of a middling height, three times as far from the Hermus, as a man, when he hollows, can be heard. His work, containing a sequel to the Iliad, in fourteen books, was found by cardinal Bessarion in the church of St. Nicholas, near Hydrus,[1] a city of Magna Græcia, and by him communicated to the learned. The name of Quintus, perhaps the owner, was inscribed on the manuscript; and the author has been since called by it, with the addition of Smyrnæus or Calaber. He appears to have been well acquainted with the country in which he lived, and has left some valuable descriptions of its antiquities and natural curiosities.

The bed of the river Meles, behind the castle, is crossed by a lofty aqueduct, which, when we saw it, had been recently repaired, and then supplied the fountains in Smyrna. Higher up is one larger, but ruinous; and near this is a remnant of an ancient paved causey [sic], which led over the hills from Smyrna toward Ephesus and Colophon. The stones are smooth, broad, and massive. By the aqueduct are several petrifications, and one, of which an aged tree was the mould. The wood has perished, but the large hollow trunk, which incrusted it, is standing. The Meles rises above the aqueducts, out of a dry course, deep-worn by torrents from the mountains.

The Smyrneans were extremely jealous of their property in Homer. They distinguished a brass coin or medal by his name; and an Homerium, his temple and image surrounded with a quadrangular stoa or portico, stood in the new city. They likewise shewed a cave, by the sources of the Meles, where they said he had composed verses. I searched for this, and in the bank above the aqueduct, on the left hand, discovered a cavern, about four feet wide, the roof a huge rock, cracked and slanting, the sides and bottom sandy. The mouth, at which I crept in, is low and narrow; but there is another avenue, wider and higher, about three feet from the ground, and almost concealed with brambles. It may be entered also from

[1] S. Nicola di Casole near Otranto, the ancient Hydruntum.

above, where the earth has fallen in. Beyond it we found a passage cut, leading into a kind of well, in which was a small channel, designed to convey water to the aqueduct. This was dry, but near it was a current with a like aperture.

The river-god Meles is represented on medals leaning on an urn with a cornucopia in his hand, to signify that he dispensed fertility; or bearing a lyre, as a friend to the muses . . .

The gulf of Smyrna, which has been computed about ten leagues long, is sheltered by hills, and affords secure anchorage. The mouth of the Hermus is on the north side, within two leagues and a half of the city. The mountain, which bounds the bay of old Smyrna on the north, extends westward to a level plain, in which the river runs. This, with the Mæander, was anciently famous for a fish called glanis, and for mullet: which came up from the sea in great numbers, particularly in spring.

The fertility of the soil by the river, and the plenty of water for the uses of gardening and agriculture, with other advantages, has occasioned the settling of numerous villages on that side of the gulf. Menimen, is the principal, and supplies Smyrna with fruits, fish, and provisions, boats passing to and fro without intermission. Near the scale or landing-place, which is three hours distant, is a large quantity of low land, bare, or covered only with shallow water. This tract is the site of a considerable fishery; being enclosed by reed fences with gates or avenues, which are shut up to prevent the shoals from retreating, when they have once entered. We saw on the beach many camels laden, or standing by their burdens; and met on the road some travellers from Arabia and other countries, going to, or returning from, Constantinople. The hills were enlivened by flocks of sheep and goats, and resounded with the rude music of the lyre and of the pipe; the former a stringed instrument resembling a guitar, and held much in the same manner, but usually played on with a bow. We were then engaged with some of our countrymen in a shooting party, and in traversing the mountains I had a distinct view of Menimen. It is situated on a rising ground by the Hermus, and appeared as a considerable place, with old castles. I have sometimes suspected it to have been anciently called Neontichos;[1] but

[1] Scholars are still not agreed on the precise location of this site.

these parts, with the whole country of Æolia, still remain unexplored . . .

Near the mouth of the river is a sand-bank or shoal. The channel there is very narrow, the land on the opposite side running out, and forming a low point, on which is a fortress erected, to secure the approach to the city, soon after the battle of the Dardanelles in 1656, when the Venetians defeated the fleet of Mahomet the Fourth. It is called *Sangiac* castle, because the grand signior's colours are on some occasions hoisted there.

It happened that our passage up and down the gulf was in the night; but when we sailed from Smyrna, the inbat met us near the entrance, and we steered our boat into a small creek on the north side, below the Hermus, and an hour from Phocæa. We had there a view of the extremity of the plain, which is wide, low, and level, encircling the rocks once called the Myrmeces and a small mountain or hill with a smooth top. This, it is believed, was the island and promontory Leuce. A long spit now runs from it out into the sea.

On the coast, after Leuce, was anciently Phocæa, situated in a bay; the city oblong, the wall enclosing a space of two miles and five hundred paces, the sides then meeting, and forming as it were a wedge which they called Lamptera, where it was one mile and two hundred paces wide. A tongue of land then running a mile out into the sea, and dividing the bay about the middle, formed two secure ports, one on each side of the isthmus; that toward the south called Naustathmos; the other, which was near, Lamptera. The present town[1] is seated on the tongue, within the isthmus, and the ancient site is called Palæa-Phoggia, or *Old Phocæa*. It has on the north four islets, one named *St. George*, lying before the harbour. Beyond Phocæa were the boundaries of Ionia and Æolia, less than two hundred stadia, or twenty-five miles, from Smyrna.

[1] *Views*. Le Brun, p. 166. [C]. Pls. 57, 58, p. 120: see *Bibliography*.

PART II

September–October 1764

Smyrna — Ephesus — Neapolis — Pygela —
Miletus — Didyma — Posidium — Iasos —
Mylasa — Stratonicea —Mylasa — Iasos —
Iakle — Myus-Heracleia — Miletus —
Ephesus — Smyrna.

[Ref. 1825 edition, chaps. XXII, XXXII–XLIV, LIV–LVIII, LII]

XVI

ON our return to Smyrna, in the evening of the 18th of September, from a small excursion with a party of our countrymen, we were agreeably surprised to find the Anglicana arrived in the bay from Constantinople. The captain brought with him a *firhman*, or *travelling command*, obtained for us from the Porte by the English ambassador. This instrument enjoined all the governors, the judges, the officers of the Janizaries and of the revenue, to whom we should present it, not to molest us or our European servants, on any pretence, nor to exact tribute from us, but to protect and defend us, and permit us to prosecute our journeys without obstruction, as they respected the imperial signature. It was dated about the middle of the moon Rebiulevvel, in the year of the Hegira 1178; or of September, 1764.

A small portion of the year yet remained not unfit for travelling. Finding our English bedding too cumbersome, we purchased thin mattresses stuffed with cotton, some tin kettles, plates, and other like necessaries; and hired a janizary, with two grooms and a cook, Armenians. One horse carried our baggage ... We left the consul's house on Sunday the last day of September [1764], in the forenoon, and passing the river Meles, rode with the castle-hill of Smyrna on our right hand, to a gap in the wall[1] of the pomœrium. We crossed the bed of the Meles, and soon arrived at Sedicui,[2] a small but pleasant village, about two hours distant. We passed the night at a house, which Mr. Lee, who had accompanied us, rented of a Turk; the asylum, where afterwards we had refuge from the plague at Smyrna.

We were on horseback again at five in the morning, before day-

[1] This wall seems to have been of an aqueduct which conveyed water to the upper part of the city. [R] [2] Now Seydıkoy.

break, going southward. A string of camels was in motion at the same time, the foremost with a bell fastened about his neck, and tinkling. The dawn soon after began to disclose the blue tops of the mountains, and the sun rising coloured the sky with a rich variety of tints. The air was soft and fragrant. We passed by an ordinary bridge or two over water-courses, then dry; and through a wet bottom, and a heath covered with pines, wild thyme, and many large thickets of myrtle in flower. On the slopes of the mountains were several villages. We dismounted about eight at a coffee-shed standing by the side of the road near a hut, called Olalanazzi. One of the rivers, which we crossed in travelling along the coast, rises there from four heads. The streams soon unite in a clear brook, and wind in the shade over a clean gravelly bed, with gentle cascades and a pleasing murmur. In it were many small fishes and tortoises. Each source is enveloped with bushes of myrtle, intermixed with plane-trees; and the hut is between two, about fifty yards asunder. The agreeable freshness and verdure produced by these lively currents afford a most grateful relief to the thirsty sun-burnt traveller. That the ancient Ionians were not insensible to the charms of the spot may be inferred from the vestiges of building near it, and from the remnants of marble.

After drinking coffee, we went on, and entering a hollow way shaded with pines, came in view of a ruined caravansera, or building for the reception of travellers, near an extensive plain. Here a stream descends through a pleasant vale, in which are some scattered cottages, named Terrenda, with a mill, by which we dined ... Among the low bushes, on a gentle rising close by, are some marble fragments; and, searching about, we found by the road an inscription,[1] which has belonged to an ancient sepulchre. It was well cut, on a square stone, and perhaps near the site of the edifice. At ten we passed by Hortená, a straggling village. On the left hand is a small Turkish burying-ground by a fountain, and vestiges of building. We arrived an hour after at Tourbali,[2] where we dined by a well near the khan under a spreading tree, and were much incommoded by dust and wind. The roof of the stable was supported by broken columns;

[1] *Inscript. Ant.*, p. 11. [C]. *CIG*, 2, p. 782, no. 3359.
[2] Now Torbalı.

and in the wall was a piece of Doric frieze, with some fragments removed, it is likely, from the ruins of Metropolis.[1]

We were told here, that the road farther on was beset with Turcomans; a people supposed to be descended from the Nomades Scythæ, or *Shepherd Scythians*; busied, as of old, in breeding and nurturing cattle; and leading, as then, an unsettled life; not forming villages and towns with stable habitations, but flitting from place to place, as the season and their convenience directs; choosing their stations, and overspreading without control the vast neglected pastures of this desert empire . . .

We set out again and had on our right Depecui,[2] a village, in which we could discern a large, square, ruinous edifice, with spaces for windows. Soon after we came to a wild country covered with thickets, and with the black booths of the Turcomans, spreading on every side, innumerable, with flocks, and herds, and horses, and poultry, feeding round them. We crossed an extensive level plain, overrun with bushes, but missed Metropolis, of which some vestiges remain;[3] our guide leading us to the left of the direct road from Smyrna to Ephesus.

About three o'clock we approached a valley, which divides two very lofty mountains. The extremity of Gallesus, or *The Aléman*, which was on our right, is covered with trees, rising beautifully in regular gradation up the slope. The other, opposite to it, as quite bare and naked. We now perceived four men riding briskly toward us, abreast, well mounted and armed. Our janizary and Armenians halted, as they passed, and faced about until they were gone beyond our baggage. We came soon after to a fountain, and a coffee-hut, above, which, on the mountain-side, is Osebanár, a Turkish village. We then discovered on our left a ruined bridge, and the river Cayster . . . the water still, and apparently stagnant, the banks steep. A castle, visible afar off, stands on the summit of Gallesus.

We turned westward at the end of the opening between the mountains, and had on our left a valley, bounded by a mountain

[1] This site is on the north slope of Alaman Dağı and consists of ruins of walls and a theatre.

[2] Now ?Derebası.

[3] See Wheler, Bk. III, p. 251; Chishull, *Travels*, etc., p. 30. [C]

called anciently Pactyas.[1] The road lay at the foot of Gallesus, beneath precipices of a stupendous height, abrupt and inaccessible. In the rock are many holes inhabited by eagles; of which several were soaring high in the air, with rooks and crows clamouring about them so far above us as hardly to be discernible. By the way was a well and part of a marble sarcophagus, or coffin, on which were carved heads and festoons. The Cayster, which had been concealed in the valley, now appeared again; and we had in view before us the round hill and stately castle of Aiasaluck,[2] very seasonably for man and horse, both jaded with heat, and wanting rest. Mount Pactyas here retires with a circular sweep, while Gallesus preserves its direction to the sea, which is the western boundary of the plain. This has been computed five miles long. The Cayster met us near the entrance on it; and we passed over an ordinary bridge, a little below which are pieces of veined marble, polished, the remnants of a structure more worthy Ephesus. The stream was shallow, but formed a basin crossed by a weir of reeds. We purchased some live mullet of the fisherman who was there. A narrow track, winding through rubbish and loose stones round the castle-hill, brought us in about half an hour more to Aiasaluck.

[1] Now Ovacık Dağı.   [2] Now Selçuk.

XVII

AIASALUCK is a small village,[1] inhabited by a few Turkish families, standing chiefly on the south side of the castle-hill, among thickets of tamarisk and ruins. It was dusk when we alighted, lamenting the silence and complete humiliation, as we conceived, of Ephesus. The caravansera, to which we had been directed, was exceedingly mean and wretched. A marble coffin, freed from the human dust, served as a water-trough to a well in the front. Some figures holding Roman ensigns have been carved on it; and, as we learn from the inscription, it once contained the bodies of a captain of a trireme, named the Griffin, together with his wife. Close by, some tall camels, just arrived, stood pensive; or, with their knees tied, to prevent their rising from the ground, mildly waited the removal of their burdens.

The caravansera being full, we were distressed for a place to lodge in, but after some time a Turk offered us a shed by his cottage, open to the south-east, the roof and sides black with smoke. Some martens had made their nests against the rafters; and we were told, their visits were deemed to portend good, and that the Turks wished them to frequent their apartments, leaving a passage for their admission. Our horses were disposed among the walls and rubbish, with their saddles on; and a mat was spread for us on the ground . . . A shrill owl, named Cucuvaia from its note, with a night-hawk, flitted near us; and a jackal cried mournfully, as if forsaken by his companions, on the mountain.

We retired early in the evening to our shed, not without some sensations of melancholy, which were renewed at the dawn of day. We had then a distinct view of a solemn and most forlorn spot; a neglected castle,[2] a grand mosque, and a broken aqueduct, with mean

[1] Now a large village of 9,000 inhabitants—took the name of Selçuk in 1914.
[2] This dates from the sixth century A.D.

cottages, and ruinous buildings interspersed among wild thickets, and spreading to a considerable extent. Many of the scattered structures are square, with domes, and have been baths. Some grave-stones occurred, finely painted and gilded, and fairly embossed, as the Turkish manner is, with characters in relievo. But the castle, the mosque, and the aqueduct, are alone sufficient evidences, as well of the former greatness of the place, as of its importance.

The castle is a large and barbarous edifice, the wall built with square towers. You ascend to it over heaps of stones intermixed with scraps of marble. An outwork, which secured the approach, con-sisted of two lateral walls from the body of the fortress, with a gateway. This faces the sea, and is supported on each side by a huge and awkward buttress, constructed chiefly with the seats of a theatre or stadium, many of them marked with Greek letters. Several frag-ments of inscriptions are inserted in it, or lie near. Over the arch are four pieces of ancient sculpture. The two in the middle are in alto-relievo, of most exquisite workmanship, and evidently parts of the same design; one, representing, it seems, the death of Patroclus; the other, plainly the bringing of his body to Achilles. The third exhibits a corpse, it is likely that of Hector, with women lamenting; is in basso-relievo, not so wide, and, besides, differs so much, that it can be considered as connected with the former only in having a reference to the Iliad. These were carefully drawn by Mr. Pars; and two of them, the first and last, may be seen, engraved by Bartolozzi, in Mr. Wood's Essay on Homer. The fourth is carved with boys and vine-branches, is narrower, and much injured.[1] Within the castle are a few huts, an old mosque, and a great deal of rubbish. If you move a stone here, it is a chance but you find a scorpion under it.

The grand mosque is situated beneath the castle, westward. The side next the foot of the hill is of stone; the remainder, of veined marble, polished. The two domes are covered with lead, and each is adorned with the Mahometan crescent. In front is a court, in which was a large fountain to supply the devout mussulman with water, for the purifications required by his law. The broken columns are remains of a portico. The three entrances of the court, the doorways of the mosque, and many of the window-cases have mouldings in

[1] Tournefort, vol. III, p. 351. [C]

the Saracenic style, with sentences, as we supposed, from the Koran, in Arabic characters, handsomely cut. The windows have wooden frames, and are latticed with wire. The inside is mean, except the kiblé, or portion toward Mecca, which is ornamented with carving, painting, and gilding. The minaret is fallen. We found a long Greek inscription, nearly effaced, in the wall of the side next to Gallesus. The fabric was raised with old materials. The large granite columns which sustain the roof, and the marbles, are spoils from ancient Ephesus.

The aqueduct, on the opposite side of the castle-hill, reaches from the foot quite across the plain, eastward to mount Pactyas. The piers are square and tall, and many in number, with arches of brick. They are constructed chiefly with inscribed pedestals; on one of which is the name of Atticus Herodes, whose statue it has supported. We copied or collated several, but found none which have not been published. The minute diligence of earlier collectors had been extended to the unimportant fragments, and even single words within reach, from the first to the forty-fifth pier. The marbles yet untouched would furnish a copious and curious harvest, if accessible. The downfall of some may be expected continually, from the tottering condition of the fabric; and time and earthquakes will supply the wand of ladders, for which the traveller wishes in vain at a place, where, if a tall man, he may almost overlook the houses. The water was conveyed in earthen pipes, and, it has been surmised, was that of a famous spring named Halitæa. It is now intercepted, no moisture trickling from the extremity of the duct on the mountain. The ruin abounds in snakes . . .

In the way from Aisaluck to Guzel-hissar or Magnesia by the Mæander,[1] about four or five miles distant, is a narrow woody valley, with a stream, over which is an ancient bridge of three arches. Two long lines, one in Latin, the other in Greek, are inscribed on it, and inform us, it was dedicated to the Ephesian Diana, the emperor Cæsar Augustus, Tiberius Cæsar his son, and to the people of Ephesus; and also that Pollio, a Roman, erected it at his own expense.[2] This fabric has been deformed by a subsequent addition;

[1] Now Morali.
[2] *Inscript. Ant.*, p. 11. [C]. *CIG*, 2, p. 603, no. 2958.

the three arches now sustaining six, extended to convey a current of water across the valley, probable to the aqueduct of Aiasaluck.

Aiasaluck has had an affinity with Ephesus similar to that of Sevrihissar with Teos. We found no theatre, nor stadium, nor temple. The whole was patchwork, composed of marbles and fragments removed from their original places, and put together without elegance or order. We were convinced that we had not arrived yet at Ephesus, before we discovered the ruins of that city; which are by the mountains, nearer the sea, visible from the castle-hill, and distant above half a mile. . .

Aiasaluck has certainly flourished chiefly, if not solely, under the Mahometans. Its origin may with probability be referred to the thirteenth century. It is related, that Mantakhia subdued Ephesus with Caria in 1313. He perhaps fortified this rock for a strong hold, and the town grew under its protection. The mosque and aqueduct, as well as the castle, are great though inelegant structures. They suggest the idea, that the place has been honoured with the residence of princes, and it is likely were erected under him and his nephew Amir. The marble materials of ancient Ephesus, then in ruins, were amassed for these buildings, which have contributed largely to the present nakedness of its site.

On the second evening of our stay at Aiasaluck heavy clouds began to arrive apace, with a southerly wind, and to settle upon the mountains round us; when all became black and gloomy. At night frequent flashes of pale lightning, each making a momentary day, gleamed into the plain; while awful thunder, prolonged by repeated reverberations, moved solemnly along upon the summits. The explosions were near, and loud, and dreadful, far beyond any I ever heard before. Well might the devout heathen, unskilled in natural causes, ascribe to a present deity so grand an operation; and while the tremendous god drove, as he conceived, his terrible chariot through the darkness, tremble at the immense display of his power, and be filled with apprehension of his wrath.

The rain, pouring down violently in large drops, soon made its way through our slender shed, and fell plentifully on us and our bedding, tinged with soot and dirt. Our horses were without shelter, and our men in an instant wet to the skin. It held up again about ten in the morning, and we crossed the plain to the ruins of Ephesus, but soon after the thunder and rain recommenced, and forced us to return. In the afternoon the plain was deluged with water, from the mountains, running down like a torrent, and rendering it in many places impassable. The aga of Aiasaluck being absent, we visited his deputy, our men carrying, as usual, some coffee and small loaves of sugar as a present. He received us sitting cross-legged[1] on the roof of an old bath, which was his habitation.

[1] In the original edition Chandler wrote that they were received 'very graciously', but Revett's manuscript note on his own copy records in the margin, 'ungraciously, being in a sullen humour'.

XVIII

EPHESUS was situated by the mountains, which are the southern boundary of the plain, and comprehended within its wall a portion of mount Prion and of Corissus.[1] Mount Prion is a circular hill, resembling that of Aiasaluck, but much larger. Corissus is a single lofty ridge, extending northward from near mount Pactyas, and approaching Prion, then making an elbow, and running westwardly toward the sea. This city, as well as Smyrna, was built by Lysimachus, who also enrolled its senate, and provided for its civil government.

We entered Ephesus[2] from Aiasaluck, with mount Prion, and the exterior lateral wall of a stadium, which fronted the sea, on our left hand. Going on and turning, we passed that wing of the building, and the area opened to us. We measured it with a tape, and found it six hundred eighty-seven feet long. The side next the plain was raised on vaults, and faced with the strong wall before mentioned. The opposite side, which overlooks it, and the upper end, both rested on the slope of the hill. The seats, which ranged in numerous rows one above another, have all been removed; and of the front only a few marbles remain, with an arch,[3] which terminates the left wing, and was one of the avenues provided for the spectators. Upon the keystone of the back front is a small mutilated figure. This part of the fabric was restored, or repaired, when the city had declined in splendour, and was partly ruinous; for it is composed of marbles which have belonged to other buildings. A bass-relief, rudely carved, is inserted in it; and several inscriptions, effaced, or too

[1] Now Panagır Dağı and Bulbul Dağı.

[2] For discussion of site and a plan see Bean, *op. cit.*, pp. 160–184. Austrian archaeologists have continued their excavations on this site since 1955.

[3] *Views*. Le Brun, p. 31. [C]. Pl. 9, p. 22: see Bibliography.

high up to be read; besides fragments, some with Roman letters.

The preaching of St. Paul produced a tumult at Ephesus, the people rushing into the theatre, and shouting "Great is Diana." The vestiges of this structure, which was very capacious, are farther on in the side of the same mountain. The seats and the ruins of the front are removed. In both wings are several architectural fragments; and, prying about the side next to the stadium, we discovered an inscription[1] over an arch, once one of the avenues, and closed up perhaps to strengthen the fabric . . .

Going on from the theatre, which had a stoa, or portico, annexed to it, as may be collected from the pedestals and bases of columns ranging along on this side, and concealed partly in the ground, you come to a narrow valley, which divides mount Prion from Corissus. Near the entrance, in a small watercourse, was a marble with an inscription, which I copied;[2] and we could discern a few letters on another stone overwhelmed with rubbish. Close by were ruins of a church, and a stone carved with the Greek cross. Within the valley you find broken columns and pieces of marble, with vestiges of an odeum, or music-theatre, in the slope of Prion. This, which was not a large structure, is stripped of the seats, and naked. Near it are some piers with small arches, each of a single stone, almost buried in soil. It is a precept of Vitruvius, that the odeum be on the left hand coming from the theatre.[3]

Beyond the odeum the valley opens gradually into the plain of Aiasaluck. Keeping round by Prion, you meet with vestiges of buildings, and come to the remains of a large edifice, resembling that with an arcade at Troas. The top of one of the niches is painted with waves and fishes, and among the fragments lying in the front are two trunks of statues, of great size, without heads, and almost buried; the drapery, which is in both the same, remarkable. This huge

[1] See *Inscript. Ant.*, p. 11. [C]. *CIG*, 2, p. 610, no. 2976.

[2] *Inscript. Ant.*, p. 11. [C]. *CIG*, 2, p. 612, no. 2983.

[3] Vitruvius speaks here of the porticoes of theatres, and among other examples gives the odeum of Pericles as one, which was situated on the left hand going out of the theatre of Bacchus, but at a distance from it, having the portico of Eumenes between them. From want of knowing this, authors have been mistaken in the sense of this passage, supposing the odeum to be a part of the theatre, or connected with it. [R]

building was the gymnasium, which is mentioned as *behind* the city. We pitched our tent among its ruins when we arrived from Claros, and were employed on it three days in taking a plan and view[1] ...

We return now to the entrance of the city from Aiasaluck. That street was nearly of the length of the stadium, which ranged along one side. The opposite side was composed of edifices equally ample and noble. The way was between a double colonnade, as we conjectured from the many pedestals and bases of columns scattered there. These fabrics were all raised high above the level of the plain, and have their vaulted substructions yet entire.

This street was crossed by one leading from the plain toward the valley before mentioned, which had on the left the front of the stadium, and the theatre, with the portico adjoining. On the right are ample substructions; and opposite to the stadium lies a basin of white marble streaked with red, about fifteen feet in diameter, once belonging to a fountain; with some shafts of small pillars near it almost buried in earth. The ruins on this side are pieces of massive wall, which have been incrusted, as appears from holes bored for affixing the marble; and ordinary arches of brick, among which are fragments of columns of red granite. These remains reach as far as the portico, and have behind them a morass, once the city-port. By the highest of them is the entrance of a souterrain, which extends underneath; these buildings having been erected on a low and marshy spot. Opposite to the portico is a vacant quadrangular space, with many bases of columns and marble fragments scattered along the edges. Here was probably the agora ...

We are now at the end of the street, and near the entrance of the valley between Prion and Corissus. Here, turning toward the sea, you have the market-place on the right hand; on the left, the sloping side of Corissus, and presently the prostrate heap of a temple,[2] which fronted east of north. The length was about one hundred and thirty feet, the breadth eighty. The cell or nave was constructed with large coarse stones. The front of the pronaos was marble, of the Corinthian order. The temple was *in antis*, and had four columns between the *antæ*. We found their capitals, and also one of a pilaster. The diameter of the columns is four feet and about six inches; their

[1] Plate III.   [2] Temple of Serapis.

length thirty-nine feet two inches, but including the base and capital forty-six feet and more than seven inches. The shafts were fluted, and though their dimensions are so great, each of one stone. The most entire of them is broken into two pieces. On the frieze was carved a bold foliage with boys. The ornaments in general are extremely rich, but much injured . . .[1]

About a mile farther on is a root of Corissus, running out toward the plain, and ending in an abrupt precipice. Upon this is a square tower, one of many belonging to the city wall, and still standing. We rode to it along the mountain-side, but that way is steep and slippery. Near it are remnants of some edifice. Among the bushes beneath we found a square altar of white marble, well preserved. On the top is an offering, like a pine-apple; perhaps intended to represent a species of cake. On the face a ram's head is carved, and a couple of horns filled with fruit; the ends twined together. The eminence commands a lovely prospect of the river Cayster, which there crosses the plain from near Gallesus, with a small but full stream, and with many luxuriant meanders.

The extent of the city toward the plain, on which side it was washed by the Cayster, cannot now be ascertained; but the mountainous region has preserved its boundary, the wall erected by Lysimachus, which is of excellent masonry. It may be traced from behind the stadium over mount Prion, standing often above twenty feet high. It crossed the valley, in which is a thick piece, with the gap of a gateway; the stones regularly placed, large, rough, and hard. From thence it ascended mount Corissus, and is seen ranging along the lofty brow, almost entire, except near the precipice, where it ceases. On mount Prion, over which I rambled, are likewise remnants of an exterior wall. This, from its direction, seems to have descended, and enclosed the gymnasium, which was without the city; forming a pomœrium by uniting with the wall on Corissus, which begins from a precipice beyond the valley.

The avenues of the ancient cities were commonly beset with sepulchres. The vaults of these edifices, stripped of their marble, occur near the entrance of Ephesus from Aiasaluck, where was once a gate; and again by the gymnasium, both on Prion and Corissus; on

[1] Of inferior taste, and the mouldings ill-proportioned. [R]

each side of the approach to the gate in the valley; and also about the abrupt precipice, without the city-wall. The vaults along the slope of Corissus, in the way thither, shew that the Ephesians buried likewise within the city . . .

Mount Pion, or Prion, is among the curiosities of Ionia enumerated by Pausanias. It has served as an inexhaustible magazine of marble, and contributed largely to the magnificence of the city . . .

In the records of our religion it is ennobled as the burying-place of St. Timothy, the companion of St. Paul, and the first bishop of Ephesus, whose body was afterwards translated to Constantinople by the founder of that city, or his son Constantius, and placed with St. Luke and St. Andrew in the church of the apostles. The story of St. John the Evangelist was deformed in an early age with gross fiction; but he also was interred at Ephesus, and, as appears from one narration, in this mountain.

In the side of Prion, not far from the gymnasium are cavities with mouths, like ovens, made to admit the bodies, which were thrust in, head or feet foremost. One has an inscription on the plane of the rock, beginning, as usual, *This is the monument*, &c. The traces of numerous sepulchres may be likewise seen. Then follows, farther on, a wide aperture or two, which are avenues to the interior quarries, of a romantic appearance, with hanging precipices; and in one is the ruin of a church, of brick, the roof arched, the ceiling plaster or stucco, painted in streaks corresponding with the mouldings. Many names of persons and sentences are written on the wall, in Greek and Oriental characters. This perhaps is the oratory or church of St. John, which was rebuilt by the emperor Justinian. It is still frequented, and had a path leading to it through tall strong thistles. Near it are remnants of brick buildings, and of sepulchres, with niches cut, some horizontally, in the rock. Going on, you come to the entrance into Ephesus from Aiasaluck. The quarries in the mountain have numberless mazes, and vast, awful, dripping caverns. In many parts are chippings of marble and marks of the tools . . .

XIX

To complete the local history of Ephesus, we must deduce it from a period of remote antiquity. Prion had in former times been called Lepre Acte; and a part behind Prion was still called *the back of Lepre*, when Strabo wrote. Smyrna, a portion of the first Ephesus, was near the gymnasium, *behind* the city of Lysimachus, and between Lepre or Prion, and a spot called Tracheia beyond Corissus. When the Ionians arrived, Androclus, their leader, protected the natives, who had settled, from devotion, by the temple of Diana, and incorporated some of them with his followers; but expelled those who inhabited the town above.[1]

The city of Androclus was by the Athenæum, or temple of Minerva, which was *without* the city of Lysimachus, and by the fountain called Hypelæus, or that *under the olive tree*; taking in part of the mountainous region by Corissus, or of Tracheia. This was the city which Crœsus besieged, and the Ephesians presented for an offering to their goddess, annexing it by a rope to her temple, which was distant seven stadia, or a mile, wanting half a quarter.

It is related, that Androclus, with the Ephesians, invaded and got possession of the island of Samos. It was then debated, where to fix their abode. An oracle was consulted, and gave for answer, "A fish "should shew them, and a wild hog conduct them." Some fishermen breakfasting on the spot, where afterwards was the fountain called Hypelæus, near *the sacred port*, one of the fish leaping from the fire with a coal, fell on some chaff, which lighting, communicated with a thicket, and the flames disturbed a wild hog lying in it. This animal ran over great part of the Tracheia, and was killed with a javelin, where afterwards was the Athenæum or temple of Minerva . . .[2] The Ionians removed to the continent, and founded

[1] Strabo, 14.1.21; Pausanias, vii.2.8. [C].   [2] Athenaeus, VIII, 361. [C]

85

their city, with a temple of Diana by the market-place, and of Apollo, Pythius by the port; the oracle having been obtained and fulfilled by the favour of these deities.

Androclus, assisting the people of Priene against the Carians, fell in battle. His body was carried away and buried by the Ephesians. Pausanias relates, that his monument, on which was placed a man armed, continued to be shewn in his time, near the road going from the temple of Diana by the Olympium, toward the Magnesian gate. His posterity had possessed hereditary honours under Tiberius Cæsar. They were titular kings, wore purple, and carried in their hands a wand or sceptre. They had, moreover, precedence at the games, and a right of admission to the Eleusinian mysteries.

The temple of Diana, which rose on the contributions of all Asia, produced a desertion of the city of Androclus. The Ephesians came down from the mountainous region, or Tracheia, and settled in the plain by it, where they continued to the time of Alexander. They were then unwilling to remove into the present city; but a heavy rain falling, and Lysimachus stopping the drains, and flooding their houses, they were glad to exchange.

The port had originally a wide mouth, but foul with mud, lodged in it from the Cayster. Attalus Philadelphus and his architects were of opinion, that if the entrance were contracted it would become deeper, and in time be capable of receiving ships of burden. But the slime, which had before been moved by the flux and reflux of the sea, and carried off, being stopped, the whole basin quite to the mouth was rendered shallow. The morass, of which I had a perfect view from the top of Prion, was this port. It communicates with the Cayster, as might be expected, by a narrow mouth; and at the water-edge by the ferry, as well as in other places, may be seen the wall intended to embank the stream, and give it force by confinement. The masonry is of the kind termed *incertum*, in which the stones are of various shapes, but nicely joined. The situation was so advantageous as to overbalance the inconveniences attending the port. The town increased daily, and under the Romans was accounted the most considerable emporium of Asia within mount Taurus.[1]

Toward the end of the eleventh century Ephesus experienced the

[1] Strabo, 14.1.24. [C]

same fortune as Smyrna. A Turkish pirate, named Tangripermes, settled there. But the Greek admiral John Ducas, defeated him in a bloody battle, and pursued the flying Turks up the Mæander. In 1306 it was among the places which suffered from the exactions of the grand duke Roger; and two years after, it surrendered to sultan Saysan, who, to prevent future insurrections, removed most of the inhabitants to Tyriæum, where they were massacred. The transactions, in which mention is made of Ephesus after this period, belong to its neighbour and successor Aiasaluck . . .

The Ephesians are now a few Greek peasants, living in extreme wretchedness, dependence, and insensibility; the representatives of an illustrious people, and inhabiting the wreck of their greatness; some, the substructions of the glorious edifices which they raised; some, beneath the vaults of the stadium, once the crowded scene of their diversions; and some, by the abrupt precipice, in the sepulchres, which received their ashes. We employed a couple of them to pile stones, to serve instead of a ladder, at the arch of the stadium and, to clear a pedestal of the portico by the theatre from rubbish. We had occasion for another to dig at the Corinthian temple; and sending to the stadium, the whole tribe, ten or twelve, followed; one playing all the way before them on a rude lyre, and at times striking the sounding-board with the fingers of his left hand in concert with the strings. One of them had on a pair of sandals of goat-skin, laced with thongs, and not uncommon. After gratifying their curiosity, they returned back as they came, with their musician in front.

Such are the present citizens of Ephesus, and such is the condition to which that renowned city has been gradually reduced. It was a ruinous place when the emperor Justinian filled Constantinople with its statues, and raised his church of St. Sophia on its columns. Since then it has been almost quite exhausted. Its streets are obscured and overgrown. A herd of goats was driven to it for shelter from the sun at noon; and a noisy flight of crows from the quarries seemed to insult its silence. We heard the partridge call in the area of the theatre and of the stadium. The glorious pomp of its heathen worship is no longer remembered; and Christianity, which was there nursed by apostles, and fostered by general councils, until it increased to fulness of stature, barely lingers on in an existence hardly visible.

XX

In the plain of Ephesus were anciently two lakes,[1] formed partly by stagnant water from the river Selinus, which ran near the Artemisium, or temple of Diana, probably from mount Gallesus. The kings had taken from the goddess the revenue arising from them, which was great; but it was restored by the Romans. The publicans then forced her to pay taxes. Artemidorus was sent ambassador to Rome, and pleaded successfully her privilege of exemption, for which and his other services the city erected a statue of him in gold. A temple in a bottom by one of the lakes was said to have been founded by Agamemnon.[2]

. . . Coming from Claros [in April 1765], we crossed the mouth of a lake, and afterwards rode along by its side. This was the lower Selenusia. Near the ferry we discovered the other, a long lake, parallel with the first, and extending across the plain. . .

The river Cayster, after entering the plain, runs by Gallesus, and crosses above the lakes, opposite the square tower. Lower down, it leaves but a narrow pass, obstructed with thickets at the foot of the mountain: it then becomes wider and deeper; and mingles, the stream still and smooth, with the sea. On the banks, and in the morass or port, and in the lake near the ferry, we saw thick groves of tall reeds, some growing above twenty feet high; and it is observable, that the river-god is represented on the Ephesian medals with this aquatic as one of his attributes. An ordinary bridge of three arches is built over the river, at the foot of Gallesus . . .

The arrangement of this portion of the coast, given by Strabo, is as follows. After Neapolis,[3] now Scala Nova, and Phygela,[4] going

---

[1] Pliny, *Nat. Hist.*, V. xxxi. 115. [C]

[2] Strabo, 14.1.27. [C]　　　　　　　　　　[3] Now Kuşadası Gü.

[4] Pygela is thought to be a small peninsular site near Kuşadası.

northward, was port Panormus, which boasted the temple of the Ephesian Diana; then the city, which had arsenals and a port; beyond the mouth of the Cayster was a lake, called Selenusia, made by water which the sea repelled; and in the same direction another, communicating with it; then mount Gallesus. Panormus, it is likely, was the general name of the whole haven, and comprised both *the Sacred Port*, or that by which the temple stood, and *the City Port*, now the morass. The former is perhaps quite filled up . . .

We would close our account of Ephesus [here], but the curious reader will ask, What is become of the renowned temple of Diana? Can a wonder of the world be vanished, like a Phantom, without leaving a trace behind? We would gladly give a satisfactory answer to such queries; but, to our great regret, we searched for the site of this fabric to as little purpose as the travellers who have preceded us.

The worship of the great goddess Diana had been established at Ephesus in a remote age. The Amazons, it is related, sacrificed to her there, on their way to Attica, in the time of Theseus; and some writers affirmed, the image was first set up by them under a tree. The vulgar afterwards believed it fell down from Jupiter. It was never changed, though the temple had been restored seven times.

This idol, than which none has been ever more splendidly enshrined, was of a middling size, and of very great antiquity, as was evident from the fashion, it having the feet closed. It was of wood, which some had pronounced cedar, and other ebony. Mutianus, a noble Roman, who was the third time consul in the year of our Lord seventy-five, affirmed from his own observation, that it was vine, and had many holes filled with nard to nourish and moisten it, and to preserve the cement. It was gorgeously apparelled; the vest embroidered with emblems and symbolical devices; and, to prevent its tottering, a bar of metal, it is likely of gold, was placed under each hand. A veil or curtain, which was drawn up from the floor to the ceiling, hid it from view, except while service was performing in the temple.

The priests of the goddess were eunuchs, and exceedingly respected by the people. The old institutions required that virgins should assist them in their office, but, in process of time, these, as Strabo has remarked, were not all observed . . .

It may be imagined, that many stories of the power and interposition of the goddess were current and believed at Ephesus. The most striking evidence of the reality of her existence, and of her regard for her suppliants, was probably furnished by her supposed manifestations of herself in visions. In the history of Massiliæ,[1] now Marseilles, it is related, that she was seen by Aristarche, a lady of high rank, while sleeping, and that she commanded her to accompany the Greek adventurers, by whom that city was founded. Metagenes,[2] one of the architects of her temple at Ephesus, had invented a method of raising the vast stones to the necessary height, but it did not succeed so well as was expected, with a marble of prodigious size, designed to be placed over the doorway. He was excessively troubled, and, weary of ruminating, fell asleep, when he beheld the goddess, who bade him be comforted, she had been his friend. The next day the stone was found to have settled, apparently from its own weight, as he wished.

Near the path, after passing the aqueduct at Aiasaluck, in our way from Smyrna, we met with a curious memorial of the importance of the goddess, and of the respect paid to her.[3] It is a decree of the Ephesians, inscribed on a slab of white marble . . .

A people convinced that the self-manifestations of the deity before mentioned were real, could not easily be turned to a religion, which did not pretend to a similar or equal intercourse with its divinity. And this perhaps is the true reason, why, in the early ages of Christianity, besides the miraculous agency of the spirit in prophetic fits of ecstasy, a belief of supernatural interposition by the Panagia, or *Virgin Mary*, and by saints appearing in daily or nightly visions, was encouraged and inculcated. It helped by its currency to procure and confirm the credulous votary, to prevent or refute the cavil of the heathen, to exalt the new religion, and to deprive the established of its ideal superiority. The superstitions derived on the Greek church from this source, in a remote period, and still continuing to flourish in it, would principally impede the progress of any who should endeavour to convert its members to the nakedness of reformed Christianity . . .

[1] Strabo, 4.1.4. [C]
[2] Pliny, *Nat. Hist.*, XXXVI. xxi. 95–97. [C]. Pliny mentions Chersiphron as architect.   [3] *Inscript. Ant.*, p. 13. [C]. *CIG*, 2, p. 600, no. 2954.

XXI

THE reputation and the riches of their Diana had made Ephesians desirous to provide for her a magnificent temple. The fortunate discovery of marble in mount Prion gave them new vigour. The cities of Asia, so general was the esteem for the goddess, contributed largely; and Crœsus was at the expense of many of the columns. The spot chosen for the building was a marsh, as most likely to preserve the structure free from gaps, and uninjured by earthquakes. The foundation was made with charcoal rammed, and with fleeces. The souterrain consumed immense quantities of marble. The edifice was exalted on a basement, with ten steps. The architects, Ctesiphon of Crete, and Metagenes his son, were likewise authors of a treatise on the fabric. Demetrius, a servant of Diana, and Peonius, an Ephesian, were said to have completed this work which was two hundred and twenty years about . . .

Ctesiphon invented a curious machine, of which a description is preserved, for transporting the shafts of the columns: fearing, if a carriage were laden with a stone so ponderous as each was, the wheels would sink deep into the soil. Metagenes adapted his contrivance to convey the architraves. These were so bulky, that the raising of any one of them to its place appeared a miracle. Perhaps it was done by forming a gentle ascent, higher than the columns, of baskets filled with sand; emptying those beneath, when the mass was arrived, and thus letting it gradually down upon the capitals. By this method, the prodigious stone, formerly mentioned, was inserted over the doorway.

This temple, which Xerxes spared, was set on fire by Herostratus; but the votaries of Diana proved so extravagant in their zeal, that she was a gainer by his exploit. A new and more glorious fabric was begun; and Alexander the Great, arriving at Ephesus, wished to inscribe it as the dedicator; and was willing, for that gratification, to defray the whole expense; but the Ephesians declined accepting this magnificent offer . . .

The temple now erected was reckoned the first in Ionia for magnitude and riches. It was four hundred and twenty-five feet long, and two hundred and twenty broad. Of the columns, which were sixty feet high, one hundred and twenty-seven were donations from kings. Thirty-six were carved; and one of them, perhaps as a model, by Scopas. The order was Ionic, and it had eight columns in front.[1] The folding-doors, or gates, had been continued four years in glue, and were made of cypress-wood, which had been treasured up for four generations, highly polished. These were found by Mutianus as fresh and as beautiful four hundred years after, as when new. The ceiling was of cedar; and the steps for ascending the roof, of a single stem of a vine, which witnessed the durable nature of that wood. The whole altar was in a manner full of the works of Praxiteles. The offerings were inestimable, and among them was a picture by Apelles, representing Alexander armed with thunder . . . The structure was so wonderfully great in its composition, and so magnificently adorned, it appeared the work of beings more than human. The sun, it is affirmed, beheld in his course no object of superior excellence, or worthier of admiration.

The temple of Diana had the privilege of an asylum, or sanctuary, before the time of Alexander; but he extended it to the stadium, or half a quarter of a mile. Afterwards Mithridates shot an arrow from the angle of the pediment, and his boundary exceeded the stadium, but not much. Mark Antony coming near him, enlarged it so as to comprehend a portion of the city; but that concession proving inconvenient and dangerous was annulled by Augustus Cæsar . . .

It appears, that the temple was distinct from the present city, and

---

[1] If the temple was two hundred and twenty feet broad, and the columns were sixty feet high, it must have had twelve columns in front; for then pieces of the architrave, from centre to centre of the columns, would be nineteen feet long, and that in the centre intercolumnation twenty-three feet in length, in order to extend the breadth of the edifice to two hundred and twenty feet. The distance of nineteen feet from centre to centre of column will exactly answer to four hundred and twenty-five feet, the length of the temple, supposing the columns to be twenty-three in number, and their diameters seven feet. [R]

the distance may be inferred; for Mark Anthony allowing the sanctuary to reach somewhat more than a stadium from it, a part of the city was comprised within those limits. It was, moreover, *without* the Magnesian gate, which, I should suppose, was that next Aiasaluck; and, in the second century, was joined to the city by Damianus, a sophist, who continued the way down to it through the Magnesian gate, by erecting a stoa, or portico, of marble, a stadium, of six hundred twenty-five feet in length; which expensive work was inscribed with the name of his wife, and intended to prevent the absence of the ministers when it rained. He likewise dedicated a banqueting-room in the temple, as remarkable for its dimensions as its beauty. It was adorned with Phrygian marble, such as had never been cut in the quarries before . . .[1]

The edifice was deemed a wonder, not for its form, as at all uncommon, but for the grandeur of its proportions, the excellence of its workmanship, and the magnificence of its decorations . . .

A writer[2] who lived toward the end of the second century, has cited a sibyl as foretelling, that, the earth opening and quaking, the temple of Diana would be swallowed, like a ship in a storm into the abyss: and Ephesus lamenting and weeping by the river banks, would inquire for it, then inhabited no more. If the authenticity of the oracle were undisputed, and the sibyl acknowledged a genuine prophetess, we might infer, from the visible condition of the place, the full accomplishment of the whole prediction. We now seek in vain for the temple; the city is prostrate; and the goddess gone.[3]

[1] Philostratus, *Lives of the Sophists*, Bk. II, chap. 23. [C]

[2] Clemens Alexandrinus, *Exhortation to the Greeks*, Chap. iv. [C]

[3] Although Chandler was aware that this temple was outside the Magnesia Gate, he failed to locate it. After a long search J. T. Wood found it and worked there from 1863 to 1874, but he did not excavate the temple to its lowest level. However in 1904, D. G. Hogarth, working under the auspices of the British Museum completed the task and the finds from his excavation are now in this museum. The site of the temple is strangely unimpressive for such a great monument, being on flat ground outside the city. See J. T. Wood, *Discoveries at Ephesus* (London, 1877), and ARTEMISIUM: D. G. Hogarth, *Excavations at Ephesus* (London, 1908).

XXII

AFTER staying at Aiasaluck four days, we set out at half past seven in the morning, with a guide on an ass, for Neapolis, or Scala Nova, distant three hours. The plain was covered with mud and slime from the recent inundation. It produces corn, cotton, sesamus, and tobacco; but in several places was swampy, and overgrown with rushes and reeds. Flocks, and herds, and camels were feeding on it . . .

We came in an hour to the gap in Corissus, and left the plain behind . . . We soon had the back of Corissus on our left hand, with the exterior front of the city-wall, high in the air, on the ridge, which is steep and inaccessible. On the mountain, between the gap and the sea, are likewise traces of a wall. Before us was a pleasant valley, with a Turkish burying-ground, and a village named Arvisia beyond a mean, ruinous aqueduct, which the road approaches, and then becomes rough and rugged; leading over the rock, in view of the sea, of the mouth of the Cayster, and of the extremity of the plain of Ephesus; into which a track descends, crossing a piece of wet low ground at the end of the mountain . . .

[Continuing] southward, we passed the vestiges of a small town, Pygela, or Phygela, upon a hill. There was once a temple of Diana, founded, as they related, by Agamemnon. He was said to have touched at this place, in his voyage homeward, and to have left behind some of his men, who were disabled by rowing. The wine of Phygela is commended by Dioscorides; and its territory was now green with vines . . .

In the Ephesian decree,[1] the city is stiled *the nurse of her own goddess*. The local story was, that Latona had been delivered of her in Ortygia, a beautiful grove of trees of various kinds, chiefly cypresses,

[1] See p. 90, n. 3.

near Ephesus, on the coast, a little up from the sea. This place was filled with shrines and images. A general assembly was held there yearly; and splendid entertainments were provided, and mystic sacrifices solemnized. The Cenchrius, probably a crooked river, ran through it; and above it was the mountain Solmissus, on which, it was fabled, the Curetes stood and rattled on their shields, to divert the attention of Juno.[1]

As the site of Ortygia is marked by a mountain and a river, we expected to discover it without much difficulty; and with that view preferred, in our second journey from Ephesus [April 1765], the lower way to Scala Nova, going from the gymnasium, where we had pitched our tent, to the extremity of the plain, and then along by the sea. We came in sight of the town sooner than before, and turned into the road near Phygela, a little beyond the broken wall, without meeting with any thing remarkable.

The improved face of a country is perishable, like human beauty. Not only the birthplace of Diana and its sanctity are forgotten, but the grove and buildings which adorned it appear no more; and, perhaps, as I have since suspected, the land has encroached on the sea, and the valley, in which Arvisis is, was once Ortygia. The houses of Damianus, in the suburbs of the city, with the pleasant plantations on his estate, and the artificial islands and portlets which he made by the seaside, are all now equally invisible.

Scala Nova is situated in a bay, on the slope of a hill, the houses rising one above another, intermixed with minarees and tall slender cypresses. A street through which we rode was hung with goat-skins exposed to dry, dyed of almost lively red. At one of the fountains is an ancient coffin, used as a cistern. The port was filled with small-craft. Before it is an old fortress[2] on a rock or islet, frequented by gulls and seamews. By the water-side is a large and good khan, at which we passed a night on our return . . .

We arrived at Scala Nova from Aiasaluck at about eleven in the morning, and drank coffee, while our men procured provisions to carry with us. We mounted again at twenty minutes before twelve, and leaving an aqueduct, with a road leading toward the sea, on our

[1] Strabo, 14.1.20. [C]
[2] Probably built by the Turks in the fourteenth or fifteenth centuries A.D.

95

right hand, passed over a broken causey to a village pleasantly situated on a hill covered with vines, called Cornea ... [By mid-afternoon they were overlooking] a beautiful cultivated plain, lying low beneath us, bounded by the sea and by Mycale, a mountain, now, as anciently, woody, and abounding in wild beasts. The promontory, once called Trogilium runs out toward the north end of Samos, which was in view, and meeting a promontory of the island, named Posidium, makes a strait only seven stadia, or near a mile wide ...

Before us were lofty mountains. Entering within the range, we had Mycale on our right hand, and on our left the termination of mount Pactyas and of mount Messogis; the latter, which was once famous for wine, reaching hither from Celænæ in Phrygia, bounding the plain on the north side of the river Mæander. The road was broken and rough. As we advanced, the passage widened; and we had on our right a water-course. We discovered the dome and minaret of a mosque, with a cypress-tree or two before us; and ten minutes after five came to Suki, a Turkish village by a plain. We were lodged in a mean caravansera, with mud walls.

In the morning it lightned and rained; with awful thunder, at intervals, on the mountain-tops, which were enveloped in fleecy clouds. We left the village at seven, and travelled along by the foot of Mycale, on the edge of the plain, which is very extensive, and skirted round with mountains. Mycale rose very high on our right hand, appearing as a single ridge, with many villages on its side. By the way were flowering shrubs, and we enjoyed the fragrance and dewy freshness of spring in autumn. We came in two hours near Kelibesh, where our guide was bemired. From this place we afterwards examined the ruins of Priene, which we now passed. At ten minutes after one we were ferried over the Mæander, now called Mendres, below it, in a triangular float, with a rope. The man was a black, and in his features strongly resembled a satyr. The stream was smooth and placid, but muddy.

XXIII

MILETUS is a very mean place, but still called Palat or Palatia, *the Palaces*.[1] The principal relic of its former magnificence is a ruined theatre, which is visible afar off,[2] and was a most capacious edifice, measuring in front four hundred and fifty-seven feet. The external face of this vast fabric is marble, and the stones have a projection near the upper edge, which, we surmised, might contribute to the raising them with facility. The seats ranged, as usual, on the slope of a hill, and a few of them remain. The vaults, which supported the extremities of the semi-circle, with the arches or avenues in the two wings, are constructed with such solidity as not easily to be demolished. The entrance of the vault of substruction, on the left side, was filled up with soil; but we examined that next the river; one of our Armenians going before us with a candle in a long paper lantern. The moment we had crept in, innumerable large bats began flitting about us. The stench was hardly tolerable; and the commotion of the air, with the apprehensions of our attendant, threatened us with the loss of our light. After we had gone a considerable way in, we found the passage choked with dry filth, and returned.

On the side of the theatre next to the river is an inscription[3] in mean characters rudely cut, in which "the city Miletus" is mentioned seven times. This a monument of heretical Christianity. One Basilides, who lived in the second century, was the founder of an absurd sect called Basilidians and Gnostics, the original proprietors of the many gems, with strange devices and inscriptions, intended to be worn as amulets or charms, with which the cabinets of the

[1] Now Balat. For discussion of site and plans see Bean, op. cit., pp. 219–230. Excavations were resumed here by the Germans in 1955.   [2] Frontispiece.
[3] *Inscript. Ant.*, pp. 16, 17 [C]. *CIG*, 2, p. 568, no. 2895.

curious now abound. One of their idle tenets was, that the appellative "Jehovah" possessed signal virtue and efficacy. They expressed it by the seven Greek vowels, which they transposed into a variety of combinations. The superstition appears to have prevailed in no small degree at Miletus. In this remain the mysterious name is frequently repeated, and the deity six times invoked, "Holy Jehovah, "preserve the town of the Milesians, and all the inhabitants." The archangels also are summoned to be their guardians, and the whole city is made the author of these supplications; from which, thus engraved, it expected, as may be presumed, to derive lasting prosperity and a kind of talismanical protection.

The whole site of the town, to a great extent, is spread with rubbish, and overrun with thickets. The vestiges of the heathen city are pieces of wall, broken arches, and a few scattered pedestals, and inscriptions,[1] a square marble urn, and many wells. One of the pedestals has belonged to a statue of the emperor Hadrian, who was a friend to the Milesians, as appears from the titles of saviour and benefactor bestowed on him. Another has supported the emperor Severus, and has a long inscription, with this curious preamble: "The senate and "people of the city of the Milesians, the first settled in Ionia, and the "mother of many and great cities both in Pontus and Egypt, and in "various other parts of the world." This lies among the bushes behind the theatre. Near the ferry is a large lion in a couchant posture, much injured; and in a Turkish burying-ground another. . .[2] Some fragments of ordinary churches are interspersed among the ruins; and traces remain of an old fortress[3] erected upon the theatre, beneath which is a square enclosure, designed, it seems, as a station for an armed party to dispute or defend the passage of the river. Several piers of a mean aqueduct are standing. . .

From the number of forsaken mosques, it is evident, that Mahometanism has flourished in its turn at Miletus. All these have been mean buildings and mere patchwork; but one, a noble and beautiful structure of marble, is in use, and the dome, with a tall palm-tree or

[1] *Inscript. Ant.*, pp. 16, 17 [C]. *CIG*, 2, p. 561, no. 2818; p. 560, no. 2876; p. 565, no. 2887; p. 559, no. 2868; p. 567, no. 2891; p. 567, no. 2893.

[2] For position of lions see Hachette World Guides, *Turkey*, p. 283.

[3] This Byzantine fortress was built in the eighth century with materials from the theatre.

v   Ruins of the Temple of Apollo Didymaeus; second view. (Cat. 11)

VI   Fragment from the Temple of Apollo Didymaeus (Cat. 12)

two, towers amid the ruins and some low flat-roofed cottages, inhabited by a very few Turkish families, the present citizens of Miletus.

The history of this place, after the declension of the Greek empire, is very imperfect. The whole region has undergone frequent ravages from the Turks, while possessed of the interior country, and intent on extending their conquests westward to the shore. One sultan in 1175 sent twenty thousand men, with orders to lay waste the Roman provinces, and bring him sea-water, sand, and an oar. All the cities in the Mæander and on the coast were then ruined. Miletus was again destroyed toward the end of the thirteenth century by the conquering Othman.

Miletus was once exceedingly powerful and illustrious. Its early navigators extended its commerce to remote regions. The whole Euxine sea, the Propontis, Egypt, and other countries, were frequented by its ships, and settled by its colonies. It boasted a venerable band of memorable men; Hecatæus, an early historian, and Thales, the father of philosophy. It withstood Darius, and refused to admit Alexander. It has been stiled the metropolis and head of Ionia; the bulwark of Asia; chief in war and peace; mighty by sea; the fertile mother, which had poured forth her children to every quarter, counting not fewer than seventy-five cities descended from her. It afterwards fell so low as to furnish a proverbial saying, "The "Milesians were once great:" but if we compare its ancient glory, and that its subsequent humiliation, with its present state, we may justly exclaim, Miletus, how much lower art thou now fallen!

XXIV

WHILE we were employed on the theatre of Miletus, the aga of Suki, son-in-law by marriage to Elez-Oglu, crossed the plain towards us, attended by a considerable train of domestics and officers, their vests and turbans of various and lively colours, mounted on long-tailed horses, with shewy trappings, and glittering furniture. He returned, after hawking, to Miletus, and we went to visit him, with a present of coffee and sugar; but were told that two favourite birds had flown away, and that he was vexed and tired. A couch was prepared for him beneath a shed made against a cottage, and covered with green boughs to keep off the sun. He entered as we were standing by, and fell down on it to sleep, without taking any notice of us. We rambled over the ruins until he awoke, when we were again admitted. He was sitting on a carpet, cross-legged, with a hooded falcon on his knee, and another, which he stroked often and caressed, before him on a stand. Round about him were dogs and horses. The Armenian, who interpreted for us, offered him our firhman; but he said, it was sufficient that he knew our country; that the English and Turks were brethren. He examined our weapons with attention; discoursed on them and our apparel, expressed regret that he was unable to entertain us so well as he wished, and promised us a letter of recommendation to the aga of Melasso. We were treated each with a pipe and dish of coffee; after which, making our obeisance, we retired, well pleased with his manly politeness and civility. In the morning he sent the letter, and a little old man, a Turk, who had been a camel-leader, and was well acquainted with the roads, to be our guide.

We set out at twenty minutes about eight for Ura, or Urada, where we expected to find the ruins of Branchidæ,[1] a place famous

[1] Didyma.

for a most magnificent temple dedicated to Apollo Didymæus.[1] Near the city-gate, going thither, on the left hand of the road, was once the monument of Neleus, a leader of the Ionians, and founder of Miletus. This was probably a barrow. We saw no traces of the city-wall. In half an hour the plain ended, and we came to the foot-hills of mount Latmus; and soon after to a poor village of Greeks named Auctui, where we stayed an hour to procure fowls, eggs, and other provisions, to be carried with us. After passing a healthy vale by the sea, and then crossing a high ridge, some columns of the temple came in view. The road was over the mountain among low shrubs, chiefly the arbutus, then laden with fruit, like strawberries, large and tempting; the colour a lively red, the taste luscious and woody.[2] Before us was a small inlet or gulf on the north side of the promontory Posidium, on which the temple is situated. We came to the head of it, and turning up in a valley, arrived about twelve at Ura, where are a few straggling huts . . .

In descending from the mountain toward the gulf, I had remarked in the sea something white on the farther side; and going afterwards to examine it, found the remain of a circular pier belonging to the port, which was called Panormus. The stones, which are marble, and about six feet in diameter, extend from near the shore; where are traces of buildings, probably houses, overrun with thickets of myrtle, mastic, and evergreens.

Some water occurring fifteen minutes from Ura, and presently becoming more considerable, I traced it to the gulf, which it enters at the head, after a very short course, full and slow. This was anciently supposed to have its source on mount Mycale, and to pass the sea in its way to port Panormus, by which it emerged opposite to Branchidæ.

The temple of Apollo was . . . two miles and a half, from the shore . . . It is approached by a gentle ascent, and seen afar off; the land toward the sea lying flat and level. The memory of the pleasure which this spot afforded me will not be soon or easily erased. The columns yet entire are so exquisitely fine, the marble mass so vast

[1] Now Yenihisar. For discussion of site and plans see Bean, op. cit., pp. 231–243. The Germans resumed excavations here in 1962.
[2] Pliny, *Nat. Hist.*, XV. xxviii. 98. [C]

and noble, that it is impossible perhaps to conceive greater beauty and majesty of ruin. At evening, a large flock of goats, returning to the fold, their bells tinkling, spread over the heap, climbing to browse on the shrubs and trees growing between the huge stones. The whole mass was illuminated by the declining sun with a variety of rich tints, and cast a very strong shade. The sea, at a distance was smooth and shining, bordered by a mountainous coast, with rocky island. The picture was as delicious as striking. A view of part of the heap, with plates of the architecture of this glorious edifice, has been engraved and published, with its history, at the expense of the society of Dilettanti.[1]

We found among the ruins, which are extensive, a plain stone cistern, covered, except an end, with soil; many marble coffins, unopened, or with the lids broken; and one, in which was a thigh bone; all sunk deep in earth; with five statues,[2] near each other, in a row, almost buried. In the stubble of some Turkey wheat were a number of bee-hives, each a long hollow trunk of wood headed like a barrel, piled in a heap. An Armenian, who was with me, on our putting up a hare, to my surprise slunk away. This animal, as I was afterwards informed, is held in abomination by that people, and the seeing it accounted an ill omen.

The temple of Apollo Didymæus seeming likely to detain us some time, we regretted the entire solitude of the spot, which obliged us to fix our quarters at Ura. Our Armenian cook, who tarried there with our baggage, sent us provisions ready dressed, and we dined under a shady tree by the ruins. Our horses were tied, and feeding by us. Our camel-leader testified his benevolence and regard, by frequent tenders of his short pipe, and of coffee, which he made unceasingly, sitting cross-legged by a small fire. The crows settled in large companies round about, and the partridge called in the stubble.

At our return in the evening to Ura, we found two fires, with our

[1] Pars made two general views of the site: see Plates IV and V. He also drew fragments of stonework; Plates VI and VII.

[2] These statues, which Chandler was the first Englishman to observe, are now in the British Museum having been removed there in 1858 by Sir Charles Newton; see F. N. Pryce, *Catalogue of Sculpture*, vol. I, pp. 101 ff.

kettles boiling, in the open air, amid the huts and thickets. A mat was spread for us on the ground by one of them. The Turks of Ura, about fourteen in number, some with long beards, sitting cross-legged, helped to complete the grotesque circle. We were lighted by the moon, then full, and shining in a blue cloudless sky. The Turks smoked, talked, and drank coffee with great gravity, composure, and deliberation. One entertained us with playing on the Turkish guitar and with uncouth singing. The thin-voiced women, curious to see us, glided as ghosts across the glades, in white, with their faces muffled. The assemblage and the scene was uncommonly wild, and as solemn as savage . . .

We retired after supper to one of the huts, which was near the fire, and, like the rest, resembled a soldier's tent, being made with poles inclining, as the two sides of a triangle, and thatched with straw. It was barely a covering for three persons lying on the ground. The furniture was a jar of salted olives . . .

XXV

THE disorders which began to prevail among us, required a speedy exchange of the thickets for some lodging less damp and chilly. We renewed our journey, after two entire days, with satisfaction and came in two hours and a half to a deep bay, formerly called *Sinus Basilicus*, on the south side of Posidium . . . [They rode along the beach for twenty minutes and went on to ascend] the lofty mountain Grius,[1] and descended by a difficult winding track. About five in the evening we arrived at Ghauzocleu, a village fronting a pleasant bay, which is land-locked. The situation is romantic, amid naked rocks, pine and olive trees, the latter then laden with black fruit. Under the trees were several wells, and women passing to and fro with their faces muffled. Some children, who were gathered about a fire, on seeing us, ran away. The aga entertained us very hospitably. We sat on a carpet after the Turkish fashion, cross-legged, the table a large salver, on which the dishes were placed one at a time, and removed in quick succession. We had been exposed this day, without any shelter, to the sun. An accidental fire had scorched the bushes by the way, and destroyed their leaves, and the ground was bare and parched . . . [Continuing next day on horseback they came to Iasus].[2]

The Iasians were a colony of Argives, and afterwards of Milesians. Their city covered a rocket islet lying near the continent, to which it is now united by a small isthmus, was a mile and a quarter in circumference. It had a port, and was maintained by the sea, which abounded in fish; its territory being rough and barren. Several stories were current of their eagerness to purchase that article, and one is recorded. A citharist or harper was displaying his skill, and the Iasians were very attentive, until a sale of fish was announced by

---

[1] Now Ilbıra Dağı   [2] Now Küren.

the sound of a bell. Immediately they all hurried away, except one person, who was hard of hearing. "Sir," says the artist to him, "I "am indeed infinitely obliged to you for the honour you do me, and "for your love of harmony. Every body besides left me on the ring-"ing of the bell." "How!" he replied, "has the bell rung? then, sir, "your servant."[1]

The north side of the rock of Iasus[2] is abrupt and inaccessible. The summit is occupied by a mean but extensive fortress. At the foot is a small portion of flat ground. On that and on the acclivities the houses once stood, within a narrow compass, bounded to the sea by the city wall, which was regular, solid, and handsome, like that of Ephesus. This, which has been repaired in many places, now encloses rubbish, with remnants of ordinary buildings, and a few pieces of marble. Single pinks, with jonquilles, grew among the thickets of mastic; and we sprung some large covies of partridges, which feed on the berries. In the side of the rock is the theatre, with many rows of seats remaining, but covered with soil, or enveloped in bushes. On the left wing is an inscription in very large and well-formed characters, ranging in a long line, and recording certain donations to Bacchus and the people.[3] Beneath, near the bottom, are several stones inscribed, but not legible. By the isthmus is the vaulted substruction of a considerable edifice; and on a jamb of the doorway are decrees engraved in a fair character, but damaged, and black with smoke; the entrance, which is lessened by a pile of stones, serv-ing as a chimney to a few Greeks, who inhabit the ruin. Opposite to the isthmus is a flat point running out into the sea, with a small square fort at the extremity.

The sepulchres of the Iasians on the continent are very numerous, ranging along above a mile on the slope of the mountain . . . They consist mostly of a single camera or vault; but one has a wall before it, and three chambers, which have been painted. Many of them have a small square stone over the entrance, inscribed, but no longer legible. In examining these, I found half of an inscription,[4] which was

[1] Strabo, 14.2.21. [C]
[2] Iasos was an island, or perhaps a peninsula site with a sheltered harbour. An Italian mission has been excavating here since 1960.
[3] *Inscript. Ant.*, p. 19 [C]. *CIG*, 2, p. 467, no. 2681.
[4] Ibid, p. 26. [C]. *CIG*, 2, p. 467, no. 2686.

copied in 1673, and has been published incorrectly. This remnant was in a fair character, on a marble lying on the rock. Below the sepulchres are broken arches, and pieces of wall, among which is a massive coffin or two of marble standing on their basements.

A marble by the isthmus records an Iasian, who was victorious at Olympia, and the first conqueror in the Capitoline games at Rome.[1] We found there likewise a piece of inscribed architrave, on which, when more entire, a stoa or portico, and Diana Civica, or the tutelary goddess of the city, were mentioned. By a wall, which seemed the remnant of a sepulchre, is a long inscription,[2] closely but handsomely engraved on a slab of white marble, in which the theatre is mentioned, with the *Prytaneum* or town-hall, and the temples of Jupiter and Diana. While I was copying it, a Greek priest came, and displaced me somewhat roughly. I was then informed that was a church, and the stone *the holy table*. I had given offence by sitting on it. The priest was wretchedly ignorant, and, among his other absurdities, told me they had a tradition, that at the last day St. Paul will rise there, shewing the place with his foot.

A vessel from the island of Stanchio was at anchor in the bay, with some small-craft, which fish, or lade with tobacco, figs, and cotton, the produce of the country. These often carry stones away for ballast. We had paid a piaster at Scio for leave to transcribe three marbles, which lay on the shore, and were transported from this place. They contained honorary decrees made by the Iasians.[3] One is of the age of Alexander the Great, and remarkable for the extreme beauty of the characters, which were as finely designed and cut as any I ever saw. These stones were part of a square pilaster before the senate-house.

On our first arrival here, a Greek, who lived in the ruin of a large sepulchre by the isthmus, declared he was commanded to suffer nobody to enter Assyn-kalesi without a written order from the aga of Melasso, to whose district the castle belonged. We offered to purchase his permission, but in vain. He knew we were going to that city, and was afraid to accept a bribe. After a short stay, finding

[1] *Inscript. Ant.* p. 19 [C]. *CIG*, 2, p. 466, nos. 2682, 2683.
[2] Ibid, p. 20 [C]. *CIG*, 2, p. 459, no. 2671.
[3] Ibid, p. 23. [C]. *CIG*, 2, p. 462, no. 2672.

him inflexible, we continued our journey, intending to return in a few days, as we did, with authority. This sepulchre was then our abode, and we lay in it, covering, with the Greek family, the whole floor. We were guarded by two large and fierce dogs, which were continually in motion round about, barking furiously at the jackals and then looking in upon us with an attention as remarkable as friendly and agreeable.

XXVI

THE frequent accessions of new land along the coast of Asia Minor will often perplex the classical traveller, especially if not aware of the alteration; and will render him suspicious of the ancient geographers whom he consults, as of false guides, on whom he cannot depend. The cities Iasus and Bargylia were situated in the recess of the same bay, which was called the Iasian, or more commonly, the Bargylietic; yet I inquired for the latter, as a place on the coast, without obtaining any information.

We set out from Iasus at half an hour after one; and, crossing the plain, ascended a very high mountain. At a quarter before three we had in view, beneath us, an extensive plain, in which was a Turkish village; and at the mountain-foot, a lake, which communicated by small meandering channels with one opposite, and that with the bay of Iasus. Within was a hillock, resembling one of the rocks by Osebashá, with ruins on it.

We led our horses down the mountain by a steep track on the left hand, into a field, in which the tall stalks of Turkey wheat were standing; and leaving behind us the distant summit of mount Titanus, came, at twenty minutes after three, to a level green, occupied by Turcomans. Their flocks and cattle were feeding round the scattered booths; and cotton, recently gathered from the pods, was exposed on the ground to dry, or on the tops of the sheds, which are flat, and covered with boughs. Beyond these we passed a wide water-course; and had the hillock again in view through an opening on the right hand.

I wish to have my omissions supplied, as well as my errors corrected, and therefore recommend this hillock to the notice of future travellers into these countries. I have no doubt that there was the site of Bargylia,[1] and there a recess of the bay, since converted into a plain, which is almost enclosed with mountains.

The Iasians had a famous statue of Vesta, which, it was the general belief, neither rain nor hail would touch, though standing in the open air. A temple of Diana near Bargylia was supposed to be distinguished, and treated with like reverence by falling snow and showers. It was at a place named Kindye.[2]

After Bargylia, on the coast, were Myndus and Halicarnassus, colonies from Troezen; and between Baryglia and Myndus was the lake Caryanda, with an island in it and a town, the birthplace of Scylax, a very ancient geographer. The traveller who shall examine the coast of Caria, will discover Caryanda, it is believed, encompassed in like manner with Baryglia, and in a plain.

Three inland cities of Caria are recorded as worthy notice, Mylasa, Stratonicea, and Alabanda. Our road to the former place lay now between mountains and by pleasant cultivated vales. The sun had set when we arrived, and the khan was shut. A Swiss . . . happened to be there, and looking out at a window, saw our hats; and some Greek or Armenian merchants of Smyrna, whom he informed that we were Franks, prevailed on the keeper to open the gate, though the khan was full. The Swiss had been in London, and had served in an English privateer in the war with France. He was now, after many adventures, with an Hungarian, an itinerant quack doctor. The bazar, or market, was closed, and we were distressed for food. He presently killed and dressed for us a couple of fowles, and the merchants permitted us to partake of their apartment, in which we all slept on the floor, as many as it could contain.

The merchants had free access to the aga as traders, and the Hungarians, as his physician. We delivered to them the letter from the aga of Suki, to be presented to him, and in the morning went to pay our visit. He was fond of the national and warlike diversion called *the jarrit*; and we found him, though in a bad state of health,

[1] Chandler was mistaken in thinking this to be Bargylia which lies much further south, towards the end of the large L-shaped inlet southwest of Güllük. Chandler's hillock is apparently the one which is still conspicuous in the marshy plain (now reclaimed and planted with tobacco) between Milâs and Güllük—it is not an ancient city.

[2] Strabo, 14.2.20: Polybius, XVI, 12. [C]

engaged in this violent exercise, with several Turks of distinction, in a large area of court before his house. The beauty and tractability of the horses, which had very rich trappings, was as surprising as the agility and address of the riders. They were gallopping from all sides at once with a confused regularity; throwing at each other the jarrit or *Blunted dart*, and recovering it from the ground, at full speed, with amazing dexterity. The music sounded, and acclamations, when any one excelled, filled the air.

We waited in a gallery, with the Hungarian and other spectators, until the game ended. We were then introduced into a spacious apartment, with a sofa, on which the aga was sitting, cross-legged, the mufti and a Turk or two on his right hand, his officers and attendants standing in a row, silent and respectful. He was a comely person, with a black beard. We made our obeisance, as usual, putting the right hand to the left breast, and inclining the head; and taking our places on the sofa, produced our firhman. The aga, on receiving it, kissed and laid it to his forehead, and then gave it to be read. We were entertained each with a pipe ready lighted, a spoonful of sweet-meat put into our mouths, and a cup of coffee; after which we retired, with full permission to employ our time at Mylasa as we pleased.

XXVII

MYLASA, or Mylassa, was the capital of Hecatomnus, king of Caria, and father of Mausolus. It has been described as situated by a very fertile plain, with a mountain rising above it, in which was a quarry of very fine white marble. This being near, was exceedingly convenient in building, and had contributed greatly to the beauty of the city, which, it is said, if any, was handsomely adorned with public edifices, porticoes, and temples. The latter were so numerous, that a certain musician entering the market-place, as if to make proclamation, began, instead of (Ἀκούετε, λαοὶ), *Hear, ye people*, with, (Ἀκούετε, ναοὶ) *Hear, ye temples*. The founders of the city were censured as inconsiderate in placing it beneath a steep precipice, by which it was commanded. Under the Romans it was a free city. Its distance from the sea, where nearest, or from Physcus, opposite the island of Rhodes, was ... ten miles. It is still a large place, commonly called Melasso.[1] The houses are numerous, but chiefly of plaster, and mean, with trees interspersed. The air is accounted bad; and scorpions abound, as anciently, entering often at the doors and windows, and lurking in the rooms. The plain is surrounded by lofty mountains, and cultivated; but was now parched and bare, except some spots green with the tobacco plant, which was in flower, and pleasing to the eye.

Our first inquiry was for the temple, erected about twelve years before the Christian era by the people of Mylasa to Augustus Caesar and the goddess Rome, which was standing not many years ago. We were shewn the basement, which remains, and were informed the ruin had been demolished, and a new mosque, which we saw on the mountain-side, above the town, raised with the marble. The house of a Turk occupying the site, we employed the Hungarian to

[1] Now Milâs.

treat with him for admission; but he affirmed we could see nothing; and added, that there was his haram, or the apartment of his women, which was an obstacle not to be surmounted. It had six columns in front, and the whole number had been twenty-two.

On the hill,[1] and not far from the basement of the temple, is a column of the Corinthian order, standing, with a flat-roofed cottage, upon a piece of solid wall. It has supported a statue, and on the shaft is an inscription "The people have erected Menander, son of Ouli- "ades, son of Euthydemus, a benefactor to his country, and descended "from benefactors".[2] The Turk who lived in the cottage, readily permitted a ladder to be placed on the terrace for measuring the capital, which was done as expeditiously as possible, but not before we were informed that several of the inhabitants murmured because their houses were overlooked. Besides this, two fluted columns of the Ionic order remained not many years since.

Euthydemus, the ancestor of Menander, was contemporary with Augustus Caesar. He was of an illustrious family, and possessed an ample patrimony. He was eloquent, and not only great in his own country, but respected as the first person of Asia Minor. His power was so advantageous to the city, that, if it savoured of tyranny, the odium was overcome by its utility. Hybreas concluded an oration with telling him he was a necessary evil. This demagogue, who succeeded Euthydemus, had inherited only a mule and its driver, employed then, as many now are, in bringing wood from the mountains for sale.[3]

Beneath the hill, on the east side of the town, is an arch or gateway of marble, of the Corinthian order.[4] On the keystone of the exterior front, which is eastward, we observed a double hatchet, as on the two marbles near Myus.[5] It was with difficulty we procured ladders to reach the top; and some were broken before we could find three sufficiently long and strong for our purpose. The going up, when these were united, was not without danger. The aga had expressed some wonder at our employment, as described to him; and

---

[1] Some scholars consider the classical city to have been on the fortress hill of Peçin and the Hellenistic city at modern Mylasa.

[2] *Inscript. Ant.*, p. 27. [C]. *CIG*, 2, p. 476g, no. 2698.

[3] Strabo, 14.2.24. [C]   [4] Plate VIII.   [5] See p. 155, n. (1).

seeing one of my companions on the arch, from a window of his house, which was opposite, pronounced him, as we were told, a brave fellow, but without brains. We desired him to accept our umbrella, on his sending to purchase it for a present to a lady of his haram, who was going into the country. By the arch was a fountain, to which women came with earthen pitchers for water, and with their faces muffled.

We saw a broad marble pavement, with vestiges of a theatre, near the Corinthian column. Toward the centre of the town we observed a small pool of water, and by it the massive arches of some public edifice. In the court of the aga's house was an altar much ornamented. We found an altar likewise in the streets, and a pedestal or two half buried, with pieces of ancient wall. Round the town are ranges of broken columns, the remnants of porticoes, now, with rubbish, bounding the vineyards. A large portion of the plain is covered with scattered fragments, and with piers of ordinary aqueducts; besides inscriptions, mostly ruined and illegible. Some altars dedicated to Hecatomnus have been discovered.

About a quarter of a mile from the town is a sepulchre,[1] of the species called by the ancients *distega*, or *double-roofed*. It consisted of two square rooms. In the lower, which has a doorway, were deposited the urns with the ashes of the deceased. In the upper, the relations and friends solemnized the anniversary of the funeral, and performed stated rites. A hole made through the floor was designed for pouring libations of honey, milk, or wine, with which it was usual to gratify the manes or spirits. The roof is remarkable for its construction; but two stones are wanting, and some distorted. It is supported by pillars of the Corinthian order, fluted, some of which have suffered from violence, being hewn near the bases, with a view to destroy the fabric for the iron and materials. The shafts are not circular, but elliptical; and in the angular columns square. The reason is, the sides, which are now open, were closed with marble pannels [sic]; and that form was necessary to give them a due projection. The inside has

[1] This fabric was ornamented with half columns both without and within, and their shafts being formed of one piece, to which is added the thickness of the pannels [sic] that enclosed them, give them the appearance of being elliptical, which has produced this mistake. See Pococke, vol. ii, pp 61–62. [R]

This Mausoleum is now called Gümüskesen and dates from Roman times.

been painted blue. This structure is the first object, as you approach from Iasus, and stands by the road. The entrance was on the farther side, the ascent to it probably by a pair of steps, occasionally applied and removed.[1]

Going down from this building, and turning from Mylasa, westward, you have the mountain on the right hand, and come, in about an hour, to another sepulchre. This is cut in the rock, high up in the side, near the top, and very difficult of access. Within the doorway on each side is a seat or bench, on which, it is likely, the urns were placed; and beyond is a smaller camera, or arched room. Over the entrance, without, is carved in basso relievo a facade; two Tuscan pillars between two pilasters, with an entablature and pediment, and a door. The slope of the mountain has been covered with innumerable sepulchres . . .

Jupiter, called by a local name Hosogo or Hogoas, had in the city a temple, in which was a well of sea-water. Jupiter, styled Carius, had also a temple, which was common to the Carians, and Lydians, and Nysians, as the same people. This was not in the town, but had once a village near it. On a steep abrupt rock, in sight from Mylasa to the south . . . is a ruined town called Paitshin, and a castle, which was repaired as a strong hold against Soley Bey. Part of the wall of this fortress, in which were a few cannon, stands on a flight of marble steps, probably belonging once to the latter temple. Near it are many deserted mosques and buildings, and a ruined church still used by the Greeks.[2]

The Mylasians were the proprietors of the famous Jupiter of Labranda. The gateway, on which his symbol, a double hatchet, is carved, was probably that leading to his temple, which was at a distance from the city. The god often occurs on medals, holding the hatchet. Hercules, it is related, killed the Amazon Hippolyte, and gave this, her weapon, to Omphale, queen of Lydia. From her it descended to the kings her successors, and was used as an ensign of royalty. Candaules delivered it, to be carried by one of his officers. Arselis, with auxiliaries from Mylasa, joining Gyges, when he

[1] Plate IX.

[2] Modern Kalin Ağıl. The church is on the site of a former temple where fourth-century B.C. inscriptions have been found.

VII Capital of a Pilaster from the Temple of Apollo Didymaeus. (Cat. 13)

VIII. An Arch at Mylasa (Cat. 1)

revolted, slew Candules and the hatchet-bearer, and returned into Caria laden with spoils. He made a statue of Jupiter, and placed the hatchet in his hand.[1]

[1] Plutarch, *The Greek Questions*, 45.302. [C]. Chandler cannot have gone to Labranda which lies 5 hours' ride to the northeast of Mylasa. Swedish archaeologists have excavated this site in recent years.

XXVIII

THE merchants preparing to leave Mylasa, and telling us we should find ruins at Eski-hissar, where they should stop next, we agreed to accompany them to that place, distant six hours eastward. We crossed the plain, with a long train of mules carrying their goods and servants, and ascended a mountain of veined marble, when the track became very steep and rough, winding by vast precipices. The slopes were covered with large firs and pines, many scorched or fallen, and some then on fire, spreading a strong smell of turpentine. The conflagration, we have before mentioned, had extended far into the country, as driven on and directed by the wind. About mid-way we alighted to refresh, near a clear murmuring brook, shaded by pines and plane-trees. In the vales farther on were stalks of Turkey wheat, with camels feeding, and booths of the Turcomans. A shepherd, whom we met in a narrow pass, was armed, and followed by two dogs, and these by his flock. We saw some of the Turcomans; the women with boots on; and one carrying a gun; and their children leading camels. After travelling an hour and an half, Mylasa bore north-west; and on our return, we had the plain in view in about four hours.

Eski-hissar,[1] once Stratonicea, is a small village; the houses scattered among woody hills, environed by huge mountains; one of which, toward the south-west, has its summit as white as chalk. It is watered by a limpid and lively rill, with cascades. The site is strewed with marble fragments. Some shafts of columns are standing, single; and one with the capital on it. By a cottage we found two[2] with a pilaster, supporting an entablature, but enveloped in thick vines and trees. In the side of a hill is a theatre, with the seats remaining, and ruins of the proscenium or front, among which are pedestals of

---

[1] Now Eskihisar. The site lies to the east of the village.   [2] Three. [R]

statues; one inscribed, and recording a citizen of great merit and magnificence.[1] Above it is a marble heap. The whole building is overgrown with moss, bushes, and trees. Without the village, on the opposite side, are broken arches, with pieces of massive wall, and marble coffins. One of these is very large and double, or intended for two bodies. Several altars with inscriptions lie about;[2] once placed in the sepulchres. The inhabitants were very civil to us; and the Greeks, some of whom accompanied us, as inquisitive as ignorant.

Stratonicea was a colony of Macedonians, and named from Stratonice, the wife of Antiochus Soter. The Selucidæ or kings had adorned it with sumptuous structures; and it was a free city under the Romans ...

The Stratoniceans had two temples in their territory; one of Hecate, at Lagina, in the way to Ephesus from Physcus, very famous, and visited by multitudes of people at the yearly congresses; the other of Jupiter, styled Chrysaoreus, or with *the golden sword*, which was near the city, and common to all the Carians; who, as well as the Ionians, met at stated times to sacrifice, and to deliberate on their affairs. This assembly was named the Chrysaorean system or body, and was composed of villages; the greater number giving the cities, to which they belonged, precedence in voting. The Stratoniceans, when the sanctuaries were reformed under Tiberius Cæsar, produced before the Roman senate, by their deputies, the decrees of Julius and Augustus Cæsar, confirming to Jupiter and Hecate their privilege of asylum.

We found Jupiter Chrysaoreus mentioned twice on one stone; and in the wall of a spacious court, before the house of the aga, was an inscription[3] relating to both deities. The preamble declares, that the city in many great and lasting dangers had been preserved by these its tutelar gods; that their statues in the senate-house furnished the most glaring evidence of their divine power and of their presence; that crowds sacrificed and burned incense before them, supplicating or returning thanks, and testifying their religious veneration of

[1] *Inscript. Ant.*, p. 29. [C]. *CIG*, 2, p. 486, no. 2719.
[2] Ibid, pp. 28, 29, 30. [C]. *CIG*, 2, p. 484, no. 2716; p. 490, no. 2724; p. 492, no. 2731; p. 492, no. 2733; p. 491, no. 2729.
[3] Chishull, *Ant. Asia*, pp. 155–160. [C]. *CIG*, 2, p. 481, no. 2715.

them; the senate therefore decrees, that thirty boys, of good families, be chosen to go daily two and two in procession, with their governors, to the senate-house, all dressed in white, crowned with olive, and bearing each a branch in their hands, with the citharist and herald, to sing a hymn, to be composed by Sosander. The stone is in two pieces, the characters large, with ligatures intermixed, and of a late age. In the same wall were other inscribed fragments[1] and near it an altar, and many marbles embossed with round shields. This aga was polite and affable beyond any Turk we had seen. His haram was impenetrable, or, as we were told, would have afforded us several inscriptions.

We have mentioned the tobacco-plant, as growing in the plain of Mylasa. Here the leaves were now gathered, and hanging in strings against the walls of the cottages to dry. The use of it and of coffee has been prohibited under some sultans. The smoking it, now so universal, was in 1610, a novel practice, even at Constantinople,[2] where a Turk had been recently led about the streets in derision, with a pipe thrust through his nose, as a punishment to deter others from following his example. The Turks were then strangers to the plant, and content to purchase the refuse of the English market, not understanding the commodity. The knowledge of coffee and of its virtues was imported from Arabia; and, by the Turkish account, the first coffee-house was established at Constantinople in 1554.

From the traveller who has remarked the inexperience of the Turks in the American weed, we learn that the English were then unacquainted with the oriental berry. He describes the Turks as sitting in houses resembling taverns, sipping a drink called coffa, in little china dishes, as hot as they could endure, black as soot, and tasting not much unlike it. To this description of coffee he subjoins, "Why not the black broth of the Lacedaemonians?" a question, I believe, hitherto unanswered. I shall reply to it, that for making their black broth, the cook was furnished with salt and vinegar, and bid to procure what was wanting from a victim. This, it has been conjectured, was blood. The epicure will not lament that the entire recipe has not reached us.

[1] *Inscript. Ant.*, p. 28. [C]. *CIG*, 2, p. 485, no. 2717; p. 487, no. 2722.
[2] Sandys, p. 52. [C]

XXIX

THE month of October was now ending. The nights, to which our men were often exposed, without any cover, grew cold; and our janizary was ill. We found it necessary to hasten to our winter quarters. We engaged the Swiss, whom we met at Mylasa on our return to the khan, in our service, pleased with his activity and intrepidity. The purchase of a horse to carry him was managed by our Turk, who, with the seller opposite, sate on the ground cross-legged, and told down some pieces of gold, and after a pause added to them, and so continued, until the price was accepted. We passed the first night, leaving Mylasa, in the sepulchre at Iasus.

On the way from Iasus to Mendelet . . . we left the level green, with the booths of the Turcomans . . . on our right hand; and, riding northward, through stubble of Turkey wheat, came in an hour to a beautiful and extensive plain covered with vines, olive, and fig-trees, and flocks and herds feeding; and skirting by mountains, with villages. We crossed it by a winding road, with the country-house of the aga of Mylasa on our right hand; and, passing a village called Iakli,[1] unexpectedly discovered the solemn ruin of a temple; but, as it was dusk, we continued our journey to Mendelet, which was an hour farther on. The merchants, our late companions, had given us a letter to some Armenians, who kindly admitted us to partake in their apartment in the khan, which was full.

We returned in the morning to the temple,[2] which was of the Corinthian order; sixteen columns, with part of their entablature standing; the cell and roof demolished. It is in a nook or recess; the front, which is toward the east, close by the mountain-foot; the back and one side overlooking the plain. The style of the architecture is noble, and made us regret, that some members, and in

[1] Now Ayalki.　　　　　　　　　　　　[2] Plate X.

particular the angle of the cornice, were wanting. Its marbles have been melted away, as it were piecemeal, in the furnaces for making lime, which are still in use, by the ruin.

A town has ranged with the temple on the north. The wall, beginning near it, makes a circuit on the hill, and descends on the side toward Mendelet. The thickets, which have overrun the site are almost impenetrable, and prevented my pursuing it to the top, but the lower portion may easily be traced. It had square towers at intervals, and was of a similar construction with the wall at Ephesus. Within it is a theatre cut in the rock, with some seats remaining. In the vineyards beneath are broken columns and marble fragments; and in one, behind the temple, two large massive marble coffins, carved with festoons and heads; the lids on, and a hole made by force in their sides. They are raised on pedestals; and, as you approach, appear like two piers of a gateway. Beyond the temple are also some ruins of sepulchres. I was much disappointed in finding no inscriptions to inform us of the name of this deserted place; which, from its position on a mountain by the way-side, and its distance from Mylasa, I am inclined to believe was Labranda . . .[1]

Our course from Mendelet was twenty-five minutes north of west, with the summits of Titanus[2] in view before us. We alighted after two hours, it being dusk, at Tarismanla, a village near the end of the plain, and waited beneath some trees, until our men could procure us a place to lodge in, when a sudden gust of wind carried away one of our hats into a deep well. In the morning we ascended the mountain by a winding track shaded with pines, myrtle, and fragrant shrubs. We enjoyed on it a fine view of the plain, which we then left in our rear. The road was rough and narrow to Bafi, where we arrived in an hour. Beyond it we passed an old castle on a hill, and soon after had the lake with Ufa Bafi, or Myus in sight . . .

We dismounted at the castle, and took a cursory survey of the ruins. It was evening before we had finished, and too late to attempt reaching Miletus.

We had consumed our whole store of provisions, which consisted of a few hard eggs, some grapes and bread, on our arrival here. We

[1] This seems to have been the site of Euromos.
[2] Latmus. [R]. Correct.

now found we could procure neither corn for our horses, nor any kind of food to allay our own hunger, which began to be importunate. We mounted, and went in quest of a lodging, passing from village to village, and inquiring, in vain, for corn. At length we were benighted among the hills on the south side of the lake, with jackals howling round us. After some time we stopped at Mersenet, a village upon mount Latmus, which afforded us a dish of boiled wheat, and some must of wine, with honey; but the quantity so small, it rather pacified the present cravings of appetite, than satisfied the stomach. Nothing remained for the morning, and both we and our horses set out fasting.

The way to Miletus, after descending the mountain, was by the lake to the plain [and after five hours they arrived there for the second time. On the previous occasion they had lodged at a smith's shop which was infested with insects, and so they decided to go on to Oranduick, but their lodgings there were so disagreeable that they would gladly have exchanged them for the inconveniences of the smith's shop.]

After a most uncomfortable night, we mounted, at seven in the morning, for Suki . . . We left the rocks or knolls which we observed in our way from Priene to the ferry, with Osebashá, upon the right hand, and twice passed the old bed of the Maeander. [Arriving at Suki, they went on to sleep at Scala Nova; the next night were at Osebanar, beyond Aiasalúck, and reached Smyrna the next day.]

PART III

March–18 August 1765

Smyrna — Clazomenae — Erythrae — Teos — Myonnesus — Colophon — Claros — Notium — Ephesus — Neapolis — Panionion — Priene — Heracleia — Alinda — Magnesia a. M. — Tralles — Nysa — Nazilli — Carura — Denizli — Laodicea — Hierapolis — Tripolis — Philadelphia — Sardis — Magnesia a. S. — Smyrna.

[Ref. 1825 edition, chaps. XXII-XXXI, XLV-LI, LIII, LIX-LXIII, LXV-LXIX, LXXII-LXXV, LXXVIII-LXXXIV]

XXX

I HAD begun early to prepare for another journey, and studied to remove, or remedy, as far as possible, the inconveniences we had before experienced, by providing a tent, and increasing the number of our attendants and horses. It was thought proper not to move until the Ramazan or Lent of the Turks, during which they are often sour and churlish, was over; and the general change or re-appointment of the governors, which is made in March, had taken place. . . .

We had agreed, on the 13th of March, to leave Smyrna on the 21st. On the 18th we were informed, that our janizary was unwilling to go then; bairam, or the Turkish holydays, beginning the next day; but was ready to set out with us either before or two days after. We then fixed on the 25th. Between the 17th and 20th we were assured that four or five persons more had been attacked by the plague, imported, it was said, from Musconisi or from Tino,[1] in which islands and in Scio, it was well known, the distemper had resided for some time. These accidents disconcerted us exceedingly, and seemed to threaten a final period to our expedition.

It may be imagined that during our abode with the consul, the plague had been a frequent topic of our conversation . . . [However,] we quitted the consul's house on Monday, the 25th of March, O.S. 1765, attended by a Swiss, and some Armenian servants, with a mule and horses carrying provision-chests, utensils for cooking, our tent, bedding, and other requisites; all together forming a very motley caravan or procession, headed by a janizary, and we did not return to Smyrna until the 8th of August. . .

The seacoast of Ionia extended from Phocæa and the Hermus, southward to Posidium, a promontory of the Milesians, and to the

[1] Macronisi and Tinos.

Carian mountains. The shape was irregular, it abounding in bays and peninsulas. The cities were all originally maritime; their number on the continent ten, besides Smyrna; their situation as uncommonly fine as their climate. It has been said of this region, that it boasted temples, such as were possessed by no other country, and many wonders hardly exceeded even in Hellas, or Greece.

The city of Ionia next to Smyrna was Clazomene. As this place was within the gulf, on the south side, and the distance anciently reckoned only twelve miles, we supposed the site known to the people of Smyrna, and the modern name to be, as they informed us, Vourla.[1] We resolved therefore to begin our second journey with that town, distant by computation six hours; hoping, if the plague did not cease at Smyrna during our absence, we might at least escape its fury; and expecting to obtain security and satisfaction, in proportion as we removed from the seat of infection, and of its sure concomitant, mortality.

We set out from Smyrna at eight in the morning, on the 25th of March, and passing through the lower portion of the city, crossed the mouth of the dry port, to a road between the burying grounds on the hill and the sea . . .

We came now to a shallow river, over which is a lofty bridge, intended to secure a passage to the traveller, when torrents descend from the adjacent mountain, formerly called Corax. On this principally the clouds seen from Smyrna reside, when the wind is southerly. Nearer the foot are vestiges of an ancient bridge, of which the piers were rebuilt, or repaired, before its final ruin; and in one of them is a maimed Corinthian capital . . .

Some fragments of architecture in the Turkish burying-grounds not far from hence, it is likely, belonged, with the relic above mentioned, to the temple of Apollo, once seated on the western bank of this stream, by the hot baths.[2] These have been computed forty stadia, or five miles from the city, and were called *the Agamemnonian*, by the people of Smyrna. It is related, that the army under Agamemnon ravaging Mysia, was engaged by Telephus near the river

[1] Urla.
[2] Strabo, 14.1.36. [C]. The so-called Baths of Agamemnon, see Bean, op. cit., p. 52.

Caicus; that many of the Greeks were wounded in the battle; that an oracle directed them for a cure to these waters; and that here, the helmets taken from the enemy were suspended. The old remains of the buildings are of brick, the masonry good, but soil and rubbish have risen to the imposts of the arches, which are closed.

You descend by steps to the bath, which is under a modern vaulted roof, with vents in it for the steam; and adjoining to this is a like room now disused. The current, which is soft and limpid, is conveyed into a small round basin of marble, and runs over into a large cistern or reservoir beneath. Our thermometer rose in the vein to one hundred and fifty. Near it is a duct which supplies a cold stream; but in January, when I saw it, was dry. A quantity of coagulated blood lay on the pavement. I was informed a sheep had been killed above, and that substance used instead of soap in shaving, which operation is often performed in the baths . . .

After passing the river and Sangiac castle, we came to the seaside, and to a coffee-hut, at which we alighted, and tarried twenty minutes. At one we opened the isthmus, or neck of the peninsula, the southern boundary of the gulf. The Clazomenians anciently inhabited on the north side, bordering on the Erythreans, who were within it. The Teians were on the south, with a port north of their city. Hitherto our course westward had been chiefly beneath the northern termination of mount Corax.

The isthmus appears as a wide pleasant valley, and the land being mostly level, we could discern across it the blue tops of the island Samos . . . Alexander the Great, to render the communication easier, ordered, that a navigable cut should be made through the plain here, intending to join the two bays, and by converting the whole cherronese into an island, to surround the city Erythræ and mount Mimas, with the sea. A dike, or canal, running up the valley, is a monument of that attempt, which failed, when the workmen came to the rock . . .

We continued our journey along the shore. The hills on our left were covered with low shrubs, and villages, some of a clean dry aspect, and several not immediately discernible, though near, the mud-built cottages being exactly of the same colour with the soil. As we approached Vourla, the little valleys were all green with corn, or filled with naked vine-stocks in orderly arrangement, about a foot and a half high. The people were working, many in a row, turning the earth, or encircling the trunks with tar, to secure the buds from grubs and worms. The shoots, which bear the fruit, are cut down again in winter . . .

Vourla is distinguished at a distance by its numerous windmills. On entering the town we saw nobody, the houses were shut up, and a silence and solitude prevailed, which, before we recollected what we had lately seen, suggested to us the terrible idea, that the inhabitants had left it, to avoid the cruel distemper from which we also were flying. It is a place of considerable extent, the buildings dispersed on eminences, with a pleasant plain toward the sea. The water and air are reputed good. The Turks have seven mosques, and the Greeks two churches. At one of these is a small bass-relief, representing a funereal supper, with a short inscription.[1] Another is fixed in the wall over a fountain . . . A cursory view of this place was sufficient to convince us, that it did not stand on the site of Clazomene.

We were assisted by a friendly Italian in our inquiries for a ruined city in that neighbourhood and in the evening procured a man to conduct us, as we supposed, to the site of Clazomene.[2] We set out early in the morning, when he carried us back to the opening of the isthmus, and shewed us, for Clazomene, a piece of ordinary wall, which has enclosed a cistern on the top of a hill, with some scattered rubbish on the slope. There, it is likely, was anciently the settlement of that Chalcidensians, probably a colony from Chalcis in Euboea, belonging to Clazomene. Above them was a grove sacred to Alexander the Great, where the games called Alexandrea were celebrated by the Ionian body.

Finding our guide ignorant, and at a loss which way to go, we adopted the surer direction of ancient history; remembering, that the Clazomenians, to be more secure from the Persians, had settled in an island, which, by command of Alexander, was afterwards changed into a peninsula by the addition of a mole. We crossed the plain of Vourla, slanting toward the sea, and soon discovered this

[1] *Inscript. Ant.*, p. 6. [C]. *CIG*, 2, p. 690, no. 3133.
[2] For discussion of site and plan, see Bean, op. cit., pp. 128–136. The archaic city is thought to be half a mile inland from the modern harbour.

monument also of that great mind, which delighted in correcting or subduing nature by filling up or forming paths for the deep; which here still bore visible marks of his royal pleasure, and now raged, as it were indignant, but in vain, against the barrier which he had appointed.

The mole was two stadia, or a quarter of a mile in length, but we were ten minutes in passing over it, the waves, which were impelled by a strong inbat, breaking over in a very formidable manner, as high as the bellies of our horses. The width, as we conjectured, was about thirty feet. On the west side it is fronted with a thick strong wall, some pieces appearing above the water. On the opposite is a mound of loose pebbles, shelving as a buttress, to withstand the furious assaults of storm and tempest. The upper works have been demolished, and the materials, a few large rough stones excepted, removed.

We computed the island to be about a mile long, and a quarter broad. The city was small, its port on the NNW side,[1] enclosed with a mole. Traces of the walls are found by the sea; and in a hill are vestiges of a theatre. Three or four trees grow on it, and by one is a cave[2] hewn in the rock, and affording water. The soil was now covered with green corn . . .

By Clazomene is a cluster of islets,[3] all once cultivated, now neglected and barren. Their number was eight but I could only count six . . .

After making the circuit of the island, we sat down by the isthmus to dine, when our attention was engaged by a large company landed at the scale or road of Vourla, which is westward from the mole, and had in it some small-craft, with a few houses and a mosque on the shore. An irregular discharge of guns and pistols followed, in compliment, as our guide told us, to the new aga or governor, who was then arrived . . .

[1] South side, enclosed with a mole. [R]

[2] Pausanias, VII.v.11 [C]: 'Nothing remains but the cave, which is cut out of firm rock, almost square, supported with four pillars of the same rock. To the eastward is part of an altar, and in the middle is a well, but the water is brackish, and not fit to be drank.' Randolph, State of the Islands in the Archipelago, 1687, p. 64. Room, the sides ornamented with niches, probably a sepulchre. [R]

[3] Pliny, Nat. Hist., V.xxxviii. 137–138. [C]

XXXI

BEYOND Clazomene the peninsula, becoming very mountainous, with narrow and difficult passes, affords many places of
refuge, inaccessible, or easily defended. Hence the Kara-
borniotes, or inhabitants of the southern cape of the gulf, were long
infamous as pirates and robbers, and had the general character of a
very bad people. We were now told, that their manners were
changed, and their disposition less ferocious and inhuman; that they
attend to the culture of the vine and the management of the silk-
worm, and frequent the market of Smyrna with the produce. We
thought it prudent, however, to increase our guard, and hire another
janizary, intending to go to Erythræ, now corruptly called Ritre,
and reckoned eight hours distant.

We set out from Vourla early in the morning, and in an hour, after
crossing a small promontory, came to the bottom of a deep bay,
which, with an island in it, is almost land-locked, lying several miles
within the cape Karavouno. We then ascended a ridge of mount
Mimas; and, passing a stream, entered on a rugged narrow track
between very lofty cliffs, and by the side of a water-course frightfully
steep. We were engaged in this straight four hours, our baggage-
horses falling, or being jammed with their burdens, where the rocks
projected. At length we arrived in view of a plain, deep sunk
among the hills which surround it. Before us was Mimas, a gray
ridge, seen at Smyrna;[1] and a little on the left, a top of the island
Scio; behind us were the two white conical summits of mount
Corax, called *The Brothers*, which served as a sea-direction in
navigating the gulf. We descended to Cerhardam, a Turkish village,
where we alighted in the afternoon. We had proposed passing the

---

[1] Mimas, now Karavouno, which forms the cape at the south side of the bay
of Smyrna. [R]

IX   Sepulchral Monument at Mylasa. (Cat. 15)

V. Temple at Idalia (Cat. 16)

night here, as our men and horses were weary, but could get neither lodging nor corn.

After dining beneath a tree, we continued our journey across a ridge to Cadoagi, a small place near an hour farther on. Here we had our tent pitched, for the first time, within an enclosure, by a cottage, and slept in it. Our bedding was a small carpet, mattress, and coverlet. Each had by his side a gun, sword, and a pair of loaded pistols. The Swiss guarded the mouth of the tent. The nights were as yet cold, and our janizary was provided with a cloak of a dark colour, shaggy, and very thick, made without a seam, with a cape, or rather cowl, for his head. Wrapped in this, he lay down, like Diomed in his bull-skin, in the open air, with his pistol and sabre, by him, and his gun in his hand. Our other attendants were likewise dispersed, mostly on the ground, round about the tent, armed as by day; and one of the Armenians watched the horses, which were fastened to stakes with the saddles on . . .

[At dawn they arose and breakfasted and set off about 6 a.m.]

In two hours we came to a vale, well watered, and stored with myrtles and evergreens. Here we observed some pieces of an ancient wall, which had been erected across it; and, after passing the ruin of mosque, which has a sepulchral inscription fixed over the doorway, an opening afforded us a view of the site of Erythræ,[1] of the sea, and of the island Scio. We entered at a gap in the ruins of the city wall, where we supposed a gateway to have been; and finding no shade, pitched our tent on a green spot, extending it as a wide umbrella to shelter us from the sun, then shining exceedingly bright and powerful.

The walls of Erythræ were erected on two semi-circular rocky brows, and had square towers at regular distances. They were very thick, the stones massive and rugged, the masonry that called *pseudisodomum.* In the middle is a shallow, lively stream, clear as crystal, which turns a solitary mill in its way through thickets of myrtle and bushes to the sea. This rivulet was anciently named Aleos, and was remarkable for producing hair on the bodies of those who drank of it.[2] Near the mouth is a piece of ordinary Mosaic pave-

[1] For discussion of site and plan see Bean, op. cit., pp. 153–159. The Turks are now excavating on this site.   [2] Pliny, *Nat. Hist.*, XXXI. viii. 14. [C]

ment. By a conical hill on the north are vestiges of an ample theatre in the mountain-side; and farther on, by the sea, three pedestals of white marble. Beyond these is an old square fortress standing on a low spot, a little inland; and by it was a short sepulchral inscription. We searched in vain for a temple of Hercules, which has been mentioned as one of the highest antiquity, and as resembling the temples of Egypt. The god was represented on a float, on which they related that he arrived at Erythræ from Phoenicia.[1]

Before the port of Erythræ are four islets, once called Hippi, *The Horses*; and beyond these are the Spalmadore islands, by which we sailed in our stormy passage from Scio to Kara-bornu. A promontory of mount Mimas, beyond Erythræ, was named Coryna; and one near mid-way, sailing toward Scio, Hera Mesate. The shore winds, and forms several bays.

Erythræ has been long deserted, and, like Clazomene, stripped even of its ruins, except some masses of hard cement, a few vaults of sepulchres, a fragment of inscribed architrave, a broken column or two, and a large stone, on which is carved a round shield. The bare rock afforded a natural foundation for the houses and public edifices; and the materials, when they were ruined lay ready to be transported to Scio and other places, which continued to flourish. Some words were visible on one of the pedestals. We would have cleared them all from weeds and rubbish, which concealed their inscriptions; but our guide had affirmed that we could not pass the night here without danger; our horses were standing ready, and we had no time to spare.

[1] Pausanias, VII.v.5–8. [C]

XXXII

ERYTHRÆ was about midway in the periplus, or circum-
navigation of the peninsula. It had to the north a village named
Cybellia, and the cape, by which was a quarry dug for mill-
stones. The lofty mountain to the south was called Corycus, and its
promontory Argennum.[1] This ran out toward Posidium, a promontory of Chios, from which it was separated by a strait, about sixty
stadia, or seven miles and a half wide. In Corycus a cave was shewn,
in which they said the sibyl Herophile was born. Its coast had several
ports, and was much infested by pirates and robbers. After Corycus
was Geræ, a small town of the Teians by the port north of their
city. The third tribe of the Erythreans had its name from a region
called Chalcitis, peopled with Chalcidensians; and the sea-baths by
a cape of that district were esteemed superior to any in Ionia . . .

Our guide, at setting out, conducted us to the shore; and, winding
southward, we ascended a lofty ridge of mount Corycus, from which
we had an extensive view of the coast, of the channel of Scio, and of
the gulf of Smyrna. *The Brothers* were before us, and behind us
Chisme.[2] The mountain was covered with low shrubs. We then
descended to the station of some goatherds, guarded by several large
and fierce dogs. In three hours and half we came unexpectedly to the
village where we lay the preceding night.

The valley beneath us, and the side of the mountain, were again
enveloped in thick shining mist when we began our journey; and,
keeping along the southern edge of a plain, reascended mount
Mimas,[3] which the ancients have described as woody, and abounding
in wild beasts. The slopes here were clothed with pines and shrubs,
and garnished with flowers, many of a bright yellow, resembling

[1] Now Argenon-Tekne Burnu.   [2] Now Çeşme.
[3] Corycus. [R]. Correct. Now Korykeion-Karaka-Burnu.

small single pinks. The wild boars had rooted up the green corn in several places. At noon we came to the bay, which we passed in going to Erythræ; and, striking off to the right, dismounted to dine under some shady trees by a copious fountain. We had suffered much from the sun, and were greatly fatigued.

After enjoying awhile the luxury of cool water and shade, we continued our journey, leaving Vourla and the villages on our left hand. As we crossed the mountain, the island Samos rose to view at a distance, and we opened the sea on the south side of the peninsula. We passed many small pleasant spots, well watered, and green with corn, or with myrtles and shrubs. We descended by a road impressed with the ruts of ancient carts which previously divided the Erythrean territory from the Clazomenian. Here the peninsula ends . . .

We rode on, and after three hours arrived at Segigeck,[1] which was before us, by the head of a shining bay, land-locked, with an islet near the mouth. We were civilly received by a party of men and boys, who were gathered about the gate on our approach, and directed to the interior fortress, which was much out of repair. Here we were lodged in an apartment over the gateway, belonging to the aga or governor, who was absent on a visit of ceremony to a superior officer, attended by most of the garrison. Our horses, servants, and baggage, were disposed in the area or court below.

Segigeck is a large square ordinary fortress, erected, it is said, by the Genoese, on a flat; with a few brass cannon toward the sea. It was anciently called Geræ, was the port of the city Teos toward the north, and had been peopled with Chalcidensians, who arrived under Geres. It encloses some mean mud-built houses. In the wall next the water are several inscribed marbles, the colour a blue-gray, transported from Teos. Another is fixed in a fountain without the south gate. In the hot bath are two large fragments placed upside down, and serving for seats, which I examined, but hastily, fearing some infection, as the plague was known to be near. All these have been published by the learned Chishull. By a mosque, and in the burying-grounds, are some scattered fragments, and a sepulchral inscription or two.[2] This place is reckoned eight hours from Smyrna. A view of it is given in the *Ionian Antiquities.*

[1] Now Segacik.   [2] *Inscript. Ant.*, p. 6. [C]. *CIG*, 2, p. 684, nos. 3106, 3107.

The cranes were now arrived at their respective quarters, and a couple had made their nest, which is bigger in circumference than a bushel, on a dome close by our chamber. This pair stood, side by side, with great gravity, shewing no concern at what was transacting beneath them, but at intervals twisting about their long necks, and clattering with their beaks turned behind them upon their backs, as it were in concert. This was continued the whole night. An owl, a bird also unmolested, was perched hard by, and as frequently hooted. The crane is tall, like a heron, but much larger; the body white, with black pinions, the neck and legs very long, the head small, and the bill thick. The Turks call it friend and brother, believing it has an affection for their nation, and will accompany them into the countries they shall conquer. In the course of our journey we saw one hopping on a wall with a single leg, the maimed stump wrapped in linen.

Segigeck stands on the north side[1] of the isthmus of a small rough peninsula, which extends westwards, and terminates in a sharp low point. This perhaps was the cape once called Macria, by which were the baths of the Teians, some on the shore in a cavity of the rock, or natural, and some made by art, and from ostentation. Teos was thirty stadia, or three miles and three quarters, from Geræ, and fronted the sea on the south side. It was equi-distant from Erythræ and Chios, sixty-one miles and a half from each by the coast.

In the morning we crossed the isthmus to Teos,[2] now called Bodrun. We found this city almost as desolate as Erythræ and Clazomene. The walls, of which traces are extant, were, as we guessed, about five miles in circuit; the masonry handsome. Without them, by the way, are vaults of sepulchres stripped of their marble, as it were forerunners of more indistinct ruin. Instead of the stately piles, which once impressed ideas of opulence and grandeur, we saw a marsh, a field of barley in ear, buffaloes ploughing heavily by defaced heaps and prostrate edifices, high trees supporting aged vines, and fences of stones and rubbish, with illegible inscriptions, and time-worn fragments. It was with difficulty we discovered the

---

[1] South side. [R]. In fact, the site lies in the middle of the isthmus between the north and south harbours.

[2] For discussion of site and plan see Bean, op. cit., 136–146. A Turkish mission has been excavating here.

temples of Bacchus; but a theatre in the side of the hill is more conspicuous. The vault only, on which the seats ranged, remains, with two broken pedestals in the area . . .

The city-port is partly dry, and sand-banks rise above the surface of the water. On the edge are vestiges of a wall, and before it are two small islets. On the left hand, or toward the continent, is a channel, which seemed artificial, the water not deep. I saw a boy wade across it . . . Beyond it, on the shore before Sevri-hissar, which stands inland, are four or five tall barrows.

The heap of the temple of Bacchus,[1] lay in the middle of a corn field, and is overrun with bushes and olive-trees. It was one of the most celebrated structures in Ionia. The remains of it have been engraved at the expense of the society of Dilettanti, and published, with its history, in the *Ionian Antiquities*; and a beautiful portico has since been erected at the seat of the right hon. lord le Despenser, near High Wycomb [sic], under the inspection of Mr. Revett, in which the exact proportions of the order are observed.[2]

The town has long been deserted. It has no ruins of churches, to prove it existed under the Greek emperors; nor of mosques or baths, to show it was frequented by the Turks. In the time of Anacreon the Teians migrated, from a love of liberty, to Thrace, but some afterwards came back, and the city reflourished. They are now utterly gone, and it is likely never to return. The site is a wilderness; and the low grounds, which are wet, produce the iris, or flag, blue and white. This flower is stamped on the money of Teos. We saw cranes here stalking singly in the corn and grass, and picking up and gorging insects and reptiles; or flying heavily with long sticks in their mouths to the tops of trees, and of the remoter houses and chimneys, on which they had agreed to fix their habitation.

The master of a Venetian snow, in the harbour of Segigeck, furnished us with a small quantity of wine, but of a poor quality; otherwise we should have drank only water on a spot once sacred to Bacchus, and able to supply a Roman fleet. The grave Turk, its present owner, predestines the clusters of the few vines it now bears for his food, when ripened; or to be dried in the sun, as raisins, for sale.

[1] This temple stood to the west of the lower town, a smaller temple has been excavated nearer to the southern port. See Plate XI.   [2] See Appendix A and B.

XXXIII

OUR apprehensions of danger from the Kara-borniotes were now at an end. We dismissed the janizary, whom we had engaged at Vourla, and on the evening of the second day after our arrival proceeded to Sevri-hissar,[1] distant one hour south-eastward. We came, soon after leaving Segigeck, between two conical rocks, one of a green aspect, the other brown and bare. The tall trees by the roadside were covered with spreading vines; and at a well was a marble pedestal perforated, and serving as a mouth. The front of it is inscribed with large characters,[2] and it once supported the statue of a great and munificent person, whose name it has not preserved.

The gray marble used by the Teians was found at no great distance from the city. The rocks above mentioned are probably remains of the quarry, to which also the high rocky mount, about a mile north of Teos, seen in the view in the *Ionian Antiquities,* belonged. This, as Pococke relates, has, on the west side, a small lake in a deep basin, which, it is imagined by the people, feeds all the fountains about the country; and to the south of the lake is a hollow ground, where are near twenty large pieces of gray marble,[3] each cut out into several steps, of a size which would be very difficult to move. On one he saw inscribed, LOCO IIII.

Sevri-hissar is an extensive straggling town, in a valley, two hours from the sea; and may be deemed the Vourla of the Teians. The country round it is pleasant and well cultivated . . . We were lodged in a wretched mud-built khan, and we had here reason to dislike,

---

[1] Now Seferihisar.

[2] *Inscript. Ant.*, p. 7. [C]. *CIG*, 2, p. 670, no. 3080.

[3] Two or three can still be seen beside the road, others are hidden in the bushes, see Bean op. cit., p. 145.

and to be alarmed at, the carriage of some of our Turkish visitants, but the janizary was our safeguard.

Many scattered remnants of the ancient city occur at Sevrihissar.[1] One, fixed in the wall of a house, mentions the two societies, the Panathenaists and the Dionysiasts.[2] At the time of the Ionic migration, a colony of Athenians took possession of Teos. These appear to have introduced the Panathenæa, the grand festival of their parent city. A crown of olive encircles the name of the community which had the care of its celebration; and one of ivy that of the Dionysiasts, who were artificers, or contractors for the Asiatic theatres, incorporated and settled at Teos under the kings of Pergamum.[3] I copied a long decree made by one of their companies in honour of its magistrates. The slab was placed as a gravestone in the Turkish burying-ground of a deserted mosque N.W. of Sevrihissar,[4] where the man who shewed it me, with some assistance, laid it flat, and a heavy shower falling, rendered the characters, which are large and uninjured, easily legible. The thanks of the community, with a crown of olive, are given as a recompense for their great liberality and trouble in office; and to perpetuate their memory, and excite an emulation of their merit, it is besides enacted, that the decrees be engraved, but at their expense; so desirable was this testimony to the individuals, and so frugal the usage in bestowing it.

The next day, April the 1st, in the afternoon, the weather proving fair, we continued our journey southward; and, soon after setting out, had a low mountain on our left hand, with an opening in it, and wide but dry watercourse, which we crossed, and then passed over hills and dales by small enclosures, regularly planted with oaks. Many of these supported vines, and between the rows was barley in ear, and other grain . . . Coming to the shore, we turned a little to the left, and ascended a very lofty hill, commanding a most extensive view of a picturesque country, of the seacoast, and islands. Near the

[1] There is no ancient city at Seferihisar—the scattered remnants seen by Chandler are ancient blocks and fragments brought from Teos.

[2] *Inscript. Ant.*, pp. 7, 8, 10. [C]. *CIG*, 2, p. 673, no. 3084; p. 653, no. 3066; p. 669, no. 3073; p. 679, no. 3090; p. 684, no. 3105; p. 682, no. 3096; p. 687, no. 3120; p. 685, no. 3111; p. 683, no. 3103; p. 683, no. 3102; p. 686, no. 3115.

[3] Strabo, 14.1.29. [C]

[4] With a deserted mosque half an hour north-west from Sevri-hisser. [R]

top is a fountain, and over it a stone, on which is cut the Greek cross. We alighted, after a pleasant ride of three hours, at Hypsile, and were very well lodged in a large apartment, in a house belonging to a Turk of Sevri-hissar.

We are now on the promontory, anciently called Myonnesus, between Teos and Lebedus. The summit has been described as conical, and standing on an ample base. It was accessible from the continent by a narrow track only, and was terminated toward the sea by wave-worn rocks, hanging over, and in some places projecting beyond the vessels, to which it furnished a safe station below. The Myonnesus was the property of the Teians.

Hypsile is a small village. The name, which is Greek, denotes its lofty situation. It was the stronghold to which Cineis retired before the army of Sultan Morat, and which he maintained gallantly, until his men began to mutiny. After surrendering, he was murdered here, sleeping in his tent.

We left Hypsile at eight in the morning, and in about an hour descended into a narrow bottom, which was filled with a thick smoke or mist, occasioned, as we discovered on a nearer approach, by steam arising from a small tepid brook, called Elijah; the bed, of a deep-green colour. The current, which tasted like copperas, is confined in a narrow channel below, and turns two over-shot mills, falling soon after into a stream, then shallow, but flowing from a rich vale between the mountains, in a very wide course; the bed, of stone and white sand.

We are now in the territory of Lebedus, which was noted, beyond any on the seacoast, for hot waters. These are on record as plentiful, beneficial to the human race, and exciting admiration. The stream now supplies two mean baths on the margin, one with a large cross carved on a stone in the pavement, and chiefly used by the Greeks.

From the baths we were conducted to some ruins called Ecclesia,[2] *The Church*, about half an hour distant, on the same side of the

[1] Now Çift Kale, or Mouse Island, but this name was transferred to Siçan Adasi, a little to the east of Lebedus. For discussion of site and sketch see Bean, op. cit., pp. 148–149.

[2] These ruins were probably baths, the walls being crusted over in some places with putrifactions. [R]. A ruined basilica still stands near the thermal baths.

river, and beneath the mountain we had descended, or Myonnesus. They consisted of naked masses of stone and of brick, with cement, besides a very few marble fragments; and a basement, with the entire floor, of a small temple; the whole environed with bushes. I rode on about a quarter of a mile to the sea, but found no port or other vestiges of buildings.

We returned to the road, and crossing a cultivated plain, with a stream or two, came in an hour and a half to the sea, and a little peninsula[1] sown with wheat. It has a fair beach, and probably is the spot on which Lebedus[2] stood. By the rocky edge are traces of ancient wall; and within it, besides rubbish, are some pieces of Doric columns. This city enjoyed a fertile territory, but was subverted by Lysimachus, who removed the inhabitants, when he peopled Ephesus, to the sea. It survived long as a village, and became, as it were, proverbial for its solitude. It is now untenanted, and not even a village . . .

The Dionysiasts, proving turbulent and seditious, were expelled from Teos. They removed to Ephesus, and from thence were translated by king Attalus to Myonnesus. The Teians sent an embassy to the Romans, requesting them not to suffer the Myonnesus to be fortified; and the Dionysiasts then removed to Lebedus, where they were received with joy. It was the custom of their synod to hold yearly a general assembly, at which they sacrificed to the gods, and poured libations to their deceased benefactors. They likewise celebrated games in honour of Bacchus. The crowns which any of the communities had bestowed as rewards of merit, were announced by heralds; and the wearers applauded. It was the business of the presidents to provide splendid entertainments, and the meeting was solemnized with great pomp and festivity. This congress, it is probable, was held at the ruins described above, and that temple dedicated to the god, their patron.

[1] Now Kisik.

[2] For discussion, sketch and plan of site see Bean, op. cit., pp. 149–153. This site is as yet unexcavated.

XXXIV

LEBEDUS was equidistant one hundred and twenty stadia, or fifteen miles, from Teos and from Colophon, near which city was Claros. We proceeded with an islet in view before us, once sacred to Diana. It was anciently believed that does, when big, swam across from the continent, and were there delivered of their young . . . We passed through lanes, olive-groves, and corn. In two hours and a half we were suddenly stopped by a wide and very turbid river, descending from between mount Gallesus or *The Alé-man*, and the southern extremity of mount Corax, the range which had continued on our left hand from near Teos. It is impossible perhaps to conceive greater visible rapidity, the water hurrying by with so precipitious and head-long a course, it was gone like an arrow from a bow. Our guide, after some hesitation, entered the stream, which proved shallow, reaching only to the belly of his horse. We were apprehensive a low mule, heavily laden with baggage, would be carried away, but it struggled through, and we all got over safe. We tarried the night at a village [Gamuldan] an hour farther on, high on the mountain-side . . .

In the morning, the wind, which had been northerly for some time, was very cutting. We rode among the roots of Gallesus, through pleasant thickets abounding with goldfinches. The aerial summits of this immense mountain towered on our left, clad with pines. We turned from the sea, and began to ascend a rough track between green hills; a clear stream falling by in murmuring cascades. At a distance was a village, which appeared almost in the clouds. Steep succeeded steep, as we advanced, and the path became more narrow, slippery, and uneven. We were instructed to let our bridle be loose, to sit steady, and to prevent the saddle from sliding back by grasping the manes of our horses, while they clambered up; their known sureness of foot was our confidence and security by fearful precipices and giddy heights; where, if, from being checked, or by accident, they chance to fall, down you tumble many a fathom, without one friendly bush or shrub to interpose and contribute to your preservation. After much labour and straining we got to the top of the ridge, which is exceedingly high.[1] Here we found the surface bare, except a few pines on one summit, beneath which some miserable cattle were standing, seemingly pinched with hunger, and ruminating on the wretchedness of their lot. We saw at a distance a vast body of water encompassed with hills, being the lake or reservoir from which the numerous rills and rivulets on the sides of the mountain are fed. Farther in the country was a white top glistening with snow; and nearly before us a summit remarkable craggy, which is by the lake of Myus, and will be often mentioned . . .

Descending Gallesus, we suddenly discovered near the bottom some mean huts, immediately beneath us, on the declivity. We inquired of the inhabitants, who were Greeks, for ruins, and they directed us to Claros, now called Zille, by the sea. We crossed a brook, which is in the middle of a cultivated vale, and entered a thick grove of olives, where some armed men started up from under a tree, and, running to the road, stopped our servants and baggage-horses. The janizary, as soon as we perceived it, gallopped back, and a short parley ensued. We were informed they belonged to the muselém, a Turkish officer of great power and extensive command, residing at Chili,[2] distant an hour and a half toward Smyrna. Cara-Elez-Oglu then possessed that high dignity. He was famous as an excellent governor, and remarkable for his civility to the Franks or Europeans. We continued our journey to Zille, which is by computation four hours from Goomulderú, where we lay . . .

We were apprised of our approach to Zille, or Claros, by vestiges of ancient sepulchres on the mountain-side, close by the way, on our left hand. One, which was hewn in the rock, has a narrow doorway leading into it; and within, a long horizontal niche or cavity, transverse, for the body. Farther on, and higher up, is a well of fine water;

[1] It appears that Chandler was here ascending the modern Siğindi Dağı, not Gallesus which is now Kuşan Dağı. [2] Now presumably Çile.

142

then full to the brim, and overflowing. This ridge is separated by a narrow vale from a small rocky promontory, which is encompassed with a ruinous wall of rough stone, the masonry that termed *pseudi-sodomum*. We rode in at a gap or gateway, and found a theatre of the same brown material as the wall, many pieces of marble, wells, and remnants of churches; and besides these an imperfect time-eaten heap of a large temple. We had a distinct view of Aiasaluck, the plain of Ephesus, and the town of Scala Nova.[1]

Claros[2] was very early the seat of a temple and oracle of Apollo. It is related, that Chalchas, after the destruction of Troy, had an interview there with the prophet Mopsus, and died of grief on finding he was excelled in his profession. The person who sustained this high office could be taken only from particular families, and was generally of Miletus, unlettered, and ignorant of composition. He was told only the number and names of the consulters, and then descended into a cave, in which was a fissure with water. After drinking of this spring, he uttered responses in verses made on the subject on which each had thought in his own mind; but this practice was prejudicial to his health, perhaps from the dampness of the place, and he was commonly short-lived. He got by rote, I conceive, or else carried down with him, the answers ready prepared; and the god would soon have lost his reputation, had the consulters been so cunning as to have kept every one his secret from the agents and spies employed to dive into their business. The temple, which was unfinished, with the sacred grove of ash-trees, is mentioned by Pausanias among the curiosities peculiar to Ionia. It is not certain whether the oracle existed after Constantine the Great, or when Apollo was finally silenced and dethroned; but Christianity succeeded, and has flourished in its turn at Claros.

In viewing the well on the ridge before mentioned, I remarked it had marble steps leading down from the top; and four or five were

[1] Chandler cannot have seen Claros, since no part of that ancient city was visible above ground in his time, and there is no theatre on that site. What he must have seen was Notium where there is a theatre and a temple which was at one time thought to be that of Clarian Apollo. Ayasoluk would also have been visible from Notium.

[2] For account of site see Bean, op. cit., pp. 190–196. French archaeologists laid bare the famous temple of Apollo and other buildings in 1950.

visible below the surface ... There, it may be conjectured, was the prophetic fountain and cave ...[1]

Colophon was situated inland. Before it, besides Claros, was Notium, a town and haven bearing the same relation to it as the Piraeus did to Athens, and distant near two miles. It is termed the Colophonian Notium, to distinguish it from that of Chios, a portion of the coast of the island, with a road for vessels. Colophon was only seventy stadia, or eight miles and three quarters, from Ephesus in a straight course; but, by the windings of the bays, one hundred and twenty stadia, or fifteen miles. Lysimachus destroyed it to enlarge that city; but some of the Colophonians remained at Notium, to whom the Romans granted immunities after their war with Antiochus. The Halys, or Halesus, ran by Colophon; and then, not far from the grove of Claros. The stream was colder than any in Ionia, and celebrated for that quality by the elegiac poets ...

Many difficulties have arisen,[2] concerning Claros, Notium and Colophon, which are removed by this account of their proximity and mutual connection. Colophon was sacrificed to the grandeur of its neighbour Ephesus. The name, as at Lebedus, survived, but without its pristine importance; and Notium suffered, as it were, by sympathy. Religion and Apollo interposed to rescue Claros, and the concourse of consulters and devotees maintained it and the temple. But now Colophon, if its site be not occupied by the wretched huts before mentioned, is extinct; and Claros, with Notium, has been long abandoned. The brook we crossed was the Halys. The vale on the north side of the promontory, which it divides, has perhaps increased toward the sea, and the old haven been filled up by soil washed from the mountains.

When we had finished our survey of Claros, we returned to some huts, and pitching our tent, lay surrounded with our baggage, men, and horses. In the morning early we passed by Zille, and over two ridges of Gallesus. We then entered on the plain of Ephesus, and travelled along the edge toward the shore, until we came to the

[1] The excavation of the temple at Claros revealed that the 'cave and sacred fountain' were located in an Oracular Chamber below it. See Bean, op. cit., pl. 48. Since the site visited by Chandler was Notium the 'well on the ridge' is clearly not that at Claros.

[2] Cellarius, pp. 47, 48. [C]

mouth of a lake, at which was a weir of reeds, and a bridge of three arches; but of one more than half was broken away. My companions, with our men, crossed below it by the sea, but seeing the water deep, I dismounted and walked over. The lake is long, and extended close by us on our left almost to the river Cayster, near which we turned up from the beach. We discovered soon after a fisherman's hut between the lake and the river. We were ferried over the latter in a triangular float; and in three hours arrived at Ephesus [where they pitched their tents near the gymnasium].

XXXV

O N the arrival of the Ionian adventurers from the European continent, the people which before possessed the country retired or were expelled. The Carians had settled about Miletus, Mycale, and Ephesus; and the Leleges on the side toward Phocæa. Their sepulchres and castles, with vestiges of their towns, remained for many ages, and some are perhaps even now extant.

The Ionian cities on the continent were, as has been mentioned, ten in number, not reckoning Smyrna. These, with Chios and Samos gloried in their name and to preserve the memory of their common origin, to promote amity and concord, and to facilitate their union for mutual defence, when occasion should require, instituted a general assembly, in which their deputies or representatives had power to propose and enact decrees, to debate and to determine on the interests of the community.

The place, where this famous council, called the Panionian, met, was on the coast named Trogilia ... It was a portion of mount Mycale, named Panionium, fronting the north, in the territory of Priene, selected by the Ionic body, and consecrated to Neptune Heliconius. The cities jointly sacrificed to that deity at the season of the congress. The ceremony is represented on the reverse of a medallion of the emperor Gallus, struck by the Colophonians. The thirteen deputies are there seen, each with his right hand uplifted, or in the act of supplication, standing round an altar, with fire, and a bull before the image and temple.[1] If the victim lowed while dragging to the altar, it was deemed a good omen.

The Prieneans were descended from the Ionians of Helice in Achaia, and introduced the worship of this god. They had petitioned

[1] *Museum C. Albani*, vol. ii, pl. 80 and p. 42. The deity is there supposed to be Apollo Clarius. [C]. *B.M.C. Ionia*, p. 45, no. 60, pls. 8, 16.

XI The Temple of Bacchus at Teos. (Cat. 17)

their mother-city to transmit to them an image of him, and a plan of his temple, intending to erect one on the same model, but were refused. They then obtained from the Achæan community a decree in their favour; and Helice not complying with it, Neptune, it is related, grew angry, and in the following winter that city was swallowed up by an inundation of the sea and an earthquake. This event happened in the night, two years before the battle of Leuctra. The Achæans then delivered to the Ionians the plan they had requested. A young man was appointed by the Prieneans to preside at the rites, as *sacrificing king*, during the festival.

[On April 8th they went on to Scala Nova and decided to proceed to Priene via Panionion by way of the sea shore.] It was dusk, and Changlee[1] lying up from the sea, escaped our observation. We expected to arrive there every minute, and rode on, until we came to the foot of mount Mycale, and the beach was at an end. There, unfortunately, we discovered a track with a gate before it, and went on, not doubting but the village was near. Steep succeeded steep; the way slippery, uneven, often winding about vast chasms, or close by the brink of tremendous precipices, with the sea rolling beneath.

We were benighted and perplexed, the track not being distinguishable, though the moon began to shine. We dismounted to lead our horses, when the janizary, who was a fat bulky man, and distressed by the bushes which entangled in his long garments, bemoaned his situation in broken Italian, with the most plaintive accents. We still persevered, suffering now from thirst even more than from fatigue, and at length heard the sound of water in a nook below us, when the moments seemed hours as we descended to it. After this refreshment we pushed on as well as we could, expecting to meet soon with some house or village, and commiserating our men and horses embroiled, as we conceived, with our baggage on the mountain behind us.

About two in the morning our whole attention was fixed by the barking of dogs, which, as we advanced, became exceedingly furious. Deceived by the light of the moon, we now fancied we could see a village, and were much mortified to find only a station of poor goatherds, without even a shed, and nothing for our horses to

[1] Now ?Güzelçamli.

eat. They were lying, wrapped in their thick capots or loose coats, by some glimmering embers, among the bushes in a dale, under a spreading tree by the fold. They received us hospitably, heaping on fresh fuel, and producing caimac, or sour curds, and coarse bread, which they toasted for us on the coals. We made a scanty meal sitting on the ground, lighted by the fire and by the moon; after which, sleep suddenly overpowered me. On waking, I found my two companions by my side, sharing in the comfortable cover of the janizary's cloak, which he had carefully spread over us. I was now much struck with the wild appearance of the spot. The trees was hung with rustic utensils; the she-goats, in a pen, sneezed and bleated, and rustled to and fro; the shrubs, by which our horses stood, were leafless, and the earth bare; a black caldron with milk was simmering over the fire; and a figure more than gaunt or savage, close by us, was struggling on the ground with a kid, whose ears he had slit, and was endeavouring to cauterize with a piece of red hot iron.

We had now the mortification to hear that our labour was fruitless, and that we must return the way we came, both we and our horses fasting. We left the goatherds, and found the track, which we had passed in the dark, full of danger even by day. We consumed near four hours on the mountain in going back. Descending from it to the beach, we . . . came to Giaur-Changlee, a small Greek village near a shallow stream. By the way was a mean church, with a ruined inscription in the portico . . .

The next morning, April the 9th, it rained; but about ten we mounted, and leaving the bay on our left hand, proceeded with a guide toward Mycale. We soon came to Turkish Changlee, which is seated higher up by a stream, then rapid and turbid. I saw by the mosque an inscription,[1] which I wished to copy, but was accidentally the last of our caravan and I was cautious of separating from the rest. There, it is likely, was the site of Panionium,[2] and of the temple of Neptune. The river was named the Gæsus or Gessus, and entered the sea on the coast called Trogilia . . .

[1] This church is now destroyed and the inscription lost.

[2] The site of Panionion has only recently been determined and has been excavated by a German mission. It appears to have been more or less where Chandler suspected as it lies on a low barren hill, Otomatik Tepe, just east of the village of Güzelçamli, a few minutes' walk from the sea.

The sacred region Panionia ending, as we supposed, a broken pavement carried us over some roots of Mycale to a pleasant valley, in which a watercourse commenced . . . At a fountain by the way is an ancient coffin with an inscription in Greek. I could read only a couple of the lines. About two we came in sight of Suki,[1] and went on, without stopping, to Giaur-Kelibesh,[2] where we arrived in the evening of April 9th.

[1] Now Soke.   [2] Now Güllubahçe.

XXXVI

GIAUR-KELIBESH is a small village, inhabited, as the name imports, by Christians or Greeks. It is situated on the east side[1] of mount Mycale, the houses rising on a slope, and enjoying a fine view over the plain. The church is mean, and was encompassed with graves. It appeared as a place recently settled. We were here not far from the ruins of Priene, on which we employed some days, returning before sunset to Kelibesh.

During our stay at the village, some of the vagrant people, called Atzincari or Zingari, the gypsies of the east, came thither with a couple of large apes, which, their masters singing to them, performed a great variety of feats with extraordinary alertness, and a dexterity not to be imagined, such as raised highly our opinion of the docility and capacity of that sagacious animal.

One evening, coming from the ruins, we found an old woman sitting by the church on the grave of her daughter, who had been buried about two years. She wore a black veil, and pulling the ends alternately, bowed her head down to her bosom; and at the same time lamented aloud, singing in an uniform dismal cadence, with very few pauses. She continued thus above an hour, when it grew dark; fulfilling a measure of tributary sorrow, which the Greeks superstitiously believe to be acceptable and beneficial to the souls of the deceased. The next morning a man was interred, the wife following the body; tearing her long dishevelled tresses in agony; calling him her life, her love; demanding the reason of his leaving her; and expostulating with him on his dying, in terms the most expressive of conjugal endearments and affection.

The Greeks now celebrated Easter. A small bier, prettily decked with orange and citron buds, Jasmine, flowers, and boughs, was

1 South side. [R]

placed in the church, with a Christ crucified rudely painted on board, for the body. We saw it in the evening; and before daybreak were suddenly awakened by the blaze and crackling of a large bonfire, with singing and shouting in honour of the resurrection. They made us presents of coloured eggs, and cakes of Easter-bread.

The weather had been unsettled. The sky was blue, and the sun shone, but a wet, wintry north wind swept the clouds along the top of the range of Mycale. We were sitting on the floor early one morning at breakfast, with the door, which was toward the mountain, open; when we discovered a small rainbow just above the brow. The sun was then peeping only over the opposite mountain, and, as it got higher, the arc widened and descended toward us; the cattle, feeding on the slope, being seen through it, tinged with its various colours as it passed down, and seeming in the bow. This phenomenon is probably not uncommon in the mountainous regions of Ionia and Greece.

Let us suppose a devout heathen one of our company, when this happened. On perceiving the bow descend, he would have fancied Iris was coming, with a message to the earth, from Jupiter Pluvius; and, if he had beheld the bow ascend in like manner, which at some seasons and in certain situations he might do, he would have confidently pronounced that the goddess had performed her errand, and was going back to heaven.

The morning after we arrived at Kelibesh, we set out to survey the ruins of Priene,[1] with the Greek, at whose house we lodged, for our guide. He led us first through the village up to the acropolis or citadel; the ascent lasting an hour, the track bad, by breaks in the mountain and small cascades. We then arrived on a summit of Mycale, large, distinct, and rough, with stunted trees and deserted cottages, encircled, except toward the plain, by an ancient wall of the masonry called *pseudisodomum*. This has been repaired, and made tenable in a later age by additional outworks. A steep, high, naked rock rises behind; and the area terminates before in a most abrupt and formidable precipice, from which we looked down with wonder on the diminutive objects beneath us. The massive heap of a temple below appeared to the naked eye but as chippings of marble.

[1] For discussion of site and plans see Bean, op. cit., pp. 231–243.

A winding track leads down the precipice to the city. The way was familiar to our guide, and a lad, his son, who was with us. We listened to their assurances, and, enticed by a fair setting out, followed them; but it soon became difficult and dangerous. The steps cut in the rock were narrow, the path frequently not wider than the body, and so steep as scarcely to allow footing. The sun shone full upon us, and was reverberated by the rugged side of the mountain, to which we leaned, avoiding as much as possible the frightful view of the abyss beneath us, and shrinking from the brink. The long-continued descent made the whole frame quiver; and looking up from the bottom, we were astonished at what we had done. We could discern no track, but the rock appeared quite perpendicular; and a soaring eagle was below the top of the precipice. At the temple we were joined by our servants, who led our horses down on the side opposite to that which we ascended; and with them came the fat janizarry, who had very wisely sneaked off on perceiving our intention.

The temple of Minerva Polias, though prostrate, was a remain of Ionian elegance and grandeur too curious to be hastily or slightly examined. An account of it, with a view and plates of the architecture, has been published at the expense of the society of Dilettanti.[1] Several inscribed marbles remain in the heap.[2] When entire, it overlooked the city, which was seated on the side of the mountain, flat beneath flat, in gradation, to the edge of the plain. The areas are levelled, and the communication is preserved by steps cut in the slopes. Below the temple are broken columns and pieces of marble, the remnants of edifices of the Ionic and Doric orders. Farther down is the ground plat of the stadium, by the city-wall. The area was narrow, and the seats ranged only on the side facing the plain. In the mountain, on the left hand, going from the temple, is the recess, with some vestiges of the theatre. Among the rubbish and scattered marbles is an inscription, with a fragment or two, and ruins of churches, but no wells or mosques as at Miletus. The whole circuit of the wall of the city is standing, besides several portions within it worthy of admiration for their solidity and beauty. It descends

[1] See Plates XII, XIII and XIV.
[2] *Inscript. Ant.*, p. 14, 15, 16. [C]. *CIG*, 2, p. 571, no. 2905. Also *B.M.* I, 403. z(1) and z(2); r(1) and r(2); u(1); y; ll. 27–33.

on each side of the precipice, and is the boundary next the plain.

Priene, not including the citadel, had three gateways; one is toward Kelibesh, and has without it vaults of sepulchres; the entrance was not wide. A part of the arch, consisting of a single row of massive stones, still remains; but those on which it rests are so corroded by age, broken, or distorted, as to seem every moment ready to yield, and let down their load. A rugged way leads to a second opening in the wall, opposite to this, and, as we guessed, about a mile from it; beyond which are likewise vaults of sepulchres. Between these was a gate facing the plain; and on the left hand going out of it is a hole, resembling the mouth of an oven, in the side of a square tower; and over it an inscription in small characters, exceedingly difficult to be read.[1] It signifies, that a certain Cyprian in his sleep, had beheld Ceres and Proserpine, arrayed in white; and that in three visions they had enjoined the worship of a hero, the guardian of the city, and pointed out the place, where, in obedience to them, he had erected the god ...

[1] *Inscript. Ant.*, p. 13. [C]. *CIG*, 2, p. 578, no. 2907.

XXXVII

[THEY then decided to make for Mount Latmus and Lake Bafa and] left the village on the 15th of April at seven in the morning. We found the torrent-bed, which occasioned our preplexity in going to Miletus, less formidable here, crossing it by a wooden bridge made for foot passengers. It has received some water from the late rains, which had also flooded the plain at the foot of the mountain. The air was sharp; and snow, recently fallen, glistened on the northern summits. About nine, we came to three distinct, bare rocks, resembling islets of the Ægæan sea, but surrounded with land instead of water. On one is a village named Osebashá, and on the side next Priene is a very wide torrent bed.[1]

We went on, and after half an hour were stopped by the Mæander. Here we were ferried over in a triangular float, with a rope, in two minutes and a half. The stream was broad, rapid, and muddy, but low within the banks, which were indented by the gradual sinking of its surface. We ascended the mountain, and enjoyed a delicious view of the river, crossing with mazy windings from the foot of mount Messogis, the northern boundary of the plain.

We were informed at the ferry, that the road to Bafí,[2] distant from thence four hours, was bad. We met on it a few camels, which carry their burdens high on their backs, or I should have described it as only not absolutely impassable. It lies over a branch of Titanus,[3] which mountain is uncommonly rough and horrid, consisting of huge, single, irregular, and naked rocks piled together; poised, as it were, on a point; or hanging dreadfully over the track; and interspersed with low shrubs and stunted oaks. Our horses suffered exceedingly, sliding down, or jammed with their burdens, or violently

[1] Forsaken bed of the Mæander. [R]
[2] Lake Bafa.   [3] Latmus. [R]. Correct.

154

forced from the road, and rolling over the steeps; and our men were much jaded with loading and unloading them, and bruised by transporting our baggage on their shoulders at the narrow passes.

We were benighted in this wild mountain, when we came to a strait, where the difficulty seemed insurmountable. Three or four of us at length pushed through; and, leading our horses into a vale beneath, committed them to the care of the janizary. We then joined our companions in distress, who were perplexed above; and lighting candles, began, all hands, to carry down our baggage piecemeal ... We pitched our tent near a tree, not far from a rill, on a green spot surrounded with brown, naked rocks.

Our toil was renewed in the morning, but about noon we got clear from the mountain. When near Bafí, we entered a small plain half-encircled with a bare ridge. This avenue had been barricaded. We pitched our tent soon after upon a pleasant green area within the city-walls of Myus.[1]

The story of Myus is remarkable, but not singular. A town by Pergamum, named Atarneus, had suffered in the same manner. Myus originally was seated on a bay of the sea, not large, but abounding in fish. Hence, this city was given to Themistocles to furnish that article for his table. The bay changed into a lake, and became fresh. Myriads of gnats swarmed on it, and the town was devoured, as it were, from the water. The Myusians retired from this enemy to Miletus, carrying away all their moveables, and the statues of their gods. They were incorporated with the Milesians, and sacrificed, and gave their suffrage with them at the Panionian congress.[2] Pausanias relates, that nothing remained at Myus in his time, but a temple of Bacchus of white stone.[3]

---

[1] On this and succeeding pages Chandler writes 'Myus' which Revett repeatedly corrects to 'Heracleia' in footnotes. This site is undoubtedly Heracleia under Latmus. Although Chandler is clearly wrong, it seems best to leave 'Myus' as he put it in the text, but readers are asked to bear in mind the correct identification. The actual site of Myus lies a short distance inland to the northwest of the lake where the foundations of a temple can be seen but little else is visible. See Bean, op. cit., pp. 244–246 for Myus and pp. 252–258 for Heracleia.

[2] This paragraph refers to the actual Myus.

[3] Pausanias, VII.ii.11; Vitruvius, IV.c.1.5–6; Strabo, 14.1.3; Diodorus Siculus, XI. 57.7. [C]

The site of Myus is as romantic as its fortune was extraordinary.[1] The wall encloses a jumble of naked rocks rudely piled, of a dark dismal hue, with precipices and vast hollows, from which perhaps stone had been cut. A few huts, inhabited by Turkish families, are of the same colour, and scarcely distinguishable. Beyond these, fronting the lake, you find on the left hand a theatre hewn in the mountain, with some mossy remnants of the wall of the proscenium or front; but the marble seats are removed. Between the huts and the lake are several terraces with steps cut as at Priene. One, by which our tent stood, was a quadrangular area edged with marble fragments; and we conjectured it had been the market-place. By another were stones ornamented with shields of a circular form. But the most conspicuous ruin is a small temple which is seated on an abrupt rock with the front only, which is toward the east, accessible. The roof is destroyed. The cell is well-built, of smooth stone with a brown crust on it.[2] The aspect was *in antis*. We measured some marble fragments belonging to it, and regretted that any of the members were missing. This edifice has been used as a church, and the entrance walled up with patch-work. The marbles, which lie scattered about, the broken columns, and mutilated statues, all witness a remote antiquity. We met with some inscriptions, but not legible. The city-wall was constructed, like that at Ephesus, with square towers, and is still standing, except toward the water. It runs up the mountain-slope so far as to be in some places hardly discernible.

Without the city are the cemeteries of its early inhabitants; graves cut in the rock, of all sizes, suited to the human stature at different ages; with innumerable stones, which served as lids.[3] Some are yet covered, and many open, and by the lake filled with water. The lids are overgrown with a short, dry, brown moss, their very aspect evincing old age. We were shewn one inscription,[4] close by a small hut in a narrow pass of the mountain westward, on marble, in large characters. It records a son of Seleucus, who died young, and the

[1] The site of Myus—extraordinary—The site of Heraclea is very romantic. [R]. See Plate XV.

[2] Of a species of red granite, but the front of the pronaos of white marble. [R]

[3] Whose surface was gradually sloped in the form of a low roof, gabled at each end. [R]

[4] *Inscript. Ant.*, p. 18. [C] *CIG*, 2, p. 570, no. 2898.

affliction of his parents; concluding with a tender expostulation with them on the inefficacy and impropriety of their immoderate sorrow. Nearer the city, among some trees, is a well with the base of a column perforated on the mouth.

A couple of peasants, who undertook to shew something extraordinary, conducted me, with one of my companions, up into the mountain on the east side of the city; on which are many traces of ancient walls and towers. We climbed several rocks in the way; our guides with bare feet, carrying in their hands their papouches, or slippers, which were of red leather; a colour not allowed to be worn except by Turks. We came in about an hour to a large rock, which was scooped out, and had the inside painted with the history of Christ in compartments, and with heads of bishops and saints. It is in one of the most wild and retired recesses imaginable. Before the picture of the crucifixion was a heap of stones piled as an altar, and scraps of charcoal, which had been used in burning incense; with writing on the wall.

Going back, I tarried with one of the Turks, while a shower fell, in a single rock, hollowed out; with the doorway above the level of the ground. It stands distinct and tall. On the dome within, Christ was pourtrayed [sic], and on the round beneath, the Panagia, or Virgin, with saints. The figures are large, and at full length; the design and colouring such as may be viewed with pleasure. On the plaster are inscriptions painted, and faint from age. One, which I carefully copied,[1] informs us, the oratory had been beautified, for the sake of the prayers and salvation of a certain subdeacon and his parents . . .

It may be inferred from the remnants of the monasteries and churches, which are numerous, that Myus became a holy retreat, when monkery, spreading from Egypt, toward the end of the fourth century, overran the Greek and Latin empires. The lake abounding in large and fine fish, afforded an article of diet not unimportant under a ritual which enjoined frequent abstinence from flesh. It probably contributed to render this place, what it appears to have been, a grand resort of fanciful devotees and secluded hermits, a nursery of saints, another Athos, or holy mountains . . .

[1] *Inscript. Ant.*, p. 18. [C]. *CIG*, 4, p. 381, no. 8861.

XXXVIII

THE Lake of Myus is visible both from Priene and Miletus and is called by the neighbouring Greeks (θάλασσα) *the Sea*. The water is not drinkable ... On the edges and round about it are square towers and ruinous castles, besides one at Myus, erected in times of war or rapine, to secure and command the passes.

The lake, which is much longer than broad, has in it several rocky islets. One, near Myus, is surrounded with an ordinary wall enclosing the ruin of a church. The water is so shallow, that we once waded across. It was chosen as the best point of view for a drawing of the city and mountain. Our servant found there the nest of some water-fowl in a hole of the wall, filled with large eggs, speckled with red. Among the rubbish was a pillar, on which a cross is carved, and a marble with a sepulchral inscription,[1] "Heraclides, son of Sotades, "temple-sweeper to Hecate." This goddess, perhaps, was wor-shipped by the Charonium near Rhymbria. The persons, who enjoyed that title, had the general care of the temples, to which they belonged. The office was accounted very honourable. It was some-times conferred on cities, and is found upon record on their medals, and other remaining monuments.

Lower down the lake is a rock, which I visited in a boat, or rather a few boards badly fastened together ... It is joined to the continent by a low sandbank, and has a wall of despicable patchwork round it. Mount Titanus[2] is the margin of the lake on that side. Our return to Myus was attended with some risk. It was evening, our float slight, the gale strong, and the water rough.

I was desirous to go down the lake to its mouth, as we supposed, eight or ten miles distant. The inbat seemed regular, and it was

[1] *Inscript. Ant.*, p. 18. [C]. *CIG*, 2, p. 570, no. 2897.
[2] Latmus. [R]. Correct.

expected would waft us pleasantly back. We embarked in the morning in a larger boat, but could procure no sail. We rowed to a picturesque islet, beyond the rock, covered with ruins of a monastery, and found an inscription in Greek over the door-way of the church, but the letters so disguised by ligatures exceedingly complicated, that I could neither copy nor decipher it. On a couple of marbles[1] in the wall is carved a double hatchet, and under it the name of the proprietor, "Jupiter of Labranda." ...

Our boat moved very heavily, but we tugged on from this islet to one in a line with it, and on the north side of the lake, overspread likewise with rubbish. On the shore we found young tortoises, lively, but so small, that we supposed they were just hatched from the eggs. The fish rose all around us, and the tops of the rocks above the surface of the water were covered with birds. We were amused with vast flights of fowl, some of a species unknown to us ... We had observed at Myus many small square niches cut; and rocks, with steps to ascend to the top. These places, it may be conjectured, were designed for the worship of the watery divinities, to receive propitiatory offerings or votive tablets: the memorials of real or imaginary perils and escapes; the tribute of their suppliants distressed and relieved in their occupation or voyages on the lake.[2]

We have already mentioned the Mæander among the rivers of Asia Minor, anciently noted for the production of new land. The stream, it was remarked, in passing through the ploughed grounds of Phrygia and Caria, collected much slime, and bringing it down continually, added to the coast at its mouth.

The Mæander was indictable for removing the soil, when its margin tumbled in; and the person who recovered damages was paid from the income of the ferries.[3] The downfalls were very frequent, and are supposed, with probability to be the cause of the curvity of the bed; the earth carried away from one part lodging in another, and replacing the loss sustained on one side, by adding to the opposite bank.

We have described the stream as crossing from near mount Mes-

---

[1] *Inscript. Ant.* p. 18. [C]. *CIG*, 2, p. 570, no. 2896.
[2] These are beds cut in the rock for the stone blocks.
[3] Strabo, 12.8.19. [C]

sogis to the foot of Titanus[1] opposite to Priene; and on that side it continues, running toward the mouth of the lake of Myus. Probably the level of the intermediate plain determined it in that course; the soil washed from Mycale, or supplied by the river, raising the surface there, and forbidding its approach. The current repelled by the rocks of Osebashá,[2] and contracted about the ferry, wore its present channel, while the mud was soft and yielding; and the bed, which we passed near them, was created from the same obstruction, the water after floods running off there more forcibly, as meeting with more resistance.

The river turns from the mouth of the lake, with many windings, through groves of tamarisk, toward Miletus; proceeding by the right wing of the theatre in mazes to the sea, which is in view, and distant as we computed, about eight miles ... The extremity of the plain by the shore appeared, from the precipice of Priene, marshy, or bare, and as mud. Such was the face of this region when we saw it. How different from its aspect, when the mountains were boundaries of a gulf, and Miletus, Myus and Priene maritime cities ...

Miletus had then four ports, one of them very capacious; and before it was a cluster of small islands. Beyond Miletus, the coast winding, was a bay called the Latmian, from Latmus, the adjacent mountain. In this bay was "Heraclea under Latmus," a small town, once called Latmos, with a road for vessels; and near that place, after crossing a rivulet, you was shewn a cave, with the sepulchre of Endymion. On this mountain, it was fabled, Luna cast that hero and hunter into a profound sleep, to have the pleasure of saluting him. After Heraclea was Pyrrha, and inconsiderable town, the distance between them by sea about one hundred stadia, or twelve miles and a half. From Miletus to Heraclea was a little more, coasting the bay; but from Miletus to Pyrrha, in a straight course, three miles and three quarters, so much longer was the voyage by the shore. From Pyrrha to the mouth of the Mæander was six miles and a quarter, the ground slimy and marshy. From thence you sailed up to Myus, in skiffs which plied. After the mouth of the Mæander was the coast against Priene. The sea had once washed the wall of this city; and it had two ports, one of which shut up; but then it was seen within land, five miles, above the shore.

[1] Latmus. [R]. Correct. [2] Now Ozbşai.

The principal island in the cluster before Miletus was Lade. There, when invaded by Darius, the Ionians assembled three hundred and sixty triremes, and engaged his fleet of six hundred. The Milesians had eighty ships, and formed the wing toward the east. Next to them were the Prieneans with twelve, and Myusians with three. The island was afterwards seized by Alexander; and, while he besieged Miletus, was the station of the Greek admiral, who blocked up the port. The Milesians, when he was about to storm the city, tried to escape; some in skiffs, some swimming on their bucklers, but were intercepted; only three hundred getting to a steep islet, which they resolved to defend. This probably was one by Lade. Two, near Miletus, called Cameliade, *the Camels*, were among the less considerable. A single one, it is likely the northermost hillock, was called Asteria, from Asterois, whose skeleton, remarkable for its size, was shewn there. He reigned, it is related, before the Ionic migration. By the Tragiæ, probably mud banks and shoals formed by the river, were other islets, the stations of robbers . . .

The bay, on which Myus was once seated, changed into a lake, when the Mæander, by lodging slime at the mouth, had cut off the ingress of the salt water. The mountains were an obstacle, or the whole recess would have been filled and converted into a plain. Their rills also supplied the fresh water, which generated the gnats. The land grew, as it were, daily, and was continually removing the sea farther from the lake. The mouth of the Mæander was then seen between Miletus and Priene; and this city had a wide plain before it. Afterwards it approached within a mile and a quarter, of Miletus; and the bays above that city were rendered firm ground. The traveller, who shall ride along the foot of mount Latmus,[1] eastward from Miletus, will, I doubt not, discover the site of Heraclea; and the rivulet may direct him even now to the cave of Endymion. Pyrrha has been mentioned as within land. The space between Priene and Miletus was added, in no long time, to the continent. The ports of this city ceased to be navigable; and by degrees Lade and Asteria, and the islets near them, were encircled with soil . . .

Miletus, deprived by the Mæander of the principal advantages of its situation, experienced, with the cities its neighbours, a gradual

[1] Grius. [R]

decay, which will end in total extinction, as it were, by a natural death after a lingering illness. The progress of the changes, as might be expected, were unattended to in the barbarous ages, as not sudden; or unnoticed, as not important. But we are informed that a place by the shore, where the river entered the sea in the year 866, was called *the Gardens*,[1] and that the Greek emperor Manuel, about the middle of the twelfth century, finding that region well watered and beautiful to the eye, resolved to refresh his army there, and to forget the toils of war in the pleasures of the chace [sic] . . .[2]

[1] Cedrenus, p. 566. *Hist. Byʒant.* t. 8. [C]. *C.S.H.B.*, 6. 198.23.
[2] Cinnamus, p. 62 [C]. *C.S.H.B.*, 10.59.13.

XIII   Capital from the Temple of Athene Polias at Priene. (Cat. 19)

XIV   Capital from the Temple of Athene Polias at Priene, with the Valley of the
Maeander. (Cat. 20)

XXXIX

T HE merchants, to whom we were recommended at Mendelet, informed us that Carpuseli was a place which afforded many antiquities. In our second tour we agreed to go thither from Myus. We set out on the 18th of April in the evening, and, after riding an hour and a half by the head of the lake, pitched our tent for the night under a spreading tree by a stream. Here we were serenaded in a disagreeable manner; frogs croaking, as it were, in chorus; owls hooting; jackals in troops howling; and the village dogs barking.

In the morning we again entered the plain mentioned before; and, crossing it near the end, came to the foot of the mountain, and began ascending with Mendelet on our right hand; the track, as may be conjectured, that which once led from Alabanda toward Miletus, and by Labranda to Mylasa. It winded northward by a small river with fish, the water forming cascades, and turning an overshot-mill or two in its way down to the lake. On the sides are furnaces for working iron . . .

In descending on the opposite side of the mountain, we passed some Turkish graves, which had each a bough of myrtle stuck at the head and feet. Beyond these were the sources of a river, probably that once called Harpasus, pellucid, and many in number. We pitched our tent below them on a brow by a Turkish village, after a continued and very laborious ride of ten hours.

We were on horseback again between six and seven in the morning, and travelled first eastward, and then south-eastward; the road good, the slopes covered with pines. The springs, which we saw the day before, had now united into a rapid transparent stream, abounding with fish. Our course lying to the south-east, we crossed it, and on the way met a Turk, a person of distinction, as appeared from his turban. He was on horseback, with a single attendant. Our janizary and Armenians respectfully alighted, and made him a profound obeisance, the former kissing the rim of his garment. He asked some questions, and went on. We arrived about noon at Carpuseli,[1] a village twelve hours north of Mylasa.

As we approached this place, many ancient graves occurred, cut on rocks as at Myus, and reaching over a tract of considerable extent; with some coffins, mostly plain, or without mouldings, of a brown coarse stone, and with holes in the sides. We rode by these, and through a ruined stadium, now the bazar, or market, the way lying between the shops, which formed a street. We pitched our tent further on, near the square basement of a large sepulchre, of handsome solid masonry, and inhabited; standing not far from one side of the city-wall, which may be traced, except toward the plain, and was of the masonry termed *pseudisodomum*. Some Turks came to us here, and one desired wine. He took his turban from his head, kissed and laid it aside; and, after drinking, replaced it with the same ceremony.

We ascended the mountain by a way paved, but rough and slippery. The remains, which we had seen from below, were a terrace-wall, with a square area, and vestiges of a colonnade. Many pedestals are standing, of a coarse, brown, ragged stone. Beyond these, in the rock, is a theatre, with remnants of the front; a cistern, a square tower, and the city-wall enclosing a summit; near which is another, with seven deep oval cisterns in a row, lined with plaster. At a distance behind them are four piers of a broken aqueduct. A pond or two carefully embanked at the mountain-foot are the present reservoirs. The plain is encompassed with hills, is pleasant, and has a stream running in it toward the Harpasus.

I was here again disappointed in finding no inscription to inform us of the ancient name of the place; but suppose it to have been Alabanda.[2] That city is described as situated beneath the summits of a mountain. The founder Alabandus was worshipped there with greater devotion than any of the noble deities. The people were luxurious and gluttonous, and the city was full of female minstrels. It was much infested with scorpions, as were in general the places lying on the range of mountains between it and Mylasa. The ridge

[1] Now Karpuzli.   [2] It must have been Alinda.

of Alabanda had been likened to an ass with a pack-saddle; and a wag added, carrying a load of these insects . . .

[They left Carpuseli early, crossed the stream of the day before, and in mid-morning came upon the banks of the Harpasus.]

. . . We were surrounded with the delightful trilling of innumerable nightingales; and the fish were visible in the crystal stream. This river is described by the shepherd-poet of Smyrna as impetuous after rain, roaring whole days at its junction with the Mæander.[1]

We passed several villages, and leaving the clear Harpasus behind us, came at one to the turbid Mæander, then deep in its bed; a side of the bank torn away by the violence of the current. We were two minutes in ferrying over in a triangular boat, the rope of vine stocks hanging down lax in water. The stream below made an elbow. An ordinary causey, across some low morassy ground, succeeded, with groves of tamarisk, and a wide road, on which we met many people. The ferry is distant about an hour from Guzel-hissar, once called Magnesia by the Mæander.[2]

[1] Q. Smyrn., X.142–146. [C]   [2] Now Morali.

XL

WE shall give here an abstract of Pococke's[1] journey into Caria from Guzel-hissar. He passed the Mæander at the ferry, when the bed was full; the stream rapid, and a furlong broad. He describes the vine-boughs, of which the rope consisted, as about an inch and a half in diameter, and from ten to fifteen feet long. Three men pulled the boat over, a post fixed in it resting against the rope. The mouth of the Harpasus, which he called the China, is, as he relates, about a mile below the ferry. The river has a wooden bridge, about eight miles further eastward, built on nine or ten large stone piers, and about three hundred feet long. He crossed there, and went on a league to Salashar, where he lodged in a miserable khan. The next day the road lay between little green hills for about a league and a half, when he came into the small fertile plain of Carpuseli, and to the ruined city on the south of it; which, he observes, exactly answers to the situation of Alabanda.

From the south-east corner of this plain, Pococke ascended southwards, about three miles, to the top of the mountain, where is a plain about a league broad. He calls the range mount Latmus, and was told it was frequented by wolves, wild boars, and jackals, and also by bears and tigers. Many herdsmen dwell on it; and in some places it was ploughed up, and the fields enclosed, with large trees laid round the edges. A low, easy descent, led into the vale of Mylasa, which he computes about four leagues long and one broad.

He set out from Mylasa for Eski-hissar or Stratonicea, distant about twelve miles, and crossed the mountains to the north-east. He describes that place as between hills, on a level spot opening to a large plain, in which the river China runs. He descended from thence, and going to a league to the north, and then about two to

[1] Pococke, vol. ii, pp. 57–66. [C]

the west, ascended near a league to a village called Lakena; about a mile from which is a ruined castle, strongly situated. The next morning he went about two leagues north to the river Paieslu, which runs into the China; and then crossing the hills to the west, for the space of three leagues, came to one of the villages called Akshouieh; and going on a league to the west, between low rocky hills, and by the side of a rivulet with a bridge, which he passed over, saw a remnant of an old aqueduct; and entering a fine plain, travelled across it two miles northward to the village of China, which is situated at the east end, to the south of the river of that name. He went up the hill, of which the top had been fortified, and saw there two or three sepulchral grots, and a cistern cased with brick, above ground, consisting of two oblong square compartments. The village Lakena seems the ancient Lagina, where Hecate had her temple. The castle near it, and that by China, are probably the two in the territory of Stratonicea, once called Tendeba and Astragon.

Crossing over to the south side of the plain from China, he came to Arabi-hissar, where are considerable ruins of an ancient city, which he describes, and supposes to have been Alinda. From hence he went about a league south-west in the plain, crossed some low hills, and returned to Guzel-hissar, after repassing the bridge over the China. The river, says Pococke, rises in the south-east part of Caria, beyond Aphrodisias; and running through the valley, which is near Stratonicea and Lagina, turns to the north a little before it falls into the Mæander. The chain of mountains between the two rivers afford fine herbage for sheep and black cattle, in which the country abounds. The reader will observe, that he has given a much longer course to the China than that assigned by us to the Harpasus.[1] He was ignorant of the transparent springs, which we discovered, and which plainly appeared the sources of this or the principal stream.

[1] Most likely he is right and ours only a rivulet that runs into it. [R]

XLI

UZEL-HISSAR, *the beautiful castle*, is a large and very populous town; the houses mean, with trees, lofty domes, and minarees of mosques interspersed; a high hill, anciently called Thorax,[1] towering behind. It is the place of residence of a basha. The air, in the hot months, is so bad as to be almost pestilential. We met many passengers on the road: and the burying-grounds were strewed with broken columns and remnants of marble. At entering the town, we were surprised to see around us innumerable tame turtle-doves, sitting on the branches of trees, on the walls, and roofs of houses, cooing unceasingly. We were conducted to a miserable khan, close, and crowded with people.

We had here alarming intelligence of the plague at Smyrna, the daily havoc it made, and the rapidity with which the fierce contagion was then propagated; threatening to overspread the whole country before the end of the summer. It was impossible a great thorough-fare, situated like Guzel-hissar, if free, could continue long without infection. We had room to be apprehensive of the malady, and to be impatient to leave so suspicious a place, where we were pent up in a small chamber and gallery, among doves and travellers, chiefly Turks; devoured by myriads of insects; and suffering alike from extreme heat and from chagrin, not daring to go out of the gate before we had permission from the basha.

This important officer lived in a despicable house on the hill; his haram, which is more shewy, standing separate, and both surrounded by an ordinary wall. Eight agas, each with a retinue of an hundred men, were then in the town, waiting his commands. We had a recommendatory letter to his mohurdar, or treasurer, which was delivered, with a present of a handsome snuff-box, by the janizary,

[1] Now Gümüs Daği.

and graciously received. He promised to mention us to the basha, but his engagements were so many, it was not easy to find an opportunity; and in the mean time we were confined to our khan.

Our unwieldy janizary had several tiresome journeys on this business up to the castle. On the second afternoon he returned with the welcome news that we were at liberty. The mohurdar had requested for us letters to the agas farther eastward, but was denied; the basha being then at enmity, and, before we left Asia Minor, at open war with some leading men in that part of the country. The janizary was pale and quivering, as with fear. He refused even coffee, and lay down to sleep with strong symptoms of violent perturbation. He had been engaged, as he afterwards related, in an insurrection of the janizaries in the island of Candia, to depose the governor, who, for some offence, had seized on six of their breathren; and when he was admitted into the presence of the basha, a privilege which the janizaries claim, to kiss his hand or garment, he immediately knew him to be that person; but fortunately was not in turn recognized. This unexpected rencounter had confounded poor Mustapha to such a degree, that he came back almost doubting whether his head was still on his shoulders.

Magnesia was peopled by a colony of Æolians from Thessaly. The city was in the plain by Thorax, at no great distance from the Mæander, but much nearer to the Lethaeus, which rose in the Ephesian mountain Pactyas, and fell into that river. Its principal ornament was a temple of Diana,[1] called Leucophyrene, or the *white-browed*, which had the privilege of an asylum or sanctuary, and was larger than any in Asia, except the two at Ephesus and at Branchidæ. It excelled the former in elegance and in the fitting up of the cell, but was inferior in the number of offerings. It was a *pseudo-dipteros*, and had eight columns in front, and fifteen on the sides, counting the angular columns. The order was Ionic; and the architect the celebrated Hermogenes, who invented that species. He was a native of Alabanda; and a treatise on the fabric was once extant, written by him. A favourite citharist was painted in the market-place, clothed with the sacred purple of Jupiter Sosipolis, or *the saviour of the city*; and had also a brass statue in the theatre. Some

[1] For description of site see Bean, op. cit., pp. 246–251.

hillocks, which we passed in our way from the ferry, were once the islets called Derasidæ and Sophonia, mentioned by Pliny as taken by nature from Magnesia. The town, which, when this happened, was not very remote from the sea, had in a more early period been maritime. The shore has since been gradually removed still farther off.

The river Lethæus divides the present town, which has a lofty but ordinary bridge over the course. It descends through a narrow and deep-worn vale, on the east side of the castle, with a mountain behind it of light brown earth, being a portion of Messogis. The stream, which in winter is a deep torrent, was now shallow. It received many brooks and rills on the sides, and was clear and rapid. Water bubbled up in several places in the bed, which was wide and partly dry. One of these springs is noted as remarkably cold and copious; and, as our guide told us, is highly esteemed and much drunk of by the Turks and other inhabitants during the hot months.

Magnesia was given to Themistocles to supply bread for his table. The goddess Ceres, standing in a car drawn by winged serpents, and bearing in each hand a lighted torch, is seen on the reverse of a medallion of the emperor Antoninus,[1] struck by this city: and in one of the streets we found a square capital, which it is likely belonged to her temple. The device on it was a poppy between two wheatears and two torches. We saw also many fragments of architecture of the Corinthian and Ionic orders. After viewing the town, we ascended to the castle, and were conducted to an eminence, about a quarter of an hour beyond it, where is a ruin which resembles the arcade at Troas; consisting or a piece of two of wall standing, and three massive arches, each painted with a garland in the centre, and two on the sides, encircling an inscription, of which some letters, with ends of fillets, are visible. The fabric has been repaired or reedified, and some inscribed marbles are inserted in it, but too high to be legible. A Turk had purchased the materials; but the arcade is too solid a building to be easily and suddenly demolished. We enjoyed from it a delicious prospect of the plain of the Mæander. We discovered no stadium but some remains of a theatre. The vestiges, if any remain, were concealed in the town by the buildings; or, without it, by stone fences, olive-trees, and nigh corn.

[1] *Museum C. Albani*, V.1, pl. 26 [C]. *B.M.C. Ionia*, p. 165. no. 56. pl. xix, 8.

In the territory of this city was a place called Hylæ, with a cave sacred to Apollo. This was of no extraordinary size, but the image of the god was one of the most ancient. It was believed that he furnished ability for every undertaking. His servants leaped down the steep rocks and precipices; or, felling tall trees, walked on them, with burdens, over the narrow passes of the mountain. The cave perhaps remains. I could get no intelligence of it or of Hylæ; but Picenini relates, that in the way to the house and garden of the basha on the hill, they were shewn a cave near the walls of the ancient city, which, they were told, extended underground as far as they could go in two days.[1]

The great road to the east from Ephesus was through Magnesia, Tralles, Nysa, and Antiochia. Magnesia, according to Strabo and Pliny, was only fifteen miles from Ephesus, but Picenini makes it eleven hours from Aiasaluck. He set out with his companions before five in the evening, going southward, and came to the vale, in which is the ancient bridge. They passed then over hills and through valleys. The next day they travelled in a pleasant plain, very extensive on their right hand, with the high tops of a mountain on their left, and arrived at Magnesia. The mountain was Messogis, and the plain that of the Mæander; but they seem not to have taken the direct road. The distance of Magnesia from Tralles was about eighteen miles. The way to it was in the plain of the Mæander. This was also on the right hand, and Messogis on the left; which arrangement was continued as far as Nysa and Antiochia.

[1] Pausanias, X 32, 6 refers to Hylae or Aulae as having a cave sacred to Apollo with a very old statue and a curious cult. See also Pauly-Wissowa, *Real Encyclopädie der Classischen Altestumswissenschaft*, XVII, Halband, p. 106. I am indebted to Prof. J. M. Cook and Dr. Sybilla Haynes for these references. Picenini remains unidentified.

XLII

TRALLES and Nysa[1] were situated alike with respect to the plain, being both above it to the north. Tralles was seated on a flat, the eminence terminating in an abrupt point, and inaccessible all around. The greater part of Nysa reclined on the mountain, which was Messogis; and the city was divided, as it were, into two, by a torrent, which had formed a deep bed. One portion of the course had a bridge over it, to connect the sides; and another was adorned with an amphitheatre, under which a passage was left for the waters. Below the theatre were two precipices; on both of them were ruins.

In the way between Tralles and Nysa was a village of Nyséans, not far from the city, Characa or Acharaca;[2] and a *plutonium* or temple of Pluto and Proserpine, with a beautiful grove above it, and a charonium or cave, of a wonderful nature. Thither sick people resorted, and the deities were their physicians, suggesting, as was believed, efficacious remedies in dreams, most commonly to the priests, who were expert in managing their patients, and would often lead them into the cave. They sometimes remained in it, as in a pit, several days fasting; but persons not guided by them perished in it. A general assembly was celebrated there yearly, when, toward noon, the youth of the gymnasium, with the boys, all naked and anointed, drove a bull with shoutings to the mouth of the cave, where he was let loose, and on entering fell down dead.

The geographer Strabo, who studied rhetoric and grammar at Nysa, mentions Tralles as inhabited, if any of the Asia cities, by wealthy persons; some of whom were always asiarchæ, or prefects of the province under the Romans. Among its eminent men, his

[1] Now Aydin and Sultanhisar.
[2] The site of Acharaka is 3 miles west of Nysa, now Savalatli.

contemporaries, was Pythodorus, a native of Nysa, and friend of Pompey. But Tralles, though an opulent and thriving place, seems then to have contained nothing very remarkable.[1] A prodigy is recorded to have happened there in the civil war. A palm-tree was seen springing from between the stones of the pavement in the temple of Victory, in which a statue of Caesar had been erected. An earthquake happening, the edifices which suffered were rebuilt by Augustus. A writer[2] who lived in the sixth century relates, that a husbandman named Chæremon, in a transport of affliction and zeal for his country, hastened to the emperor, who was then in Cantabria, and by his entreaties prevailed on him to restore the city, which, he observes, had retained its form unaltered from that period. He found in a field near Tralles a pedestal, which had supported a statue of this person, and copied from it the inscription, which he has preserved. It is in the Doric dialect, which was spoken there, and introduced by the Argives, who, with some Thracians, founded Tralles.

The Turks in 1175 making an irruption into the Roman empire on this side, and laying it waste, Tralles and Antiochia capitulated. In 1266 they seized many towns and monasteries; but Tralles, with other advanced places, was secured by the Roman general. In the following year the Turks extended their frontier to the river Sangarius. Michael Paleologus was then emperor. The garrisons by the Mæander, in Caria, Antiochia, and the interior region, were exceedingly weak; and the fortresses by the Cayster, with Priene and Miletus, taken.

Andronicus, son of Paleologus, and his associate in the empire, arriving with succours in 1280, was charmed with the situation of Tralles, and resolved to rebuild the city, and replace in it the families which had been driven out. He intended calling it Paleologopolis or Andronicopolis; and it is related, that on a marble dug up by the workmen an oracle was found inscribed, foretelling this restoration of Tralles, and promising long life to its new founder. When the

[1] Probably an Ionic temple dedicated to Æsculapius, the work of Argelius, on which he wrote a treatise. [R]. Tralles has a large theatre with a tunnel in the orchestra which Prof. Bean informs me that when he saw it in 1945, it was already almost obliterated by the long-standing military occupation.

[2] Agathias. [C]. *C.S.H.B.* I. 101, 18.

walls were raised, it became one of the most considerable places by the Mæander; people, it is likely, flocking to it as a strong hold. It had thirty-five thousand inhabitants; but was destitute both of reservoirs to receive rain, and of wells, which it seemed impossible to dig sufficiently deep. An army of Turks suddenly appeared, and intercepted the supply of water from the river. The citizens persevering in their defence, they entered by storm, and put them all to the sword; Andronicus not moving from Nympheum, near Smyrna. The Turks had before subdued Nysa.[1]

[1] Pachemyrus, p. 320 [C]. *C.S.H.B.* 35.469, 7.

XLIII

WE set out from Magnesia on the 23d at noon, going eastward. By the road near the town were several wells in a
row, with Attic bases of columns perforated and placed
over the mouths. These we supposed remnants of the famous temple
of Diana. The way was straight and wide in the plain; the soil light
and sandy, like that of Messogis, the mountain on our left hand. On
each side of us were orchards of fig-trees sown with corn; and many
nightingales were singing in the bushes. We passed some dry
water-courses and rivulets running down to the Mæander; which was
once in view, the stream winding, with a ferry. It was dusk when we
pitched our tent by Sultan-hissar, which is about five hours from
Magnesia.

Sultan-hissar is an old fortress with houses in and by it, standing
in the plain; the site corresponding neither with that of Tralles nor
with Nysa. It has, however, some marble fragments, which have
been removed from adjacent ruins; and on inquiry, we were informed
that the eminence before us had on it some remains of old buildings;
that the place was called Eski-hissar, and distant about half an hour.
We now expected to find Tralles or Nysa there . . .

In the morning we ascended from the plain to the foot of the
eminence . . . going toward the body of mount Messogis. The road
up it was stony, and carried over a deep but dry water-course by an
arch. Then followed broken vaults of sepulchres, and distinct
remnants of buildings, all stripped of their marble; standing on a
flat covered with corn, trees, fences and walls. This immediately
appeared to me to be the site of Tralles, which had a river or
torrent near it called Eudon.[1]

---

[1] The site of Tralles was flat on an eminence surrounded by a precipice on all
sides, to which this has no resemblance. [R]

Leaving these ruins, the road, still on the eminence, carried us eastward, and then to the south . . . [Passing by a few cottages they came to other ruins,] plainly of Nysa . . . Here we found a large theatre in the mountain-side, with many rows of seats, almost entire, of blue-veined marble, fronting southward. By the left wing is a wide and very deep water-course, the bed of the river once called Thebaites, making a vast gap into the plain, but concealed in the front of the theatre, where is a wide level area, with soil, supported by a bridge by the end of the stadium situated in a hollow . . . with the seats resting on the two slopes. The bottom of this structure is destroyed, and only some masses of brickwork remain, with some marble fragments by the end next the theatre, where you have a view of the lofty and solid piers, with arches, sustaining the area. The eminence terminates on each side of the stadium in a precipice and on one side are other ruins . . .[1]

The ruins on the eminence, though separate, are at a very small distance from each other in a straight line . . .

We set forward again about noon, and riding through Sultan-hissar, came to Nosli-bazar, or *the market of Nosli*, the town called Nosli-Boiuc, or *Great Nosli*,[2] appearing with white minarees at a distance on our right hand toward the Mæander.

The road which we took from Sultan-hissar was that which anciently led to Carura and to Laodicea in Phyrgia . . . We met on it many passengers, and mules, and long strings of camels. The ground was dry, the soil fine, and covered with corn, with fig and olive trees. Our course was a little north of east. After five hours we pitched our tent. A summit of the mountain Cadmus, on the south side of the Mæander, or of Taurus, which was opposite to us, had snow on it. On our left was a rising ground beneath the hilly range of Messogis, with a large village; and on the level in the front were many deep wells, each furnished with a tall pole supporting a long lever, from which hung a rope and a wooden bucket to raise water for the caravans.

---

[1] It is evident that Chandler is mistaken in thinking he had found Tralles which lies about 15–20 km to the west on the hill above Aydin, formerly Güzelhisar. The first lot of ruins which he found must have been Acharaca and thereafter his identification of Nysa is correct.   [2] Now Nazilli.

Mount Messogis, beyond Nosli-Bazar, becomes less wide and lofty than before, and is overtopped by mount Tmolus. I observed a remarkable gap in the range of Messogis, opening a view into a green plain, at some distance on our left hand. I wished to explore this pleasant region; but our route was settled, and the sudden changing it might have been attended with inconveniences, if not with danger. That was the place, if I mistake not, called Leimon, or *the Meadow*, which is described as lying above mount Tmolus, and the southern parts of Messogis, three miles and three quarters, from Nysa. The inhabitants of this city, and all around it, held there a general assembly. They said it was the Asian meadow of Homer; and shewed the monument of Asius, and also of Cayster, with the source of the river named from him; and not far off was the mouth of a cave sacred to Pluto and Proserpine, supposed to communicate with that at Characa ...

[After several hours' riding they] approached the site of Carura, anciently a village with Khans or inns for travellers; in one of which a large company, while revelling, had been swallowed up by an earthquake. It was remarkable for surges or eruptions of hot waters in the river or on its margin;[1] and was the boundary of Caria toward Phrygia.

Riding along the bank of the river, we discovered the ruin of an ancient bridge. The remnant was on the farther side, and consists of half of the central arch, with one smaller arch entire. This bridge was probably broken before the year 1244; when an interview being agreed on between the emperor of Nice and the Turkish sultan, the latter passed the river, in his way to Tripolis, on a temporary bridge made of rafts for the occasion.

The existence of Carura, it is likely, was determined by the loss of the passage. We saw no traces of that place; but, going near the ruin, one of our horses turned short, which led us to observe a vein of hot water boiling up out of the ground, like a jetté, some inches perpendicular, and forming a small quagmire. We now enter Phrygia.

[1] Strabo, 12.8.17. [C]

177

XLIV

CONTINUING our journey, we lost sight of the river; the plain widened again, and was cultivated, but not enclosed, as before. Messogis was now of a chalky aspect; and the mountain on our right green with trees. We saw a few scattered booths of Turcomans. At four our course inclined to east-south-east. We observed many jays, and upupas, and a beautiful bird, like a hawk, with blue glossy plumage. We had travelled eight hours and three quarters, when we pitched our tent by a village under a summit [Cadmus] covered with snow.

The following day our course was as before, the river not in view. The sun shone very comfortably, and the melted snow ran in dirty rills down the slopes. On the way some stones and vestiges of a building occurred; perhaps of a temple once between Carura and Laodicea, called that of Men Carus,[1] and held in high veneration. In Strabo's time a great school of physicians flourished there ... We arrived at Denisli[2] in four hours.

Denisli is fortified with an ordinary wall, which encloses a few cottages, and resembles Segigeck. The gateway, on our approach, was crowded with men and boys. Our janizary and Swiss tarried there to purchase provisions and other necessaries, while we dismounted in a meadow at a small distance, expecting their return. Our baggage-horses were scarcely unloaded, when both rejoined us; the Swiss complaining that the Greeks understood only the Turkish language, in which he was not expert; the other, to inform us we were required by the owner of the ground to change our conác or *resting-place*. We removed to a tree, under which we dined, by a muddy stream, and were wetted by a smart shower.

---

[1] Strabo, 12.8.20. [C]   [2] Now Denizli.

XV   The Lake and Theatre at Heraclea. (Cat. 21)

XVI   The Stadium at Laodicea. (Cat. 22)

We had lately perceived an alteration in the carriage of the Turks; who, in the interior regions, seldom see strangers, and are full of ferocity. A general want of cordiality toward us had been apparent, and some trifling insults we had received on the road were fore-runners of more inconvenient incivilities. Some Turks here told us, we had no danger to apprehend on this side of the plain; but if we proceeded to Pambouk, on the farther side, we must be cautious, for the Turcomans in that quarter were robbers and murderers.

We set out again for Eski-hissar, or Laodicea,[1] then distant an hour northward, the way between hills. A Turk, whose dress and mien bespoke him above the common rank, overtook us; and our men inquiring, courteously directed them to a commodious situation for our tent, which we pitched in the evening on a small rising, on the edge of the plain, by the junction of two streams.

We were in general very much fatigued, and about sunset lay down to rest; an Armenian or two watching our horses, which were staked and grazing by the tent. Some time after it was dark, we were suddenly surrounded by armed men, conducted by the Turk who had recommended this spot. Their business was to demand bac-shish for their aga. They pried into our baggage, prancing their long-tailed horses, and threatening if they were not immediately gratified. We were too soundly asleep within the tent to be easily awakened. The Swiss, shaking the relater by the hand, informed him of the quality and importunity of these unwelcome visitants. He was bid to tell their chief, that the aga should be satisfied in the morning; and the janizary urging that the hour was unseasonable, and that we purposed staying, they were prevailed on to depart, taking him with them to pacify their master.

At the dawn of day a Turk was sent to observe if we were stirring, and the janizary set out with our firhman, and a present of coffee, sugar, and money; but the aga declared he would have at least an hundred and thirty piaster; and Mustapha, pleading our firhman, and presuming to remonstrate, was seized, disarmed, and thrown into prison. In the mean time we were very uneasy at the tent, presaging no good from his long stay. After some hours we saw him coming without his gun, pistol, or sabre; terrified and dejected. He exclaimed,

[1] Now Goncali.

we were among rebels and robbers, that the roads were beset to prevent our escape, and the aga, if we hesitated to comply with his demand, was determined to cut us in pieces, and take possession of our baggage.

The janizary described this aga as uncommonly fierce and haughty, and bade us apprehend the very worst consequences from his intemperance and savage disposition. The impression made on him was communicated to our Armenians, and we all disliked our situation. After a short consultation, I gave him twenty zechins, affirming truly that we had no money to spare, but might want even that sum before we reached Smyrna. He ventured back, with some reluctance, into the presence of the aga, who was prevailed on to receive it, but with difficulty; and then inquired about our firhman, which he before had refused to hear named. The janizary returned to him again with it, and, after it had been read, he refunded nine of the zechins; believing, as he was told, that we belonged to the English ambassador, and were going from Smyrna to Constantinople, and fearing we might complain there of his behaviour. He now said he would be responsible for our safety.

As soon as this business was adjusted, we began to examine the site of Laodicea, which was close by us. On the first day we were attended by one of the aga's men, a mean, ill-looking fellow, who required a piaster, his pay, and in the evening left us. The janizary, who by that time had slept away his fatigue and chagrin, went back with him to the village, about an hour distant, for his bridle, which had been exchanged for one of no value. We were visited at our tent, during our stay here, by several of the natives and Turcomans, who manifested so savage and bad a disposition, that our men established a regular watch. They stole our pipes, and took even earthen bowls; a species of petty larceny, which exceedingly distressed some of our company.

The Mæander, running between the hill of Laodicea and mount Messogis, divides the plain, which there becomes narrow. Our view eastward was terminated by mountains, not very remote. The summits on the south and south-east were covered with snow. From the first quarter we had a very sharp piercing breeze at the dawn of day; and from the latter, as soon as the sun was risen. At noon the atmosphere was smoky, the sky hot and fiery; and then cloudy, with showers. It thundered in the north and north-west. We experienced, as it were, winter and summer in the space of twenty-four hours.

XLV

THE city Laodicea was named from Laodice, the wife of its founder Antiochus, the son of Stratonice.[1] It was long an inconsiderable place, but increased toward the age of Augustus Cæsar, after having suffered in a siege from Mithridates. The fertility of the soil, and the good fortune of some of its citizens, raised it to greatness. Hiero, who adorned it with many offerings, left the people his heir to more than two thousand talents. After that benefactor followed Zeno, the rhetorician; and his son Polemo, as renowned a sophist as ever lived. This person flourished at Smyrna; but was buried here, by the Syrian gate, near which were the sepulchres or coffins of his ancestors.[2] Laodicea, though inland, grew more potent than the cities on the coast, and became one of the largest towns in Phyrgia. The other was Apamea Cibotos.

We had crossed the hill, on which Laodicea[3] stood, coming from Denisli. On our approach to it, we had on either hand traces of buildings; and on our right, of a low duct, which has conveyed water. The first ruin was of an stadium,[4] in a hollow, the form oblong, the area about one thousand feet in extent, with many seats remaining. At the west end is a wide vaulted passage, designed for the horses and chariots; about one hundred and forty feet long. The entrance from without is choked up, except a small aperture, at which a glimmering light enters; and the soil has risen above the imposts of the interior arch. This has an inscription on the mouldings, in large characters, in Greek . . .[5]

1 Strabo, 12.8.16. [C]
2 Philostratus, *Lives of the Sophists*, Bk. II.25.
3 A Canadian mission has excavated this site in recent years provisionally locating the sanctuary of Isis.
4 Plate XVI.
5 *Inscript. Ant.*, p. 30. [C]. *CIG*, 3, p. 39, no. 3935.

The city increasing, the stadium, it should seem, was not suffic-iently capacious; but Nicostratus enlarged or lengthened it, and converted it into an amphitheatre. A structure of so vast a circum-ference, when filled with the Laodiceans sitting in rows, must itself have been a very glorious and striking spectacle.

On the north side of the stadium, towards the east end, is the ruin of a most ample edifice. It consists of many piers and arches of stone, with pedestals and marble fragments. At the west end lies a large stone, with an inscription; the city or people "has erected "Asad, a man of sanctity and piety, and recorder for life, on account " of his services to his country." This fabric was perhaps the reposi-tory of the laws, and contained the senate-house, the money-exchange, and public offices. It has been remarked, that the waters of Laodicea, though drinkable, had a petrifying quality; and at the east end of this ruin is a mass of incrustation formed by the current, which was conveyed to it in earthen pipes by the duct before mentioned.

From this ruin you see the odeum, which fronted southward. The seats remain in the side of the hill. The materials of the front lie in a confused heap. The whole was of marble. Sculpture had been lavished on it, and the style savoured less of Grecian taste than Roman magnificence.

Beyond the odeum are some marble arches standing, with pieces of massive wall; the ruin, as we conjectured, of a gymnasium. This fabric, with one at a small distance, appeared to have been re-edified, probably after an earth-quake to which calamity Laodicea was remarkably subject. Westward from it are three marble arches crossing a dry valley, as a bridge. Many traces of the city-wall may be seen, with broken columns and pieces of marble used in its later repairs. Within, the whole surface is strewed with pedestals and fragments. The luxury of the citizens may be inferred from their other sumptuous buildings, and from two capacious theatres in the side of the hill, fronting northward and westward; each with its seats still rising in numerous rows one above another. The travellers in 1705 found a maimed statue at the entrance of the former, and on one of the seats the word ZHNωNOE, *of Zeno*.

The hill of Laodicea consists of dry, impalpable soil, porous, with many cavities, resembling the bore of a pipe; as may be seen on the sides, which are bare. It resounded beneath our horses' feet. The stones are mostly masses of pebbles, or of gravel consolidated, and as light as pumice-stone. We had occasion to dig, and found the earth as hard as any cement. Beneath, on the north, are stone coffins, broken, subverted, or sunk in the ground.

The two streams, which united by our tent, were the Lycus and the Caprus. The Lycus flows from a mountain called Cadmus, above Laodicea, or to the east. It is seen in the plain, north of the hill, and was now shallow, and about two yards over. After its junction with the Caprus, on the north-west, it becomes a sizeable river. The Caprus descends on the west, through a narrow valley, in which are four tall piers of a bridge once crossing it, and leading to a gate of the city. These rivers are represented on medals. The Asopus, which ran on the opposite side, was dry. Laodicea, with Colossæ, its neighbour, was enriched by sheep, which produced fleeces exceeding Milesian in softness, and the jetty raven in colour. The river Xanthus, or Scamander, was supposed the author of the yellow hue observable in the Troad. This region was said to be indebted to the Lycus. The breed perhaps has been neglected. Some shepherds came with their flocks to the ruins, and in the evening to the water by our tent. I remarked only one or two, which were very black and glossy.

Laodicea was often damaged by earthquakes, and restored by its own opulence, or by the munificence of the Roman emperors. These resources failed, and the city, it is probable, became early a scene of ruin. About the year 1097 it was possessed by the Turks, and submitted to Ducas, general of the emperor Alexis. In 1120 the Turks sacked some of the cities of Phrygia by the Mæander, but were defeated by the emperor John Commenus, who took Laodicea, and built anew or repaired the walls. About 1161 it was again unfortified. Many of the inhabitants were then killed, with their bishop, or carried with their cattle into captivity by the Turks. In 1190, the German emperor, Frederick Barbarossa, going by Laodicea with his army toward Syria on a croisade, was received so kindly, that he prayed on his knees for the prosperity of the people. About 1196, this region, with Caria, was dreadfully ravaged by the Turks. The sultan, on the invasion of the Tartars in 1255, gave Laodicea to the Romans; but they were unable to defend it, and it soon returned to the Turks. We saw no traces either of houses, churches, or mosques. All was silence, and solitude. Several strings of camels passed eastward over the hill; but a fox, which we first discovered by his ears, peeping over a brow, was the only inhabitant of Laodicea.

XLVI

PAMBOUK,[1] or the ruined city of Hierapolis, which we could see, is seated upon Mt. Messogis, beneath the summits of the mountain. The distance was one hour and a half, north-north-eastward. The aga, with whom we had lately been embroiled, told the janizary, that he commanded at Pambouk, the aga of the district being absent, and that we had nothing to fear there, as we were under his protection. We relied on his assurances, and left Laodicea on the 30th of April in the afternoon; crossing the plain toward Pambouk.

We passed the Lycus on the west of Laodicea, near an ordinary bridge, and in about three quarters of an hour the Mæander; which here had two beams laid across it, with planks; the water deep in its bed, muddy, as usual, and rapid. Some men, who were digging a trench in the plain, left off, and waited our approach. They were headed by a chiaush, or *the messenger* of an aga, who commanded in a small village to the west of Pambouk. He stopped us at a narrow pass, seizing the bridles of the horses which were foremost. Our janizary galloped up, and interposing, was informed the aga insisted on bacshish.

We rode on to Pambouk, and, while our tent was pitching, the janizary went to the aga with our firhman, and a present of coffee and sugar. He was civilly received, the aga commiserating our late ill usage, of which he had heard, and complaining, that the same person had extorted from him an extravagant ransom for a stray beast; saying, he was a man of a bad character, of an imperious temper, and, from his superior power, the tyrant of that country. He demanded five okes of coffee; and some other claims were made for

[1] Now Pamükkale.

his officers, amounting in the whole to ten okes, for which money was accepted. He declared we had no danger to apprehend by day at Pambouk, but recommended our leaving the ruins early in the evening. We enjoyed by anticipation the security he foretold.

Our tent stood on a green dry spot beneath the cliff. The view before us was so marvellous, that the description of it, to bear even faint resemblance, ought to appear romantic. The vast slope, which at a distance we had taken for chalk, was now beheld with wonder, it seeming an immense frozen cascade, the surface wavy, as of water at once fixed, or in its headlong course suddenly petrified. Round about us were many high, bare, stony ridges; and close by our tent one with a wide basis, and a slender rill of water, clear, soft and warm, running in a small channel on the top. A woman was washing linen in it, with a child at her back; and beyond were cabins of the Turcomans, standing distinct, much neater than any we had seen; each with poultry feeding, and a fence of reeds in front.

It is an old observation, that the country about the Mæander, the soil being light and friable, and full of salts generating inflammable matter, was undermined by fire and water. Hence it abounded in hot springs, which, after passing underground from the reservoirs, appeared on the mountain, or were found bubbling up in the plain, or in the mud of the river; and hence it was subject to frequent earthquakes; the nitrous vapour, compressed in the cavities and sublimed by heat or fermentation, bursting its prison with loud explosions, agitating the atmosphere, and shaking the earth and waters with a violence as extensive as destructive, and hence, moreover, the pestilential grottos, which had subterraneous communications with each other, derives their noisome effluvia; and, serving as smaller vents to these furnaces or hollows, were regarded as apertures of hell, as passages for deadly fumes rising up from the realms of Pluto. One or more of the mountains perhaps has burned. It may be suspected, that the surface of the country has, in some places been formed from its own bowels; and in particular, it seems probable, that the hill of Laodicea was originally in irruption.

The hot waters of Hierapolis have produced that most extraordinary phenomenon, the cliff, which is one entire incrustation.

They were anciently renowned for this species of transformation.[1] It is related they changed so easily, that being conducted about the vineyards and gardens, the channels became long fences, each a single stone. They produced the ridges by our tent. The road up to the ruins, which appears as a wide and high causey, is a petrification; and overlooks many green spots, once vineyards and gardens, separated by partitions of the same material. The surface of the flat, above the cliff, is rough with stone and with channels, branching out in various directions; a large pool overflowing and feeding the numerous rills, some of which spread over the slope, as they descend, and give to the white stony bed a humid look, resembling salt or driven snow, when melting. This crust, which has no taste or smell, being an alkaline, will ferment with acids; and Piccenini related, that trial of it had been made with spirit of vitriol. The waters, though hot, were used in agriculture.

Tamerlane, when he invaded this country, encamped for the summer at Tangúzlik, where many of his men were destroyed by drinking of a spring, which stagnated and petrified. I should have supposed that place to have been Hierapolis; but other hot waters, with a similar cliff, will be mentioned in a following chapter. The Turkish name Pambouk signifies *cotton*, and, it has been said, refers to the whiteness of the incrustation.

The shepherd-poet of Smyrna, after mentioning a cave in Phrygia sacred to the nymphs, relates, that there Luna had once descended from the sky to Endymion, while he was sleeping by his herds; that marks of their bed were then extant under the oaks; and that in the thickets around it the milk of cows had been spilt, which men still beheld with admiration; for such was the appearance, if you saw it very far off; but that from thence flowed clear or warm water, which in a little while concreted round about the channels, and formed a stone pavement.[2] The writer describes the cliff at Hierapolis, if I mistake not, as in his time, and has added a local story, current when he lived. It was the genius of the people to unite fiction with truth; and, as in this and other instances, to dignify the tales of their

[1] Strabo, 13.4.14; Pausanias, VIII.vii.3; Vitruvius, VIII.c.iii,10; Ulpian, *Pandect.* lib. xliii. [C]

[2] Q. Smyrn., X.125–137. [C]

mythology with fabulous evidence, taken from the natural wonders in which their country abounded.

We ascended in the morning to the ruins,[1] which are on a flat, passing by sepulchres with inscriptions, and entering the city from the east. We had soon the theatre on our right hand, and the pool between us and the cliff. Opposite to it, near the margin of the cliff, is the remain of an amazing structure, once perhaps baths, or, as we conjectured, a gymnasium; the huge vaults of the roof striking horror as we rode underneath. Beyond it is the mean ruin of a modern fortress; and farther on are massive walls of edifices, several of them leaning from their perpendicular, the stones distorted, and seeming every moment ready to fall, the effects and evidences of violent and repeated earthquakes. In a recess of the mountain, on the right hand, is the area of a stadium. Then again sepulchres succeed, some nearly buried in the mountain-side, and one, a square building, with an inscription in large letters. All these remains are plain, and of the stone created by the waters. The site has been computed about two hundred paces wide, and a mile in length.

After taking a general survey, we returned to the theatre, intending to copy inscriptions and examine more particularly as we changed our station. We found this a very large and sumptuous structure, and the least ruined of any we had seen. Part of the front is standing. In the heap, which lies in confusion, are many sculptures well executed in basso-relievo; with pieces of architrave inscribed, but disjointed; or so encumbered with massive marbles, that we could collect from them no information. The character is large and bold, with ligatures. The marble seats are still unremoved. The numerous ranges are divided by a low semicircular wall, near midway, with inscriptions on the face of it, but mostly illegible. I copied a short but imperfect one, in which Apollo Archegetes or *the Leader* is requested to be propitious. In another compartment, mention is made of the city by its name Hierapolis; and on a third is an encomium in verse . . .[2]

The waters of Hierapolis were surprisingly attempered for tinging wool with a colour from roots rivalling the more costly purples,

[1] Recent excavations have taken place here.
[2] *Inscript. Ant.*, p. 31. [C]. *CIG*, 3, p. 32, no. 3909.

and were a principal source of the riches of the place. The company of dyers is mentioned in the inscription,[1] on the square building among the sepulchres. That heroum, or monument, was to be crowned by them with garlands or festoons of flowers. The springs flowed so copiously, that the city was full of spontaneous baths, and Apollo, the tutelar deity of the Hierapolitans, with Æsculapius and Hygiea, on their medals, bear witness to the medicinal virtues which they possess. The people, in some of their inscriptions, are styled *the most splendid*, and the senate *the most powerful*.

The pool before the theatre has been a bath, and marble fragments are visible at the bottom of the water, which is perfectly transparent, and of a briny taste. The women of the aga, after bathing in it, came to the theatre, where we were employed, to see us, with their faces muffled. They were succeeded by the aga, with several attendants. He was a young man of good deportment and uncommon affability. He discoursed with our janizary, sitting cross-legged on the ruins, smoking and drinking coffee; and expressed his regret, that no water fit to drink could be discovered there; wishing, if we possessed the knowledge of any from our books, we would communicate it to him; saying, it would be a benefit, for which all future travellers should experience his gratitude.

Hierapolis was noted, besides its hot waters, for a *plutonium* This was an opening in a small brow of the adjacent mountain, capable of admitting a man, and very deep, with a square fence before it, enclosing about half an acre; which space was filled with black thick mist, so that the bottom could be scarcely discerned. The air, to those who approached it, was innocent on the outside of the fence, being clear of the mist in serene weather; it remaining then within the boundary; but there death abode. Bulls, as at Nysa, dropped down, and were dragged forth without life; and some sparrows, which Strabo let fly, instantly fell senseless. But eunuchs, the priests of Magna Mater, or Cybele, could go in quite to the aperture, lean forward, or enter it unharmed; but they held their breath, as their visages testified, and sometimes until in danger of suffocation. Strabo, the relater, was in doubt, whether all eunuchs could do this, or only they of the temple; and whether they were preserved by

[1] *Inscript. Ant.*, p. 31. [C]. *CIG*, 3, p. 37, no. 2924b.

divine Providence, as in cases of enthusiasm, or were possessed of some powerful antidotes. But it is likely this mist was the condensed steam of the hot waters,[1] made noxious by the qualities of the soil; and that the whole secret of the priests consisted in carrying their faces high in the air, as another spectator has observed they always did; and in avoiding respiration when they stooped. I had hoped the description of this spot would have enabled me to find it, but I searched about for it unsuccessfully.

We descended to our tent at the approach of evening, by a steep track down the cliff, beginning beyond the pool, in which we also bathed with pleasure, on the side next the gymnasium. Our way was often rough and slippery, resembling ice, and our horses with difficulty preserved their footing. When arrived at our tent I renewed my inquiries for the *plutonium*, and an old Turk, with a beard as white as snow, told me he knew the place, that it was often fatal to their goats; and, accounting for the effect, said, it was believed to be the habitation of a demon or evil spirit. We ascended again early in the morning to the theatre, where he had promised to join us; and a live fowl was intended to be the martyr of experiment. But we met this day with some unexpected interruption, which made us leave Hierapolis in haste ... [They had intended to journey eastward to the sources of the Maeander.]

[1] Pausanias, V.v.9. [C]

XLVII

WHILST we were busy at the theatre, the aga of a village eastward came to bathe with a considerable retinue, and two of his men summoned our janizary to appear before him. He was sitting beneath a wall, in the shade of the large ruin; and among the Turks with him were a couple, whom we had treated on the preceding day with coffee. He alleged, that we had knowledge of hidden treasure, and had already filled with it the provision chests, which he had seen by our tent; and demanded one of them for his share. He treated the janizary as mocking him, when he endeavoured to explain the nature of our errand, and the manner in which we had been employed. The janizary returned to us, exclaiming, as at Ezki-hissar, that we were among rebels and robbers; that neither equity, our firhman, or the grand signior would avail us; that, unless we would repent too late, it behoved us to hasten away. He was prevailed on, however, to remonstrate again; but the aga insisted on his claim with threatenings, if we did not speedily comply.

It seemed an exorbitant sum would be requisite to glut this extortioner and his dependents; and, if he were gratified, we might still expect other agas to follow his example, and be harassed until we were quite stripped of our money. The dispute growing very serious, we were apprehensive of immediate violence; and it was deemed prudent to retire by the causey to our tent. At the same time, his two men, who had tarried by us, mounted their horses with visible chagrin, and rode off, as was surmised to the village with orders.

On our arrival at the tent we held a consultation, when the janizary warmly urged the peril of our present situation; that the frontier of the Cuthayan[1] pashalike, in which we were, was inhabited by

[1] Cutheya, ancient Cotyæium in Phyrgia. [C]

a lawless and desperate people, who committed often the most daring outrages with impunity. He recommended the regaining, as fast as possible, the pashalike of Guzel-hissar. It was indeed the general desire that we might remove from a region in which we had already experienced so much solicitude, and where our safety for a moment was deemed precarious. Our men were alert in striking the tent, and loading our baggage; and at nine in the morning we fled from Pambouk, under the conduct of our janizary.

We forded the Mæander by a wooden bridge for foot passengers, with the water up to the bellies of our horses. We rode through a court before the house of the aga, with whom we had first treated and saw there some marble fragments, probably removed from the adjacent ruins. The village is exceedingly mean and small.

Keeping up the plain to recover the road from Laodicea west-ward, we had on our left a narrow and deep water-course. The stream, at an over-shot mill, was turned from its channel, and per-mitted at intervals to run into the corn fields. The rills also from the mountain were conducted into lands recently ploughed, on which cranes were stalking to devour insects or reptiles distressed by the moisture. We hurried on, apprehensive of being pursued, until we were opposite the snowy summit, beneath which we had pitched our tent, going to Denisli. We found there a company of Turks, and alighted to dine near them under some trees, which grow by a fountain. These repasts were usually followed by sleep on a carpet in the shade.

The travellers, with whom our men conversed, informed them, that the Turcomans, encamped in the plain on the other side of the Mæander, had very lately plundered some caravans, and cut off the heads of the people who opposed them. We disliked this intelligence, and set out again after two hours, fearing we might be benighted among them. Leaving the road to Magnesia on the left hand, we came in half an hour to a crazy wooden bridge, over a rapid stream, falling, lower down, into the Mæander. This river had also a wooden bridge on piles, which we crossed; with one of stone, in view, higher up, consisting of a single arch. The plain was here very wide and smooth, and covered with the black booths of the Turcomans. Our janizary appeared as one half frantic, if he saw any of the company straggling, or loitering on the way. We pushed briskly through, and then travelled westward in a green and pleasant recess of the mountain Messogis.

On entering the recess, we had on our right hand, at a distance, the ruins of Tripolis.[1] Smith[2] relates, that he saw there only huge stones, lying confusedly in heaps, besides vestiges of a theatre and of a castle. We could plainly discern the naked site of the former on the slope of Messogis, and beneath it masses of wall, remnants of the fortress. About half an hour to the west is a flourishing town or village. A stream, of which we had a distinct view from the mountains the next morning, winds not far off in the plain, and has been mistaken by several travellers for the Mæander. Smith forded it near Tripolis, in his way to Pambouk, where he arrived about four hours after.

Tripolis is the place where St. Bartholomew taught, and St. Philip is said to have suffered martyrdom. It was afterwards the see of a bishop. John Ducas, the second emperor of Nice, had an interview there with the Turkish sultan in 1244. It was enlarged and fortified for a bulwark to cover Philadelphia. In 1306 it was in the possession of the Turks, who had besieged and taken it by stratagem; and Alisuras made from it his incursions into the empire. Its buildings were later destroyed and its inhabitants emigrated to Buldan.

We rode on by fine crops of barley, with a large water-course on our left hand; and, after nine hours, arrived in the dusk of evening at Bullada, a Turkish town; the houses numerous and scattered on slopes, with a bridge crossing the bed of a torrent, then dry. We were lodged in a new khan, small, but unusually neat; and from the windows, in the morning, had an extensive view over the plain. We could see part of the white cliff of Hierapolis. On inquiry, we found that we were now only a journey of about four days from Smyrna, going the direct road; and were assured, that the plague raged there with uncommon fury.

[1] Tripolis on the Maeander.
[2] *Survey of the Seven Churches*, p. 245. [C]

XLVIII

OUR mode of living in this tour had been more rough than can well be described. We had endeavoured to avoid, as much as possible, communicating with the people of the country; and had commonly pitched our tent by some well, brook, or fountain, near a village; where we could purchase eggs, fowls, a lamb or kid, rice, fruits, wine, rakí or white brandy, and the like necessaries; with bread, which was often gritty, and of the most ordinary kind. We had seldom pulled off our clothes at night; sleeping sometimes with our boots and hats on, as by day; a portmanteau or large stone serving instead of pillow or bolster. But one consideration had softened the sensations of fatigue, and sweetened all our hardships. It was the comfortable reflection, that we enjoyed our liberty, and were, as we conceived, at a distance from the plague; but now we were about to lose that satisfaction, and at every stage to approach nearer to the seat of infection.

We had agreed to visit Ala-shahir,[1] or Philadelphia; and, setting out in the morning, ascended the mountain, which is Messogis, and turned to the north-west, through a cultivated tract, the way good, to hills green with flowering shrubs, and in particular with labdanum. The air partook of their fragrancy, and dispensed to us the sweet odours of mount Tmolus.[2] The manner of gathering the gum from the leaves, with the whip or instrument made use of, is described by Tournefort.[3] After five hours we alighted, and dined beneath a tree in a burying-ground by a well. We then entered a deep narrow track, and came in two hours more to a village, and pitched our tent on a dry spot; with an old castle on the mountain on our left hand, and before us an extensive plain, in which the river Hermus runs.

[1] The City of God. [C]. Now Alasehir.
[2] Now Boz Daği.   [3] Tournefort, vol. I, pp. 58–60. [C]

This region, which is above, or to the east of Philadelphia, was called Catakekaumene, or *the burned*; . . . anciently bare of trees, but covered with vines, which produced the wine called by its name, and esteemed not inferior to any in goodness. The surface of the plain, which is now turf, was then spread with ashes; and the range of mountains was stony and black, as from a conflagration, which some, who fabled that Typho was destroyed there, supposed to have been occasioned by lightning; but earth-born fire was concerned, instead of the giant and Jupiter. This was evident from three pits, which they called Physæ, or *the bellows*, distant from each other about five miles, with rough hills above them, formed, it was believed, by cinders from their volcanoes. The wits of old, observing such places peculiarly fertile in vines, affirmed, alluding to the story of Semele, it was no fiction that Bacchus was begotten by fire.[1]

The river Hermus, which divides this plain, begun near Dorylæum, a city of Phrygia; rising on the mountain Dindymus, which was sacred to Cybele, the mother of the gods. From this region it flowed into the Sardian, and received the Phrygius, which separated Phrygia from Caria; and also many other streams from Mysia and Lydia, in its way to the sea.

In the morning we descended from the mountain, and winding toward the left, soon after met a cow laden with the dwelling, the goods, and chattels of a Turcoman family; a very grotesque and risible figure. A woman followed, trudging on foot, with a child at her back, her naked breasts hanging down before her. In half an hour we crossed a stream rising near, and running eastward; and then passed by a spot where a number of the Turcomans were loading their camels, and busied in removing their booths, their wives, children and cattle. The plain was cultivated. We entered the caravan road from Angora to Smyrna, when our course, became west, with mount Tmolus on our left; and arrived in three hours and a half at Ala-shahir.

Attalus Philadelphus, brother of Eumenes, was the founder of Philadelphia, which stood on a root of mount Tmolus, by the river Cogamus. The frequent earthquakes, which it experienced, were owing to its vicinity with the region called Catakekaumene. Even

[1] Strabo, 13.4.11. [C]

the city-walls were not secure, but were shaken almost daily, and disparted. The inhabitants lived in perpetual apprehension, and were always employed in repairs. They were few in number, the people residing chiefly in the country, and cultivating the soil, which was fertile.[1]

John Ducas, the Greek general to whom Laodicea submitted, took Philadelphia with Sardes by assault in 1097. It was again reduced, about the year 1106, under the same emperor, without difficulty. Two years after, the Turks marched from the east, with a design to plunder it and the maritime cities. In 1175 the emperor Manuel, falling into an ambuscade of the Turks not far from the sources of the Mæander, retired to this place. In the division of the conquests of sultan Aladin in 1300, the inner parts of Phrygia, as far as Cilicia and Philadelphia, fell by lot to Karaman. The town in 1306 was besieged by Alisuras, who took the forts near, and distressed it, but retired on the approach of the Roman army. It is related, that the Philadelphians despised the Turks, having a tradition, that their city had never been taken. The Tripolines requested succour from the general, the grand duke Roger; who, after defeating the enemy, returned hither, by the forts of Kula and Turnus, and exacted money. In 1391 Philadelphia singly refused to admit Bajazet; but wanting provisions was forced to capitulate. Cineis, on his reconciliation with Amir, prince of Ionia, drew over to his interest this place, with Sardes, Nympheum, and the country as far as the Hermus.

It was anciently matter of surprise, that Philadelphia was not abandoned, and yet it has survived many cities less liable to earthquakes, and continues now a mean, but considerable town, of large extent, spreading up the slopes of three or four hills. Of the wall which encompassed it, many remnants are standing, but with large gaps. The materials of this fortification are small stones, with strong cement. It is thick and lofty, and has round towers. On the top, at regular distances, were a great number of nests, each as big as a bushel; with the cranes, their owners, by them, single or in pairs. The bed of the Cogamus, which is on the north-east side, was almost dry . . .

Going a little up the Cogamus, between the mountains, in the bank

[1] Strabo, 13.4.10. [C]

on the right hand, is a spring of a purgative quality, much esteemed and resorted to in the hot months. It tasted like ink, is clear, and tinges the earth with the colour of ochre. Farther up, beyond the town, on the left hand, is the wall, which, it has been said, was built with human bones, after a massacre, by one of the sultans. That wonder is nothing more than the remnant of a duct, which has conveyed water of a petrifying quality, as at Laodicea.[1] This incrusted some vegetable substances, which have perished, and left behind, as it were, their moulds. It was now partly fallen, but served as a fence between two corn fields. The whole is much decayed, the pieces easily breaking, and crumbling.

The bishop of Philadelphia was absent, but the proto-papas or chief priest, his substitute, whom we went to visit, received us at his palace, a title given to a very indifferent house, or rather a cottage, of clay. We found him ignorant of the Greek tongue, and were forced to discourse with him, by an interpreter, in the Turkish language. He had no idea that Philadelphia existed before Christianity, but told us it had become a city in consequence of the many religious foundations. The number of churches he reckoned at twenty-four, mostly in ruins, and mere masses of wall decorated with painted saints. Only six are in a better condition, and have their priests. The episcopal church is large, and ornamented with gilding, carving, and holy portraits. The Greeks are about three hundred families, and live in a friendly intercourse with the Turks, of whom they speak well. We were assured that the clergy and laity in general knew as little of Greek as the proto-papas; and yet the liturgies and offices of the church are read as elsewhere, and have undergone no alteration on that account.

The Philadelphians are a civil people. One of the Greeks sent us a small earthen vessel full of choice wine. Some families beneath the trees, by a rill of water, invited us to alight, and partake of their refreshments. They saluted us when we met; and the aga, or governor, on hearing that we were Franks, bade us welcome by a messenger.

Philadelphia possessing waters excellent in dying, [sic] and being situated on one of the most capital roads to Smyrna, is much

[1] Hierapolis. [R]. Correct.

frequented, especially by Armenian merchants. The khan in which we lodged was very filthy, and full of passengers. Mules arrived almost hourly, and were unladen in the area. As a caravan goes regularly to Smyrna, and returns on stated days, we were uneasy here, and afraid of infection. The accounts now given us of the plague, and of the havock it was making, were such, that the most intrepid person might reasonably shudder with horror and apprehension.

We set out at nine in the morning from Philadelphia for Sardes, distant twenty-eight miles, according to the Antonine Itinerary. The way is by the feet of mount Tmolus, which was on our left; consisting of uneven, separate, sandy hills, in a row, green and pleasant, once clothed with vines, but now neglected. Behind them was a high ridge covered with snow. The plain, besides the Hermus, which divides it, is well watered by rills from the slopes. It is wide, beautiful and cultivated; but has few villages, being possessed by the Turcomans, who, in this region, were reputed thieves, but not given to bloodshed. Their booths and cattle were innumerable. We stopped, after an hour, at a handsome fountain. The cistern was a marble coffin, carved with festoons, and inscribed in Greek, "Of Appius." In an old burying ground near it were marble fragments. We travelled three hours and a half north-westward, and as long westward. We met numerous caravans, chiefly of mules, on the road; or saw them by its side feeding on the green pasture, their burdens lying on the ground; the passengers sitting in groups, eating or sleeping on the grass. We pitched our tent about sunset, and the next day, after riding two hours in the same direction, arrived at Sardes, now called Sart.

XLIX

LYDIA was celebrated for its city Sardes,[1] which was of great antiquity, though posterior to the war of Troy.[2] It was enriched by the fertility of the soil, and had been the capital of the Lydian kings. It was seated on the side of mount Tmolus, and the citadel was remarkable for its strength. This was on a lofty hill; the back part, or that toward Tmolus, a perpendicular precipice. One of the kings, an ancestor of Crœsus, it is related, believed that by leading a lion about the wall, he should render the fortress impregnable, and neglected that portion of it as totally inaccessible.

Crœsus, who was tyrant or king of all the nations within the river Halys, engaging Cyrus, who had followed him into Lydia, was defeated in the plain before the city, the Lydian horses not enduring the sight or smell of the camels. Cyrus then besieged him, and offered a reward for the person who should first mount the wall. One of his soldiers had seen a Lydian descend for his helmet, which had rolled down the back of the citadel. He tried to ascend there, where not even a sentinel was placed, and succeeded. Afterwards the Persian satrapas, or commandant, resided at Sardes, as the emperor did at Susa.

In the time of Darius, the Milesians sailed to Ephesus, and leaving their vessels at mount Corissus, marched up by the river Cayster, and crossing mount Tmolus, surprised the city, except the fortress, in which was a numerous garrison. A soldier set fire to one of the houses, which were thatched, and presently the town was in flames. The Ionians retreated to Tmolus, and in the night to their ships.[3]

The city and fortress surrendered on the approach of Alexander,

[1] Now Sart. For discussion and plan of site of Sardis see Bean, op. cit., pp. 259–272. The Americans have been excavating here since 1958.
[2] Strabo, 13.4.5: Herodotus, I, 7. [C]   [3] Herodotus, V.101. [C]

after the battle of the Granicus. His army encamped by the river Hermus, which was twenty miles stadia, or two miles and a half, distant. He went up to the citadel, which was then fortified with a triple wall, and resolved to erect in it a temple and altar to Jupiter Olympius, on the site of the royal palace of the Lydians.[1]

Sardes under the Romans was a large city, and not inferior to any of its neighbours, until the terrible earthquake, which happened in the time of Tiberius Cæsar. Magnesia by Sipylus, Philadelphia, Laodicea, Ephesus, and several more cities partook largely in that calamity; but this place suffered prodigiously, and was much pitied. The munificence of the emperor was nobly exerted to repair the various damages, and Sardes owed its recovery to Tiberius.[2]

The emperor Julian made Chrysanthius, a Sardian, of a senatorial family, pontiff of Lydia. He attempted to restore the heathen worship; erecting temporary altars at Sardes, where none had been left, and repairing the temples, if any vestiges remained. In the year 400, the Goths, under Tribigild and Caianas, officers in the Roman pay, who had revolted from the emperor Arcadius, plundered the city. In the subsequent trouble in Asia, the natives in general were compelled to retire for safety to the hills and strong holds. At Sardes they permitted the Turks, on an incursion of the Tartars in 1304, to occupy a portion of the citadel separated by a strong wall with a gate, and afterwards murdered them in their sleep.

The site of this once noble city was now green and flowery. Coming from the east, we had the ground-plot of the theatre at some distance on our left hand, with a small brook near us, running before it. The structure was in a brow, which unites with the hill of the citadel, and was called Prion. Some pieces of the vault, which supported seats, and completed the semicircle, remain.

It was on this side the effort was made, which gave Antiochus possession of Sardes. An officer had observed, that vultures and birds of prey gathered there about the offals and dead bodies thrown into the hollow by the besieged, and inferred that the wall, standing on the edge of the precipices, was neglected as secure from any attempt. He scaled it with a resolute party, while Antiochus

[1] Arrian, *Anab.*, 1.17.4–9. [C]
[2] Strabo, 13.4.8; Tacitus, *Ann.*, ii.47. [C]

called off the attention both of his own army and of the enemy by a feint; marching as if he intended to attack the Persian gate. Two thousand soldiers rushed in at the gate opened for them, and took their post at the theatre, when the town was plundered and burned.[1]

Going on, we passed by remnants of massive buildings; marble piers sustaining heavy fragments of arches of brick; and more indistinct ruins. These are in the plain before the hill of the citadel. On our right hand, near the road, was a portion of a large edifice, with a heap of ponderous materials before and behind it. The walls are standing of two large, lofty, and very long rooms, with a space between them, as of a passage. This remain, it has been conjectured, was the house of Crœsus, once appropriated by the Sardinians, as a place of retirement, to superannuated citizens. It was called the Gerusia, and in it, as some Roman authors have remarked, was exemplified the extreme durability of the ancient brick.[2] The walls in this ruin have double arches beneath, and consist chiefly of that material, with layers of stone. The bricks are exceedingly fine and good, of various sizes, some flat, and broad. We employed a man to procure one entire, but the cement proved so very hard and tenacious, it was next to impossible. Both Crœsus and Mausolus, neither of whom could be suspected of parsimony, used them in building their palaces. It was a substance insensible of decay; and it is asserted, if the walls were erected true to their perpendicular, would, without violence, last for ever.

The hill, on which the citadel stood, appears from the plain to be triangular. It is sandy, and the sides rough. The fortress is abandoned, but has a double wall, as in 1304, fronting the plain, besides outworks, in ruins. The eminence affords a fine prospect of the country, and in the walls are two or three fragments with inscriptions. Not far from the west end is the celebrated river Pactolus, which rises in the mountain behind, and once flowed through the middle of the market-place of Sardes in its way to the Hermus, bringing down from Tmolus bits of gold. Herodotus, observes, that, except this one and the barrow of Alyattes, Lydia was not remarkable for wonders. The Treasures of Crœsus and of his ancestors were collected chiefly

[1] Polybius, VII. 15–18. [C]
[2] Vitruvius, II.c.viii.10; Pliny, *Nat. Hist.*, XXXV.171–172. [C]

from the Pactolus; but in time that source failed.[1] After snow or rain a torrent descends; but now the stream was very shallow; the bed sand or gravel, in colour inclining to a reddish yellow.

Beyond the supposed Gerusia, we turned from the road to the left. We passed the miserable village Sart, which stands, with a ruinous mosque, above the river, on a root or spur of the hill of the citadel, and crossing the Pactolus, pitched our tent in a flowery meadow. Not far from us were booths of the Turcomans, with their cattle feeding. Some of them joined us, and one or two wanted rakí or brandy, but were told we had none. A small gratuity was required for the aga of the village, which was opposite to our tent.

After resting a while, we were conducted toward Tmolus, and suddenly struck with the view of a ruin of a temple, near us, in a most retired situation, beyond the Pactolus, between the hill of the citadel and the mountain. Five columns are standing, one without the capital; and one with the capital awry to the south. The architrave was of two stones. A piece remains on one column, but moved southward; the other part, with the column, which contributed to its support, has fallen since the year 1699. One capital was then distorted, as was imagined, by an earthquake; and over the entrance of the naos, or cell, was a vast stone, which occasioned wonder by what art or power it could be raised. That fair and magnificent portal, as it is styled by the relater,[2] has since been destroyed; and in the heap lies that most huge and ponderous marble. Part of one of antae is seen about four feet high. The soil has accumulated round the ruin; and the bases, with a moeity of each column, are concealed; except one, which was cleared by Mr. Wood. The number in the front, when entire, was eight. The order is Ionic. The shafts are fluted, and the capitals designed and carved with exquisite taste and skill.

It is impossible to behold without deep regret this imperfect remnant of so beautiful and glorious an edifice; which however is, I believe, unnoticed by the ancient authors now extant. Herodotus mentions a temple dedicated to Cybebe, or Cybele, as damaged in the conflagration of Sardes by the Milesians. The same goddess is invoked in Sophocles as inhabiting by the great Pactolus, abounding

[1] Strabo, 13.4.5.[C]   [2] Chishull, *Travels*, p. 16. [C]

in gold. Crœsus, king of Sardes, contributed to the building of the temple at Ephesus, where a similar mass of marble was placed over the entrance by Metagenes; and if this fabric be not coeval, it was perhaps planned and erected by some of the successors of that bold and enterprising architect.

L

BEFORE Sardes, on the opposite side of the plain, are many barrows on an eminence, some of which are seen afar off. We were told, that behind them was a lake, and agreed to visit it. We left Sardes in the afternoon, and repassed Pactolus, farther on; the stream foul and dull. In an hour we came to the banks of the Hermus, which was also muddy, but wide and rapid. We forded with the water up to our girths, and then rode among huts of the Turcomans; their large and fierce dogs barking vehemently, and worrying us. The plain now appeared as bounded with mountains. The view westward was terminated by a single, distinct, lofty range, the east end of mount Sipylus.

We approached near to the high green ridge, on which the barrows are, and going on beyond its eastern extremity, pitched our tent after three hours by a village called Bazocleu. A continual noise or hooting was made, to drive away the small birds, which lodged in the corn. We saw them changing their quarters, as soon as molested, in troops. A large dog had followed our men, who fed him, from Sart.

We were on horseback again at seven in the morning, and going northwestward for half an hour, came to the lake, which lay behind the ridge, extending westward, and was anciently called Gygæa.[1] It is very large, and abounds in fish, its colour and taste like common pond water, with beds of sedge growing in it. We saw a few swans with cygnets, and many aquatic birds; in particular, one species resembling a gull, flying about in flocks, or lighting on the ground. These were white, but with the whole head black. The air swarmed with gnats.

Some very ancient historians had related, that this lake was made as a receptacle for the floods, which happened when the rivers were

---

[1] Now Marmara Gölü.

swollen. The Lydians asserted it was perennial, or never dry. The name had been changed from Gygæa to Coloe. By it was a temple of Diana, called Coloene, of great sanctity. A story is recorded as current, that on the festivals of the goddess certain baskets danced . . .[1]

By Gygæa, which was within five miles of Sardes, is the burying place of the Lydian kings.[2] The barrows are of various sizes, the smaller made perhaps for children of the younger branches of the royal family. Four or five are distinguished by their superior magnitude, and are visible as hills at a great distance. The lake, it is likely, furnished the soil. All of them are covered with green turf; and as many as I observed, in passing among them, retain their conical form without any sinking in of the top.

One of the barrows on the eminence, near the middle, and toward Sardes, is remarkably conspicuous. This has been described by Herodotus as beyond comparison the greatest work in Lydia; inferior only to the works of the Egyptians and Babylonians. It was the monument of Alyattes, the father of Crœsus; a vast mound of earth heaped on a basement of large stones by three classes of the people; one of which was composed of girls, who were prostitutes. Alyattes died, after a long reign, in the year 562 before the Christian era. About a century intervened, but the historian relates, that to his time five stones, (οὖροι *termini*, or *stelæ*,) on which letters were engraved, had remained on the top, recording what each class had performed; and from the measurement it had appeared, that the greater portion was done by the girls. Strabo likewise has mentioned it as a huge mound raised on a lofty basement by the multitude of the city . . .

It was customary among the Greeks to place on barrows either the image of some animal, or *stelæ*, commonly round pillars with inscriptions. The famous barrow of the Athenians in the plain of Marathon, described by Pausanias, is an instance of the latter usage. An ancient monument in Italy by the Appian Way, called, without reason, the sepulchre of the Curiatii, has the same number of *termini* as remained on the barrow of Alyattes; the basement, which is square, supporting five round pyramids.

[1] Strabo, 13.4.5. [C]　　　　[2] Strabo, 13.4.7. [C]

The barrow of Alyattes is much taller and handsomer than any I have seen in England or elsewhere. The industry shewn in carrying earth for its elevation was probably excited by the pay which Crœsus offered; for it is not likely that the sepulchres, of a regal family, which possessed immense riches, should be raised by public contribution or gratuitous labour. The mould, which has been washed down, conceals the stone-work, which, it seems, was anciently visible. The apparent altitude is diminished, and the bottom rendered wider and less distinct than before . . .

The reader, it is likely, will wonder at the great number of girls which were employed in this work; and will conceive a bad opinion of the morals of the Sardians. The historian relates, it was the custom of the Lydians to permit their daughters to procure their own dowries; deviating in this from the Greek laws, which were established among them. They were an ingenious people, the inventors of gold and silver coin, of wine-taverns, and of several games in general use. The female Lydians were much admired for the elegance of their dress, the beauty of their persons, and their wonderful performance of a grand, choral, circular dance, in honour of Bacchus.

LI

AFTER riding an hour by the side of the calm and noble lake, we turned to the south-west, passing by a fountain with an inscription,[1] to recover the road from Sardes to Magnesia by mount Sipylus. We crossed the ridge, and at eleven again forded the Hermus. The stream was very wide, rapid, and turbid. We entered on the road by three barrows, ranging on the side close by each other. We stopped, after two hours more, near a green barrow, at a neat coffee-hut by Uran-lui,[2] four hours from Sardes. Our dog, which we had named Sart, here very wisely forsook us, and, as we supposed, returned to the Turcomans, his old masters.

The mountains, when we moved from Bazocleu in the morning, were all clear, except Sipylus, which was enveloped in mist. On the way a shower or two fell, which cooled the air, and occasioned a delicious freshness and fragrancy. Now Sipylus was quite hid; and thunder, with violent rain, proceeded from the thick black clouds in which it was enwrapped. At half after four the sun broke out, the clouds brightened, and above them its summit was discernible. Thin fleeces were yet hanging low on the side of the mountain beyond the Hermus.

After dining under a tree by a clear stream we rode briskly on, and arrived in two hours at Durguthli, or Casabar. This is a town of considerable extent, in the plain, with many minarees of mosques rising amid trees. The khan was most exceedingly wretched, and our stay, though for a single night, seemed tedious. The place was a great thoroughfare; and the accounts we received of the malady raging at Smyrna, became at every stage, as we advanced, more terrible, as well as more authentic.

[1] *Inscript. Ant.*, p. 30. [C]. *CIG*, 2, p. 820, no. 3468.
[2] Now ?Turgutlu.

Early in the morning we went on toward mount Sipylus. On our left was an opening into a plain, between that mountain and the end of mount Tmolus; and beyond it was a lofty ridge covered with snow. Magnesia, with the river Hermus, is on the north side of Sipylus ... We passed a wide watercourse, and a river, and then a stream, after which we came to the extremity of the mountain.

Mount Sipylus was anciently noted for frequent thunder. At Smyrna I had often listened to the rumbling, and marked the remote lightning, which gleamed from that quarter. A city of the same name as the mountain was once the capital of Mæonia or Lydia. It was recorded, that, in the time of Tantalus, prodigious earthquakes had happened. Then many villages were absorbed, the city Sipylus was subverted, and marshes were changed into lakes. The credibility of this relation was demonstrated, as Strabo remarks, by the dreadful effects of the earthquake under Tiberius, and the overthrow of Magnesia. Where Sipylus had stood was a marsh called Sale. The mountain, terminating on the north-east in a vast naked precipice, has now beneath it a very limpid water, with a small marsh, not far from a sepulchre cut in the rock, and there perhaps was Sale, and the site of Sipylus.

We travelled on at the foot of the mountain, with the plain of the Hermus, which is very extensive, on our right hand. Our horses were much jaded, and we fatigued, when, after eight hours, we reached Magnesia.

The famous story of the transformation of Niobe the daughter of Tantalus, had for its foundation a phenomenon extant in mount Sipylus ... The phantom may be defined, "an effect of a certain "portion of light and shade on a part of Sipylus, perceivable at a "particular point of view." The traveller, who shall visit Magnesia after this information, is requested to observe carefully a steep and remarkable cliff, about a mile from the town; varying his distance, while the sun and shade, which come gradually on, pass over it. I have reason to believe he will see Niobe.[1]

Magnesia[2] surrendered to the Romans, immediately after the decisive battle between Scipio and Antiochus. It was a free city, and

[1] See Bean, op. cit., pp. 53–55.
[2] Now Manisa—Bouverie died here in 1750.

shared in the bounty of Tiberius Cæsar, next to Sardes, as second in its sufferings from the earthquake. While the Turks made incursions in to the field of Menomen by Smyrna, ruining the country, in 1303, the emperor Michael was shut up in this place; from which he escaped by night. The grand duke Roger garrisoned it with Italians. The inhabitants rose and killed some of them; when he besieged the city, but was forced to retire. In 1313 it ranked among the acquisitions of Sarkhan, afterwards sultan of Ionia. It was the city chosen for his retreat by Morat, of Amurath the Second, in 1443, when he resigned the empire to his son Mahomet the Second, the conqueror of Constantinople.

Soon after our arrival at the khan, we were visited by a Frenchman, a practitioner in physic; who told us that he had attended Mr. Bouverie in a pleurisy at Sanderli. He conducted us about the town, which retains its ancient name, and is still very extensive; spreading in the plain at the mountain foot, on the acclivity of the castle hill, and up a valley on each side.[1] It is populous, and has a great trade. The mosques are numerous; and the Greeks have a large and handsome church, and also a monastery.

Among the mosques at Magnesia, two have double minarees or turrets, and are very noble structures, of marble. Each has before it an area with a fountain. We were permitted to enter one of them which had been lately beautified, leaving our boots or shoes at the door. The inside was as neat as possible; and the floor covered with rich carpets. The ornamental painting pleased by an odd novelty of design, and a lively variety of colour. The dome is lofty, and of great dimensions. The lamps, which were innumerable, many pendant from the ceiling, with balls of polished ivory[2] intermixed, must, when lighted, amaze equally by their artful disposition, their splendour, and their multitude. These edifices, a college of dervises, and a bedlam, were erected and endowed by sultan Morat and his queen.

Sultan Morat intended to lead a private life at Magnesia. We were shewn the site of his palace, his seraglio, and garden. The remains are some pieces of wall, with several large and stately cypress trees. Near them is a neat mausoleum, with a dome, over the tombs of his

[1] *Views.* Le Brun, p. 37 [C]. Pl. 21, p. 26: see Bibliography.
[2] Ostrich eggs. [R]

wives and children, in number twenty-two, of different sizes, disposed in three rows, all plain, and of stone.

The castle hill is exceedingly high, the ascent steep and tiresome, with loose stones in the way. By the track is a fountain, with a broken inscription, and earthen pipes, which convey water down to the city. It is a mean fortress, abandoned, and in ruins. The cannon, it is related, were removed to the Sangiac castle in the gulf of Smyrna. The recompense of our toil, in gaining the summit, was an extensive view of a fine verdant plain, divided by the Hermus shining like silver. Chishull relates, that the needle of a sea-compass placed on different stones, after pointing various ways, quickly lost its whole virtue. We tried with our pocket compass, but discovered no such magnetic quality in the rock . . .

LII

OUR situation was now become very critical and distressing. We were only eight hours north-eastward from Smyrna. We were all sufficiently wearied with wandering, and desirous of a respite. Several of our horses were spoiled by the rough service they had undergone; and some of our men were anxious for their families, and uneasy from their long absence. The disabled condition of our little corps, with the general disquietude, and the risk in journeying, as well from the season as from the distemper, made us ardently wish for a secure retreat, but the difficulty was to find one.

The malady, it was believed, had not yet reached Magnesia; but caravans were continually arriving from Smyrna, and it could scarcely fail of being speedily imported. In a khan we were exposed among the foremost to infection. If we obtained admission into the Greek monastery, or a private house, horror and momentary peril would be our portion as soon as the plague commenced; at a distance from our countrymen, without friends, among people fatally ignorant and negligent; in whom we could place no confidence; and from whom we, if attacked, could have little room to expect any attention and regard, or indeed even sepulture.

An Italian quack-doctor had visited us at the khan, and accompanied us up to the castle. He had just arrived from Akhissar or Thyatira, and assured us that place was free from contagion. We determined, rather than enter Smyrna without absolute necessity, to extend our tour thither, and to Pergamum; hoping, while we were employed on that side of the Hermus, a favourable alteration might ensue. The janizary and Armenians acquiesced, with some reluctance, and our baggage was loading, when a papas, or Greek priest, informed one of my companions, that he had recent intelligence from Thyatira, and that the plague was then in the house of the aga. Our whole arrangement was in an instant overturned; but we agreed immediately to abandon Magnesia; and fortunately, as the evil presaged became manifest there very soon after, and the civil Frenchman, our guide, perished among the first victims.

We are now on the road to Smyrna. After riding for some time at the foot of mount Sipylus, we entered on a track on the left hand, and crossing the mountain, arrived in the plain of Hadgilar, a village two hours from Smyrna. We met a few travellers, whom we passed with caution, inquiring of them at a distance, and hearing a most dismal tale. Our terror and perplexity increased as we advanced. We were assured many of the villages were infected. We were ignorant whether we could be admitted into the house of the English consul, and whether he had remained at Smyrna. Various methods of giving and procuring the intelligence necessary for our mutual security were devised, and proposed, and rejected, as unsafe; when, being exceedingly embarrassed, we turned aside from the road to deliberate, and to repose awhile among the olive-trees.

Seeing the village of Hadgilar near us, I rode on, followed by the Swiss, and meeting a peasant, asked him whether any Frank or European lived there; and was answered, Mr. Lee. I gallopped up to his house, and was received with his accustomed cordiality. A prudent regard to the safety of his family forbidding our admission within his gate,[1] he ordered liquors and plenty of provisions for our refreshment, and with Mr. Maltas his partner, and the abbé D. Giuseppe Icard, who had been educated at the college De Propaganda at Rome, and had attended us as our instructor in the Greek and modern languages, accompanied me back to the tree, where joy was already diffused through our tattered and sunburnt troop.

Mr. Lee had reserved for us the house which he occupied the summer before at Sedicui.[2] We crossed to it in the evening, leaving Smyrna, where the plague was very furious, on our right hand. The next day we dismissed our men, except the Swiss and an Armenian, our cook, who had a couple of horses, which we kept for some time. The janizary resumed his station at the consul's gate, with the same composure as if unattended with any danger; and the Armenians

---

[1] *Views*, Le Brun, p. 400 [C]. See Bibliography.
[2] Now Seydiköy.

retired to a spot near another village, where many of their nation were assembled, waiting under tents and sheds until the malady should abate.

We remained five in number, besides a Greek, who had the care of the garden, and had been indulged with the privilege of vending its produce to the villagers; but this occasioning a more free intercourse than was consistent with our safety, a separation followed; after which his place of abode was on some planks laid over a cistern beneath a shed, at some distance from the house; the furniture, a very few utensils and tools, a coverlet, a garment or two, some dry gourds, and his gun. The danger of infection increasing, he accepted a compensation, and ceased to sell. He was intrusted with a key of the garden door solely for his own use, but at times admitted other Greeks, and sat drinking with them to a late hour, disturbing us with droning songs, and the melancholy tinklings of a rude lyre.

Sedicui is a small village with a mosque and a fountain.[1] It was inhabited by a few Turks and Greeks, and by two Franks, with their families; the count de Hochpied the Dutch consul, and Mr. Fremaux a merchant of that nation. It is seated by a flat plain, on which are scattered fig, almond, and olive trees, with some bushes; the surface then parched, no verdure, neither weeds nor a blade of grass. On the west side are mountains, branches of Corax; and on these the jackals howled every night, beginning about sunset. We were informed that an old Turk, with a snow-white beard, had foretold that Sedicui would not suffer from the plague, for their hunting near it was a favourable prognostic, which in his memory had never failed.

A gentle ascent led from the village to the roots of mount Corax, through a corn-field, in which is a fountain fed by clear rills, carefully conveyed to it along the slopes. Close by is a square reservoir sunk in the ground; from which in the morning and at evening, when the stoppage was removed, a streamlet ran babbling over pebbles down to the village, to water the gardens. We had it in our turn, and the garden was ingeniously disposed for its reception, a small trench branching out over the whole area, and each bed having its furrows, with the plants standing on their edges. The

1 *Views.* Le Brun, p. 29 [C]. Pl. 7, p. 20: see Bibliography.

current enters at a hole in the wall, and the gardener attends and directs it with a spade or hoe; damming across the general communication to turn it into the parterres, and conducting it about, until the soil is saturated.

When it happened that the springs were dry, or the allowance not sufficient, the necessary fluid was raised by a machine, as in the orange-orchards of Scio. It is a large broad wheel furnished with ropes, hanging down and reaching into the water. Each rope has many cylindrical earthen vessels, fastened to it by the handles with bands of myrtle or of mastic. This apparatus is turned by a small horizontal wheel, with a horse or mule blinded and going round, as in a mill. The jars beneath fill and arrive in regular succession at the top of the wheel, when they empty, and return inverted to be again replenished. The trough, which receives the water, conveys it into a cistern to be distributed, at a proper hour, among the drooping vegetables. A like engine is in use in Persia and in Egypt.

Above the corn-field the mountain rose, brown and arid; the wild sage and plants crumbling when touched. In the side are narrow retired vales worn by torrents, and filled with spontaneous evergreens, thickets of myrtle in blossom, and groves of calodaphne or oleander, the boughs then laden with flowers of a pale red colour. Amid these a slender current trickled down a rocky precipice, like tears, to invert the poet's simile, from the eyes of sorrow. The slope afforded a pleasing view of our little village and of the country; and from a summit may be seen part of the gulf of Smyrna. I discovered a goat-stand in a dale, on the top, when I was too near to retreat. The savage-looking shepherds called off and chid their dogs, which were fierce, and barked furiously. They were sitting at the mouth of a pen, seizing the ewes and the she-goats, each by the hind leg, as they pressed forward to milk them. Some of the flock or herd were often by the fountain below, with their keeper, who played on a rude flute or pipe.

Our house was two stories high; chiefly of wood and plaster, which materials are commonly preferred, not only as cheap, but for security in earthquakes; the joists and nails swaying and yielding as the undulation requires. The lower story was open in the centre. On the right hand was a magazine or store-room; and opposite to it, an apartment with old fashioned lackered chairs. Between these our servants slept, on the ground. A door communicated with the offices, which were behind. The ascent to the upper story was by stone stairs, as usual, on the outside. The gallery extended the whole length of the front. It sheltered us from the sun, which darted fiery rays from a cloudless sky, and was agreeable as a place to walk and sleep in. We had three apartments, with wooden lattices to admit the air, while cool; and with shutters to exclude it, when inflamed. That in the centre was small. The end rooms, one of which we reserved for our meals, were large, with their doors opposite. The walls were all white-washed. Our furniture consisted of three or four broken or infirm chairs, a couple of unequal tables, and the utensils, bedding and baggage, with which we had travelled. We lay on boards placed on stools, and moveable.

We endeavoured, by reducing our wants to as small a number as we could, to avoid communicating with Smyrna. Our village supplied us with fowls and eggs, and with flesh, as often as a cow was killed. The garden furnished a variety of articles, particularly a species of fruit called melinzane, and gourds, which are eaten stewed. But wine, candles, and many other requisites, could be purchased only in the city; and for these a Turk was to be sent, as seldom as possible, with our provision-chests on a horse. He unloaded in the court, received his pay, and left us without touching any person or thing. The chests were then washed with water and vinegar, and the contents exposed in the air, or fumigated as their quality directed. This was done before they were handled or used, with the most minute attention; and, as a check on negligence, generally under our immediate inspection.

The reader perhaps will imagine, that we tempted the Turk to go on these errands by the offer of a great reward; but we had no difficulty in procuring a messenger to Smyrna, even when the malady raged most, and appeared inevitable. Our market-man, who likewise served the other Frank families at Sedicui, did not once hesitate. Fear was overcome by a sentiment of duty, and of obedience to his law. He had liberty to avoid the infected city; but, if he entered, might not afterwards refrain. His hire was one piaster, or about half a crown. The good mussulman persevered, and repeatedly underwent, for this trifling gratuity, such immediate risk, as the wiser European would not once incur for all the treasures of the grand signior.

Soon after our arrival at Sedicui, we wanted some articles from our apartments in the consuls' house, for which my companions determined to go in person, escorted by a janizary. It was dusk when they left the village. They arrived at night, and did their business; but one of our servants getting in liquor proved unmanageable, and detained them so long, that in coming back they met some Turks who had been burying a corpse. The caution of the Franks is offensive to the Mahometans, as implying a distrust of the Supreme Being. The man was embroiled with them, and one striking him with a spade, he drew a pistol, and it was with difficulty a fray was prevented. Besides the danger on the spot, our general safety was deeply interested in his misconduct, which indeed was without excuse.

Our confinement proved sufficiently irksome. We had some books and our papers with us, and full leisure for study or meditation. A very few kind visitants, among whom was Mr. Lee, called on us now and then, and inquired of our welfare, at a distance; condoling with us on the necessity of mutual estrangement, or relating the progress of the malady and its daily havock, which afforded but too much room for strenuous exertions of fortitude and resignation. The brightness and power of the sun, with the extreme heat of the air, made us seldom stir out, unless early in the morning, and in the evening. The languor of noon demanded sleep. The body, though arrayed as thinly and loosely as possible, was covered during the day with big drops of sweat, and dissolved, as it were, in a mighty and universal perspiration. Then followed a milder sky, lengthening shadows, and a gradual coolness, grateful and pleasing beyond imagination. Then was the comfortable hour for change of linen and of apparel, to enjoy the garden, or to wander on the mountain. These privileges of our situation were not inconsiderable in their value, as some of our acquaintance testified, whose lot it was to be pent up in the city, tormented by insects, drooping, and dispirited, with nothing to alleviate or divert their melancholy. The castle hill of Smyrna was an object plainly in view in these our walks, and beheld not without emotion. The plague and death were busy near us, and the intelligence which we received from the Franks and Greeks was dreadful to hear. We had personal liberty, but it became more and more necessary to use it with extreme caution, by avoiding the near approach of any whom we chanced to meet, and all intercourse, which could produce danger or suspicion. The sun setting behind the summits of mount Corax, left the sky serene, and stained with rich and varying tints. A chorus of jackals ensued; and the cucuvaia, or night-hawk, flitted in the air.

We found Sedicui free from the insects which had molested us at Smyrna, except a few stray mosquittoes, and some of the small flies, which were very teasing; but the tettix, or cicada, in the day-time is extremely troublesome. It is a brown insect resembling a chafer. with wings much longer than its body, and thin like those of a fly. It sits on the bushes and trees, making with its wings ... a very loud, ugly, screaking noise. When one begins, others join, and the disagreeable concert becomes universal; then a dead pause ensues; and then, as it were on a signal, it commences again. Dionysius of Syracuse signified his resolution to burn and lay waste the territory of a people, with whom he had a quarrel, when he said, that, *if they refused to comply with his demands, their tettixes should sing on the ground.*

We had excessive heat in the latter end of May, the wind northerly; as also during the harvest in June. From that quarter it blowed fiery as from a furnace, coming over mountains scorched by the sun. We endeavoured to exclude it by closing our shutters and doors, though gasping for breath. The thermometer, which at other times was commonly between eight-four and eighty-six, then rose at noon to ninety-five. The harvest was presently over. The sheaves were collected in the field, and the grain trodden out by buffaloes. In the morning the wind was often southerly, before the inbat from the bay reached us. This frequently continued to a late hour, rustling among the trees. We had thunder, with distant lightning, in the beginning of June; and, in the latter end of July, clouds began to appear from the south. The air was repeatedly cooled by showers, which had fallen elsewhere, and it was easy to foretell the approaching rain. This was the season for consuming the dry herbage and undergrowth on the mountains; and we often saw the fire blazing in the wind, and spreading a thick smoke along their sides.

On the eleventh of July we had an earthquake, which agitated the whole house, the beams and joists of the roof crashing over our heads. It happened about seven in the morning, and was preceded by a hollow rumbling noise, which was mistaken by several persons for the report of cannon; the captain basha or Turkish high admiral then waiting with a fleet in the gulf of Smyrna, to receive on board the revenues of the grand signior. The sound seemed to come from the south-east. The sensation was such as would be felt, I imagine, if the earth were set suddenly afloat. It occasioned a great alarm. Some lesser shocks succeeded, but their centres were remote.

LIII

THE beginning of the plague was, as we have related, in the spring. The first sufferers were from the island Musconisi, or from Tino.[1] An uncertain rumour preceded its manifestation. One sickened, then two or more; until, the instances multiplying, the Franks shut their gates, or prepared to retire into the country. It was no new ememy, and as yet produced no great terror. When we were about to quit Smyrna, three English gentlemen, Mr. Fitzgerald, Mr. Skipwith, and Mr. Wilbraham, arrived from Athens, with Mr. Turnbull,[2] a very worthy physician, who had lived many years at Smyrna, and was highly esteemed there by the Europeans in general. They were visited, and received, and no danger apprehended.

The kindly temperature of the weather gave vigour to the disease, while we were absent, and it was propagated amazingly. The consul then appointed a market-man from among his domestics; and his station was at the gate near the janizary. After about three weeks he was attacked, carried with his bedding to the hospital, and died the same day. A maidservant next complained that she had taken cold by sleeping on the terrace. She had a slight fever with the head-ache. Half a paper of James's powder purged and sweated her. The fever returned every afternoon. Another half paper vomitted her; but neither eating nor sleeping, she grew costive and weak. An Italian, who was physician to the factory, came on the ninth or tenth day from the country, and standing below, ordered the patient to be brought to the stair-head. He observed a vein, under her tongue, black and very turgid; pronounced her disorder to be the plague;

---

[1] The islands of Macronisi and Tinos.

[2] Mr L. P. Wilkinson, British Consul General at Smyrna, informs me that the Consular records which survived the fire of 1922 only go back to the year 1850 and it is therefore not possible to give further information about Dr Turnbull.

and advised sending her to the hospital, where his opinion was confirmed by a Greek. She was then removed to the Roman Catholic hospital, and died after lingering on ten days. The welfare of a large family was rendered suspicious by this alarming incident. We had reason to rejoice both that we did not tarry in Smyrna, and that we had met with our friend at Hadgilar.

The malady did not abate in May, when we took possession of our asylum. Four persons were seized in the family of the cadi, the deputy chancellor of the French nation died, and a dragoman, or interpreter, was attacked. Turks, Jews, Greeks, Armenians, and the like, perished without number. Of the Greeks alone sometimes above an hundred and thirty were buried in a day. It was generally agreed the calamith [sic] had not been severer in the memory of man. In July, when the captain pasha arrived to receive the taxes and tribute-money, some hundreds of houses, it was said, were unoccupied or without owners. A fire, which began to rage near the Frank quarter, seemed, amid all this misery, to threaten new affliction, but was fortunately subdued.

The plague might perhaps be truly defined, a disease arising from certain animalcules, probably invisible, which burrow and form their nidus in the human body. These, whether generated originally in Egypt or elsewhere, subsist always in some places suited to their nature. They are imported almost annually into Smyrna, and this species is commonly destroyed by intense heat. They are least fatal at the beginning and latter end of the season. If they arrive early in the spring, they are weak; but gather strength, multiply, and then perish. The pores of the skin, opened by the weather, readily admit them. One or more tumours, chiefly in the glandular parts, ensue, with a variety of the most afflicting symptoms. If the patient survive suppuration, he is dreadfully infectious; and the calamity is wofully augmented by the consideration that one recovery is no security from future attacks. Seycuse, an Armenian, who had been our cook, and at my request revealed his unsightly scars, perished now; and, as I was assured, it sometimes happens, that in one season an individual is twice a sufferer.

The plague is a disease communicated chiefly, if not solely, by contact. Hence, though it encircle the house, it will not affect the persons within, if all are uniformly discreet and provident, as experience has demonstrated. Tranquility of mind and freedom from apprehension cannot be expected. They are most disagreeably, and without the minutest care most dangerously circumstanced. Iron, it is observed, and the like substances, which are of a close hard texture, do not retain, or are not susceptible of the contagion. In bodies soft or porous, and especially in paper, it lurks often undiscovered but by its seizing some victim. The preservatives are fumigation, and washing with water or vinegar. In particular a letter is taken up with a pair of tongs, and in a manner singed before it can be opened with safety. Domestic animals, which are prone to wander, must be excluded or destroyed. A large family will require many articles to be procured from without, and is exposed in proportion to its wants. If in the city, a clandestine intercourse of debauched servants is ever to be feared; if in the country and detached, some untoward accident, or trivial but important inadvertency. Unremitting attention is necessary to avert horror and suspicion from either situation.

The streets of Smyrna are so narrow and filthy, the houses so crowded, and the concourse of people in spring so great, that during the summer heats distemper could not fail to riot there, if the town were not regularly perflated by the inbat and land-breezes; but the plague is not the offspring of the atmosphere. It perhaps could not even exist long in a pestilential air. The natives retire to rest about sunset, and rise with the dawn, when the dead are carried on biers to be interred. The Frank, who has business to transact, goes from the country to his house in the town in the interim, or returns without fear. Solitude and the sacred night befriend him.

The progress of the plague at Smyrna is utterly uncontrolled. The people, except the Franks, are in general as negligent as ignorant. Their dwellings are crowded, many inhabiting in a small compass; and their chambers are covered with matting or carpets, sofas, and cushions, adapted as well to retain as to receive contagion. Besides this, the Turk deems it a meritorious office to assist in carrying the dead; and, on perceiving the funeral of a mussulman, hastens to put his shoulder under the bier, on which the corpse lies extended and in its clothes. He perseveres in the pious work, until relieved by one equally mad and well-meaning. Several succeed by turns, and concur to rescue the living plague from being interred with the carcase, its prey. This kind of infatuation is not, however, without some utility. It ensures burial, the sick are tended, and the markets supplied.

The plague might be wholly averted from these countries, or at least prevented from spreading, if lazarettoes were erected, and salutary regulations enforced, as in some cities in Europe. Smyrna would be affected as little perhaps as Marseilles, if its police were as well modelled. But this is the wisdom of a sensible and enlightened people. The Turk will not acknowledge the means as efficacious, or will reject them as unlawful. A bigotted predestinarian, he resolves sickness or health, pleasure or pain, with all, even the most trifling, incidents of life, into the mighty power and uncontrollable will of the Supreme Being. He views the prudent Frank with insolent disdain, and reproaches him with timidity or irreligion. He triumphs in superior courage and confidence, going out or coming in during the malady with a calm indifference, as at other times; like the brute beast, unconscious of the road which leads to his security or destruction.

It is an established opinion among the Greeks, that soon after St. John's day, O.S. the fury of the plague decreases, and that the term of its duration does not extend beyond the 10th or 15th of August. About that time the Frank Merchants commonly unlock their gates, drooping trade revives, and a free intercourse is restored. We looked forward, as may be imagined, to that period, with the most earnest desire and impatience.

The villages round Smyrna suffered sooner or later with the city; nor was Sedicui wholly exempted. A Greek, eager to secure the trifling effects of a deceased brother, went to the town, returned and sickened; was carried back, and presently expired. A Frenchman, valet to count de Hochpied, who lived opposite to us, a wall separating our gardens, complained of indisposition in the beginning of July. A swelling appeared, and a poultice applied to it was attended with sharp pain, and raised a fiery bladder. Suspicion was then exchanged for unwelcome certainty. He was removed to Smyrna, and recovered. This family was well regulated; and the man, who had a good character for his care and circumspection, could not account for his contracting the malady; unless it were communicated by a sheathed knife, which in following his master he had picked up, and instantly on recollection thrown down again. These accidents disturbed our quiet, removed all confidence in our retreat, and made us redouble our vigilance and caution. A fire also happened, which destroyed a house by our garden.

We were happy, when the month of August arrived, in finding the popular remark on the continuance of the plague verified. The city was said to be free from that disease, but a contagious and mortal fever raged, principally among the Greeks. This was attributed to their diet, which in the summer season consists almost wholly of fruits. We engaged a number of horses and mules to carry us and our baggage once more to Smyrna; and the 8th of August was fixed for our departure from Sedicui, where we had resided from the 11th of May.

It was striking, as we passed the Turkish cemeteries, on our way into Smyrna, to contemplate the many recent graves of different sizes, exhibiting the uncertain tenure of a frail body at every stage of life; and furnishing melancholy evidence that death had been glutted with as little distinction of age as of condition. Farther on were the half-burned ruins of houses, which had lately menaced a general conflagration. In the Frank street, which had been crowded in the winter, we now met a few persons wearing a pensive look; and the comparative solitude of that quarter added force to the dismal ideas which intruded on us. All had been involved in public misery and in private distress, but some were wonderfully spared. We were heartily greeted by the fat janizary at the gate. The consul welcomed us again, and soon after we had the satisfaction of seeing our other friends, and Mr. Lee.

It was natural to wish for a speedy removal from a country, in which we had been exposed to so many dangers. We resolved to proceed immediately to Athens. We found on inquiry that we could not draw on Leghorn for money from thence; and that to obviate much future difficulty and solicitude, we must carry specie with us. Mr. Lee accepted our bills on London for 800L. at the usual discount. The animosities which had subsisted between the governors in the district of Cuthaya, and the basha of Guzel-hissar, had now produced hostilities; and on the north side of the gulf of Smyrna some great men were seizing cannon, horses, and arms, and preparing to decide their disputes by battle. These troubles would have prevented our making any farther excursions from Smyrna. We hired a boat to sail in ten days; and had reason to rejoice that our long stay on this continent was so near a conclusion.

APPENDIXES

APPENDIX A

Notes on the Members of the
Society of Dilettanti who signed the instructions to
the Ionian Mission

"Charlemont"

James Caulfeild, 4th Viscount Charlemont (1728–1799). Irish states-
man and patron of arts and letters in Ireland. Went to the Continent in
1746 where he spent a year at Turin and thereafter visited Rome, the
Greek islands, Constantinople, the Levant and Egypt. Created Earl of
Charlemont 1763. In 1768 m. the d. of Robert Hickman of co. Clare.
Elected to the Society 1756. F.R.S., F.S.A., K.P. In 1822, after his death,
appeared *Select Sonnets of Petrarch, with Translations and Illustrative
Notes.*

"Rob Wood"

Robert Wood (1717?–1771). Eldest s. of Rev. James Wood of Summerhill,
co. Meath, m. Ann d. of Thomas Spottowe or Skottowe. Traveller and
Politician. Made expeditions to the Troad, Asia Minor, Palmyra and
Baalbec with James Dawkins. In 1753 accompanied the young Duke of
Bridgewater to Italy. Elected to pocket Borough of Brackley, Northants
1761 and held it until his death. Under-Secretary of State, 1756–1763.
Groom Porter 1764–1766. Recommended Chandler to lead the Ionian
Mission. Died at Putney in the house formerly occupied by Gibbon.
Elected to the Society 1763. Noted for his publications; *Ruins of Palmyra*
(1753); *Ruins of Baalbec* (1757), *An Essay on the Original Genius of Homer
with a Comparative View of the Antient and present state of the Troad* (1767).

"Tho. Brand"

Thomas Brand of The Hoo, Herts (1717–1770). Son of Thomas Brand and
Margaret d. of John Nicol of Chipping Barnet, Herts, m. 1749 Lady
Caroline Pierrepont d. of Evelyn 1st Duke of Kingston. 1747 M.P. for
Tavistock, 1754 M.P. for Gratton and travelled in Italy, 1768 M.P. for Oke-
hampton. Elected to the Society 1741.

"*Wm. Fauquier*"

William Fauquier. Banker and Director of the South Sea Company. Registrar and Secretary of the Order of the Bath 1785. Elected to the Society 1736 and its Secretary 1771–1774. Died 1788.

"*James Stuart*"

James Stuart (1713–1788). Painter and Architect. Was the son of a Scottish mariner. Made measurements and drawings at Athens for *The Antiquities of Athens*, published by the Society. Elected to the Society 1751 and appointed its Painter in place of George Knapton, but executed no work although he held the post until 1769. See Appendix B.

"*Middlesex*"

Charles Sackville, Earl of Middlesex (1711–1769). M.P. for East Grinstead 1734. High Steward of the Honour of Otford 1741. Lord of the Treasury 1743–1747. Master of Horse to Frederick Prince of Wales 1747–1751. Succeeded his father as 2nd Duke of Dorset 1765. P.C. 1766. Married 1744 Hon. Grace d. of Richard Boyle, Viscount Shannon. Wrote a History of the Opera. Elected to the Society 1736.

"*Le Despencer*"

Sir Francis Dashwood, Bart. (1708–1781). Only s. of Sir Francis Dashwood, 1st Bart. and his 2nd wife Mary d. of Vere Fane, Baron Le Despencer and 4th Earl of Westmorland. Succeeded his father as 2nd Bart. 1724. Was married 4 times. Was in Parliament from 1741 to 1763, first as member for New Romney and then for Weymouth. Member of the Household of Frederick Prince of Wales. Chancellor of the Exchequer 1762–1763. Joint Paymaster General from 1766 until his death. Confirmed in his mother's barony as Baron Le Despencer 1763. Elected to the Society 1736. D.C.L., F.R.S., F.S.A. See Appendix B and *Sir Francis Dashwood. An Eighteenth Century Independent* by Betty Kemp (London, Macmillan, 1967).

"*J. Gray*"

Sir James Gray, Bart., (1708?–1773). Son of Sir James Gray, 1st Bart. In 1744 went to Venice with Robert D'Arcy, 6th Earl of Holdernesse and remained there as British Resident till 1753 when he was transferred to Naples as envoy extraordinary to the King of Naples and the Two

Sicilies. Appointed minister plenipotentiary to the King of Spain 1761 and made K.B., but owing to the outbreak of war did not take up residence at Madrid till 1766 where he remained until his death. P.C. 1769. Elected to the Society 1736. See Appendix B.

"Bessborough"

Hon. William Ponsonby (1704–1793). Son of 2nd Viscount Duncannon and 1st Earl of Bessborough. Elected to the Irish House of Commons 1725. Appointed Secretary to his father-in-law, the Duke of Devonshire then Lord Lieutenant of Ireland, 1739. Irish P.C. 1741. Elected to British House of Commons as member for Derby 1742. Lord of the Admiralty 1746. Succeeded his father as 2nd Earl of Bessborough 1758. Joint Postmaster General 1759 but resigned 1762. Married Lady Caroline Cavendish, eld. d. of William 3rd Duke of Devonshire 1739. Elected to the Society 1736 and known as its 'Father'.

APPENDIX B

Note on Nicholas Revett

Nicholas Revett (1720–1804) was the second son of John Revett of Brandeston Hall, near Framlingham in Suffolk. He determined to become an artist, and in September 1742 left England for Leghorn and went on to Rome where he studied under Cavaliere Benefiale, an established painter. In April 1748 he joined Matthew Brettingham (later the architect of Holkham Hall), James Stuart and Gavin Hamilton in an expedition on foot to Naples. Later that year these young men put forward a scheme for publishing an accurate description of the antiquities of Athens: Hamilton and Revett being its originators and Stuart supporting it enthusiastically. Their proposals were well received in England and financial aid was forthcoming from such personages as Lord Charlemont and the Earl of Malton, later Marquess of Rockingham, both of whom were later to be admitted to the Society of Dilettanti. Revett and Stuart left Rome for Venice in March 1750 intending to take ship to Athens, but they were delayed for several months and spent three months of this time at Pola on the Dalmatian coast where they studied the classical antiquities. These results were eventually published in *The Antiquities of Athens*, vol. IV.

Later in 1750 Sir James Gray, who was Secretary at the Embassy and then British Resident at Venice, and with whom Revett and Stuart had been in touch, proposed these two young artists for election to the Society, this election being duly confirmed in March 1751. In January 1751 Revett and Stuart embarked from Venice and arrived at Piraeus on 17 March having visited Zante and other places in Greece on the way. They remained there studying the antiquities of Athens until political unrest caused them to leave for Smyrna in March 1753—they visited Delos and Chios *en route*. They returned to Athens in June but continued political troubles and an outbreak of plague forced them to leave again for Smyrna. The continuance of the plague made it impossible for them to return to Greece and they went back to England arriving early in 1755.

On their return Revett and Stuart were formally admitted to the Society of Dilettanti, and the two artists set to work to arrange their notes and drawings for intended publication putting forward a scheme for this.

They had been receiving financial aid from many members of the Society; and in March 1757 the Society agreed to present 'the Authors of the Antiquities of Attica with the sum of Twenty Guineas for their first Volume', and further agreed to contribute the same sum for succeeding volumes.

The Antiquities of Athens, measured and delineated by James Stuart, F.R.S. and F.S.A., and Nicholas Revett, painters and architects was eventually published in 1762 and achieved remarkable success. Stuart soon found himself famous and became known as 'Athenian Stuart'. The publication of this work for 'the first time revealed to the educated public the important place in the history of art which the existing remains of Greek sculpture and architecture still have a right to hold'. As a result of this success the Society began to consider a project for similar researches in Asia Minor, and in May 1764 Mr Richard Chandler was appointed to lead an expedition for this purpose. Revett and Pars were appointed to accompany him as architect and artist respectively.

On the return of this mission in November 1766, Revett set to work on his material which was to appear in the Society's publication *Ionian Antiquities*. After the first volume was issued in 1769, Revett still had much unpublished material, not only of his work in Asia Minor but also at Athens. He seems to have made little progress, but in March 1774 was granted by the Society 'Ninety nine pounds nineteen shillings out of the General Fund' to assist him in 'the compleating the Publication of the Asiatic and Grecian drawings'. Revett still delayed, and Stuart, who had earlier on purchased all Revett's rights in *The Antiquities of Athens*, contemplated a continuation of this work and applied to the Society for the use of their drawings in order to complete his work. In March 1777 Revett was ordered to attend a Committee of the Society who 'are appointed to meet to take into consideration whether Mr Stewart [sic] is to be permitted to have any of them for his use'. However, all schemes for further publication, both of *The Antiquities of Athens* and *Ionian Antiquities* hung fire, and it would seem that Revett still had not handed over his material, because in March 1780 he was again ordered 'to deliver all the drawings belonging to them finished and unfinished into the hands of the Secretary before the next meeting'.

It is clear that difficulties arose between Stuart and Revett which caused long delays and it was not until 21 April 1782 that £200 was paid to Revett 'as a full compensation for all his Claims upon the Society including his payment for finishing his Drawings by order of the Society and for work done upon and paid for an unfinished plate'. At the same time certain Athenian drawings were lent to Stuart 'for the space of one year in order for their publication in the second volume of the Antiquities of Athens'. This second volume, which was prepared by Stuart in collaboration with William Newton was finished in 1787, but was not issued until 1788 owing to Stuart's ill-health and eventual death in February of that year. The volume bears the date of 1787.

Some time after the publication of *Ionian Antiquities* Revett bought up all the remaining stock from the Society, but since the Society wished to be released from all obligations to Revett, they decided in May 1782 to buy back all the 'Remaining perfect Copies of the Ionian Antiquities now in the hands of Mr Revett' at fifteen shillings a piece. Revett produced 200 copies a year later and there his association with the Society seems to have ended so far as publications were concerned.

However, in May 1771 it was recorded that the marbles brought home by the Ionian expedition which had been entrusted to the care of a member of the Society, Mr Thomas Brand, had been handed over by Mr Brand to Revett who had 'delivered them to the care of Lord Clanbrassil'. The only other commission which Revett appears to have been asked to undertake on behalf of the Society was when in February 1767 he was asked to prepare a design for Bacchus's Tomb (the box in which the Society's books are kept) because 'Bacchus's backside appear'd bare, there should be some decoration for it'. It does not seem that this work was ever carried out.

So far as Revett's other activities are concerned, it is known that he designed the Greek ionic west portico at West Wycombe Park for Sir Francis Dashwood who arranged a 'jubilee' and opened the gardens to the public for three days in September 1771. Revett also designed the small temple near this portico and the Temple of Flora on the island in the lake. In 1776 Sir Francis Dashwood rented Round Tar Island between Marlow and Cookham and Revett was commissioned to undertake some work there in 1780–1781. He is also noted for his work on the church at Ayott St Lawrence in Hertfordshire. A *Memoir* of him was published in vol. IV of *The Antiquities of Athens*. See also Lesley Lawrence: *Stuart and Revett*, JWCI, II, 1938 and Dora Wiebenson: *Sources of Greek Revival Architecture*, London, Zwemmer, 1969, pp. 118-20.

APPENDIX C

Published Works of Richard Chandler

Elegiaca Græca, Oxford, 1759.

Marmora Oxoniensia, Oxford, 1763.

Ionian Antiquities, Pt. I for the Society of Dilettanti, 1769.

Inscriptiones antiquæ, plenæque nondum edital in Asia Minor et Græcia, presentum Athenis collectæ (cum appendice), Oxford, 1774.

Travels in Asia Minor, or an Account of a Tour made at the Expense of the Society of Dilettanti, Oxford, 1775.

Travels in Greece, Oxford, 1776.

The History of Ilium including the adjacent Country, and the opposite coast of the Chersonesus of Thrace, London, Nichols, 1802.

The Life of W. Waynflete, Bishop of Winchester, London, 1811. Published after his death and edited by C. Lambert.

BIBLIOGRAPHY

For readers wishing to know more about the archaeological sites visited by Chandler the following works are recommended.

Bean, George E., *Aegean Turkey. An Archaeological Guide*. London, Ernest Benn, 1966.
Blegen, Carl W., *Troy*. London, Thames and Hudson, 1963.
Cook, J. M., *The Greeks in Ionia and the East*. London, Thames and Hudson, 1962.
Stark, Freya, *Ionia. A Quest*. London, John Murray, 1954.

These books contain good bibliographies, maps, plans and illustrations. Hachette World Guides, *Turkey* can also be consulted, and the following periodicals.

Annual of the British School at Athens. Articles on 'The Cnidia', 'The Halicarnassas Peninsula' and 'Researches in Caria', by G. E. Bean and J. M. Cook appear in vol. XLVII (1952), pp. 171–212; vol. L (1955), pp. 85–171 and vol. 52 (1957), pp. 58–146 respectively; also vol. 56 (1961), 'Some sites of the Milesian Territory', by J. M. Cook.
Archaeological Reports published by the Society for the Promotion of Hellenic Studies and the British School at Athens. No. 1959–60, pp. 27–57, 'Archaeology in Western Asia Minor', by J. M. Cook, and under the same title No. 1964–65, pp. 32–62 by J. M. Cook and D. J. Blackman.
Journal of Hellenic Studies, vol. LXXIII (1953), pp. 10–35 and vol. LXXIV (1954), pp. 85–110 contain relevant articles by G. E. Bean; vol. LXXVIII (1958), pp. 102-20, 'Alexander's March from Miletus to Phrygia' by Freya Stark.

For scholars, who will know where to look for them, there are specialised studies by Turkish and foreign missions on the results of their archaeological explorations, and an account, 'Recent Archaeological Research in Turkey', appears annually in *Anatolian Studies*.

In addition to references to Classical and Byzantine Texts, the following works are cited by Chandler in abbreviated form in the footnotes to his text.

Chishull, Edmund: *Antiquitates Asiaticæ* etc., London, Bowyer, 1728.
— *Travels in Turkey and back to England*. London, W. Bowyer, 1747.

Montague, Lady Mary Wortley: *Letters. Written during her Travels in Europe, Asia and Africa.* London, Becket and De Hondt, 1748. 3 vols.

Pococke, Richard: *A Description of the East and Some Other Countries.* London, Bowyer, 1743. 2 vols.

Randolph, Ber.: *The present State of the Islands in the Archipelago (or Arches).* Oxford, 1687.

Sandys, George: *Travels containing a History of the Original State of the Turkish Empire,* etc. London, John Williams Jun., 1670 (1st edition) and 1673 (7th edition).

Smith, Thomas: *Remarks upon the manners, religion, and government of the Turks, together with a survey of the seven churches of Asia.* London, 1678.

Tournefort, M.: *A Voyage in the Levant.* London, Midwinter, Ware, Rivington etc., 1741. 3 vols.

Wheler, Sir George and Spon, Dr Jacob: *A Journey into Greece.* London, Cademan, Kettlewell and Churchill, 1682.

Wood, Robert: *An Essay on the Original Genius and Writings of Homer with a Comparative View of the Antient and Present State of the Troade.* London, H. Hughs, 1767.

On several occasions, Chandler refers to 'Views. Le Brun', but I have not been able to find any book with this specific title. However, in 1702 an English translation of Cornelius Le Bruin's *Voyage au Levant* was published entitled *A Voyage to the Levant; or Travels in the principal parts of Asia Minor, the islands of Scio, Rhodes, Cyprus, and done into English by W. J.,* London, 1702, and all except one of the illustrations cited by Chandler are published in it. The references which I have given in this edition refer to the above-mentioned English translation; the unidentified reference remains as Chandler quoted it.

According to E. G. Cox, *A Reference guide to the literature of travel* (Seattle, 1935), vol. I, p. 251, a three-volume edition of Le Bruin's *Travels* was published in London in 1720 entitled *Voyage to the Levant and travels in Moscovey, Persia and the East Indes.* It is possible that Chandler used this text and the missing reference to the 'house of Mr Lee at Hadgilar' may be found in it, but I have not succeeded in locating this edition.

I am indebted to officials of the Department of Printed Books at the Bodleian Library at Oxford for help over this problem.

HELLESPONT

Abydos
Eleüs •Çanakkale

Yeniköy •Sigéum
Troy
SCAMANDER R.

TENEDOS •Alexandria Troas
•Colonae
IDA M.

CAPE
BABA

LESBOS

•Mytilene

Pergamon

•Cyme
•Phocaea

KARA
BURUN
Menemen •Manisa
HERMUS R.

MYAS M. •Bayraklı
Smyrna OLYMPUS M. Sardıs Magnesia a.S.
CHIOS •Erythrae Clazomene SIPYLUS M.
•Çeşme •Seydiköy Philadelphia
Urla Seferihisar •Torbalı
Teos Metropolis•
CORYCUS M. •Sığacık Lebedos CAYSTER R.
Myonnesus •Colophon
CAPE MACRIA •Notium Claros •Selçuk MESSOGIS M. Nazilli •Tripolis
Ephesus Tralles Nysa MAEANDER R.
•Pygela •Neapolis THORAX M. Carura Hierapolis
Kuşadası Laodicea •
•Söke Denizli •
SAMOS •Magnesia
•Panionion Priene Ozbası a.M.
MYCALE M. •Myus Alinda
Miletus •Heracleia
Didyma L.BAFA Labranda
LATMUS M. •Jakle
GRION M. •Mylasa
CAPE POSEIDEUM •Iasos Stratonicea

A E G E A N

S E A

RHODES

238

INDEX

Note:

The system of indexing is not always consistent but, in general, place names are indexed as in Chandler's text with the modern equivalent following in parentheses. Turkish place names are usually indexed as such where they appear in the footnotes to the text and are normally confined to the most important places. Small villages which have not been identified have not always been included.

Page references only are given to Authors of Classical texts; these appear in italics.

The main headings only of Appendix A have been indexed.

Chandler does not appear to have been as familiar with Byzantine history as he was with that of the Classical world and some of the persons mentioned, and dates, are inaccurate. To provide adequate amendments to Chandler's text would have added considerably to the footnotes and to the expense of production. Minor clarifications only have therefore been attempted in the Index.

INDEX A

Persons and Places

The section on William Pars is indexed separately below—see Index B)

INDEX B

William Pars (pp. xxi–xlv)